*Roots of Crime*

PATTERSON SMITH REPRINT SERIES IN
CRIMINOLOGY, LAW ENFORCEMENT, AND SOCIAL PROBLEMS

*A listing of publications in the* SERIES *will be found at rear of volume*

PUBLICATION NO. 68: PATTERSON SMITH REPRINT SERIES IN CRIMINOLOGY, LAW ENFORCEMENT, AND SOCIAL PROBLEMS

# Roots of Crime

## PSYCHOANALYTIC

## STUDIES

BY

### FRANZ ALEXANDER, M.D.

*Institute for Psychoanalysis, Chicago*

AND

### WILLIAM HEALY, M.D.

*Judge Baker Guidance Center, Boston*

*Montclair, New Jersey*
**PATTERSON SMITH**
*1969*

SBN 87585-068-5

Library of Congress Catalog Card Number: 69-14908

# *Preface*

THIS research was financed by a grant from the Julius Rosenwald Fund which enabled Dr. Alexander to spend a large share of his time for nine months in 1931–2, on the actual psychoanalysis of offenders. The trustees of the Judge Baker Guidance Center, with their usual fine support of scientific investigation, authorized Dr. Healy's part in the work. Two years later, with interim knowledge of the cases, the extensive material gathered has been carefully evaluated and foreshortened for publication.

An advisory committee for the enterprise, consisting of Dr. C. Macfie Campbell, Professor Sheldon Glueck, Mr. Herbert Parsons, Dean Roscoe Pound, and Dr. A. W. Stearns, willingly offered to serve, but since the study advanced without too many difficulties, the committee was called upon for nothing except to express approval of the plans of the investigation.

Anticipated difficulties in meeting with the offenders who were under sentence became largely dissolved through the fine attitude of helpfulness taken by Dr. Stearns, then Commissioner of Correction for Massachusetts. His assistant, Mr. E. C. R. Bagley, very kindly aided much by transfers of individuals to a conveniently situated institution. Five of the cases were seen while serving sentences; one of these continued with the psychoanalysis after release. All cases have been followed as much as has been practicable.

v

The actual psychoanalytic studies and this publication represent a co-operative endeavor divided between the authors. The major part of the analytic work was done by Dr. Alexander. The transcripts from the earlier case records have been mainly contributed by Dr. Augusta F. Bronner, and her assistance at every stage is gratefully acknowledged.

That these studies shall prove readable for all who would acquaint themselves with fundamental causations of certain very important types of delinquent and criminal careers, the technical terminology of psychoanalysis has been largely avoided. The more theoretical considerations can easily be derived by analysts from the material presented. Our subject-matter and our findings challenge a wider public that may have interest in the prevention or checking of antisocial behavior.

*April, 1935*

# Contents

*Roots of Crime*

# CHAPTER ONE

# *Introduction*

ANY task, however difficult, would seem to be pre-eminently justified if science can gain ground anywhere for the better understanding of human behavior. Our efforts, recorded here, have been directed toward gaining knowledge that might lead to better control of delinquency and crime, so shockingly important in our present civilization. Because of the practical importance of the problem of criminality, any scientific discussion of this topic may arouse great expectations. The control of crime is a major interest for society in America and recently the attention of almost everyone has been focused upon it. At the outset it should be clearly understood that this book attacks the problem of crime from only one angle and offers no single remedy. It is written with the conviction that crime is a complex phenomenon, a certain type of reaction of an individual to the general social organization and to his special social situation, and that this reaction is determined by the personality characteristics—congenital or acquired—of the offender.

Also it is our conviction that any great reduction of crime will result neither from assuming a *laissez-faire* attitude nor by deductive speculations, nor through superficial statistical studies (such as computing the coincidences of crime with some external and easily obtainable data), but solely by a better understanding of the psychological processes which underlie human behavior in general and crime in particular. These

3

processes determine the individual's reactions to his situation, even though this situation itself is often beyond the offender's control. The natural consequence of these considerations is that we make no attempt to offer any immediate practical solution of the crime problem, but, on the other hand, we do insist that a better understanding of the causes of criminal behavior is necessary for an intelligent program of prevention.

Our work represents mainly an etiological study of delinquency and crime. It approached this aim by the method of careful investigations of a limited number of careers. We established step by step how these individuals actually became delinquent and criminal, considering their character-formation in the light of their life-history and particularly as the result of a causally connected chain of psychological processes.

This book will in the first place demonstrate that those factors which, statistically considered, are commonly regarded as major determinants in the causation of crime (such as unfavorable environmental conditions—slum districts, broken homes, alcoholism of the parents, economic uncertainty, etc.) are factors which become effective only in a special setting and in combination with the reactive tendencies of certain personalities. It will also demonstrate that apart from these more tangible factors, other less obvious ones are at least of equal importance. We refer to those ideological trends characteristic of any civilization, trends which determine the individual's attitude to collective life, toward authority, toward law, and which determine his evaluations and ideals. To mention only one example of such ideologies: if in a civilization material success is considered above everything as the highest value, all members of such a society who accept this attitude will be inclined to sacrifice such other values as respect for law if they have to choose between the two. The existence of slum districts alone does not explain the high frequency of criminality; this also requires a certain psychological attitude on the part of the inhabitants. In some other centers of civilization, with a more passive and contemplative attitude toward life, people live under even harder economic conditions than in the poorer parts of American cities and yet criminality may be almost entirely absent. Again, in other civilizations discontent is more likely to lead to collective expressions, such as politically organized revolutionary movements, than to the individualistic form of rebellion which is represented by crime. These psychological group-attitudes which are of such prime importance cannot be studied by methods which consider only surface data, but only by the thorough analysis of individual cases representative of certain groups.

Although this book represents primarily an etiological study of crime, it was possible because of the nature of the psychoanalytic approach to combine the study of causation with some modest attempts at therapy or, more precisely, at readjustment. Since the effect of psychoanalytic treatment is based on a better understanding by the individual of his own motives, the aim of understanding the motives of crime coincides to a high degree with the therapeutic aim.

In projecting our research we agreed for the above reasons to take some apparently exceedingly difficult cases of offenders whom we had long known as being failures under police and court procedure, probation, and the régime of correctional institutions. Only two, one of them a very severe offender, had not received some such forms of treatment at the hands of society. Other kinds of treatment also had been given before and after they were originally seen at the clinic. In most of the cases parents or guardians had stated in the juvenile court or at the clinic that after trying various methods they were at their wits' end to know how to handle the young offender. Indeed, several of the delinquents had been removed from apparently inimical environmental conditions to good foster-homes by child-welfare agencies, a procedure which, as shown elsewhere,[1] has in general seemed relatively to be a most valuable therapeutic measure.

Moreover, most of these offenders at an earlier age had been offered at least some psychiatric help which may untangle, from the standpoint of causation, the interweaving of experience, circumstance, ideas, and emotional attitudes which together form the patterns of delinquent behavior. The social and personal treatment undertaken in a number of the cases, as judged by good standards, was well considered and prolonged, but to very little avail. Evidently the bottom of the difficulty had never been reached.

For psychoanalysis only a few cases could be taken, but even so, it was realized that the body of material that might give insight into deeper motivations of delinquency through this research would be greater than any that heretofore has been presented. Detailed records were made from notes directly after each interview. The publication of these would require several volumes; it has been no small work to epitomize without omitting important issues that appear in the vast amount of ideational and emotional life that was brought to the surface in the analytic sessions.

In order to avoid a mélange of human material, we agreed to exclude mentally defective or mildly psychotic individuals or those classifiable in the ordinary categories of neuroses and psychoses. On the other hand, we selected offenders whose criminal careers apparently were due primarily to internal mental conflicts rather than to external circumstances. These individuals, even if they do not exhibit pronounced neurotic or psychotic symptoms, belong to the larger group of neurotic

[1] Healy, Bronner, Baylor, and Murphy: *Reconstructing Behavior in Youth.* New York: Alfred A. Knopf, 1929.

personalities, since their behavior is to such a high degree determined by their inner conflicts. The unsuccessful effort at previous treatment had seemed to indicate something of the nature of the trouble, and in some instances the story of the individual himself had given intimation that affairs were far from right in his emotional life, even though the difficulty never was verbalized by the delinquent. It would be erroneous to believe that these more or less emotionally unadjusted individuals, whose behavior is largely determined by their inner conflicts, constitute very unusual cases. Though there are no reliable statistical data available, we should be inclined to consider them far more numerous than is ordinarily considered.

The individuals taken for analysis had all been well known earlier, some of them eight or more years previously, to the Judge Baker Guidance Center (formerly the Judge Baker Foundation). The usual careful case studies had been made, including all available social data as well as the family and developmental histories, medical and psychological studies, together with psychiatric interviews—all obtained through the co-operation of members of the family, school authorities, probation officers, and others. In some instances these studies were already voluminous, and in most cases the life of the offender has been fairly well known during the intervening years.

Neither of the analysts at the time of the analysis was acquainted with the full material that had been obtained in the previous case study. For orientation, only a short review of the outstanding data was utilized, with no transcription of the offender's earlier statement of his own problems, attitudes, or conflicts.

An essential part of the research project avowedly was confrontation of material gained through psychoanalysis with the data obtained by the previous more or less thorough study of the individual—and vice versa. This seemed to offer the advantage of comparing the psychoanalytic exploration of the mental processes of the offender with the different type of material contained in the earlier records and obtained through clinical interviews with the delinquent, with parents, agency visitors, and others.

One of the questions we put to ourselves was: could we by delving into genetics learn more about the period or periods of character- and personality-formation as these were related to the development of such unfortunate and costly lives as were exhibited in the cases to be studied? In other words, could we discern what situations and influences and attitudes, if any, might have been altered, and at what age could these alterations have been accomplished, that the development of delinquent trends might have been thwarted? Much of the success of efforts for the prevention of delinquency and crime may depend upon gaining such knowledge.

As far as direct therapeutic aims are concerned, our expectations naturally had to be extremely modest under the time limits and conditions at our disposal: ten months for the whole research project. In only exceptional cases is this length of time considered sufficient to effect satisfactory therapeutic results by the technique of psychoanalysis. To the majority of our cases even considerably less time could be devoted. What has developed during the two years following the analysis is set forth in the epilogues to the individual case records.

Nothing can better illustrate the complexity of the causes leading to criminality than cases where continued criminal behavior appears to be entirely irrational and cannot be explained by the motives which ordinarily induce individuals to violate the law. The following case well illustrates the futility of legal and penal treatment where deep psychological issues are not uncovered—that of an offender whom we particularly had hoped to investigate by the psychoanalytic approach.

More than ten years ago a very mannerly, intelligent boy of sixteen who had been held in jail for three weeks on account of stealing a suitcase which he had pawned was seen for a day at the clinic. In court he first gave the age of nineteen and then acknowledged his true age and that he was on parole from a boys' correctional institution. Physical examination showed a splendid physique; psychological examination gave him full average intelligence. In the juvenile court he told the judge that two correctional institutions had failed to cure him and that he needed more severe punishment and desired to go to the reformatory for adults, whereupon he was committed to that institution.

The history that he gave to us was corroborated later by his father and authorities of the correctional schools. He had begun thieving when he was eight years old, and when he was ten he told his father that there was something, he could not tell what, that drove him to steal. By the time we saw him, there had been an enormous amount of such stealing, with four or five commitments to correctional institutions, where he was always found courteous, well-behaved, and industrious. He readily made friends everywhere by his upstanding qualities. Whenever he was confronted with his delinquencies, he stated that his own behavior was a puzzle to himself.

At the present time his case has become so notorious and has been so much in the newspapers that there is no breach of confidence in giving a very brief sketch of his history with proper disguises. At the reformatory he behaved well and was highly regarded. Paroled from there, he speedily got into more trouble, but then settled down again for a year or so, living at home and being advanced in a certain business concern on account of his good working qualities. This boy came from a fairly well-to-do family where he had all normal advantages. He was an active, outgoing youngster. We learned of no peculiarities in his upbringing. He was the eldest of five children, and no other members of his family had been delinquent. His home and school satisfactions on the surface seem to have been equal to those of any of the others.

After his period of doing well he married and was very proud of his young wife. After his first child was born (by this time he has three), he began again his unreasonable delinquencies while he was doing well in business. He frequently told his wife that he acted under some strange impulse that he could not understand. He stole from his father and from other people and repeatedly took automobiles, travelling long distances in them. He entered the Navy under an alias and soon deserted, was arrested for more stealing and placed in a disciplinary institution, and escaped, getting into more and more trouble. During this time he wrote affectionate letters to his wife begging for forgiveness. It must be emphasized that he might have been living comfortably at home earning a good salary. His father and his wife's parents spent a great deal of money getting him out of various difficulties and tried hard to reform him. He had won the affections of his wife's people by his gentlemanly conduct and ordinarily good attention to business, being a modest fellow and nothing of a high flyer.

Then began more serious affairs. He was arrested in a Western state for burglary because in senseless fashion he stole cheap jewelry from apartments which he entered. He was given a long sentence to the penitentiary, where he was always a hard-working, well-behaved inmate; on the occasion of a catastrophe there he proved himself a hero. A pardon was forthcoming and he was allowed to work on the outside. His wife went to be near him. A few days before the pardon was to become effective and after he had joyously sent word to his parents, he ran away from his wife and pardon. His going away also broke up a new business arrangement which, much to his avowed liking, had been made for him. In another state he soon committed a series of thefts and burglaries which were very easily traced to him and he was given a very long sentence. Once more people became interested in him because of his unusual qualities. A psychiatrist who studied him now felt, as did one who saw him earlier in the other penitentiary, that here was a case out of the ordinary, a man not of a usual criminal type, but rather one who seemed criminal through inner compulsion. Again all attempts to get him placed where he could be studied by psychoanalytic methods were frustrated.

The young man made his escape from a road gang where he was working under atrocious conditions; with aid he then established himself in an Eastern city under an alias. However, he speedily entered into other crimes, taking automobiles and engaging in bizarre stealings and burglaries. With a woman of some standing who was earning well he contracted a bigamous marriage; she knew him only under his alias, and thought him well-to-do. At this time he did such foolish things as having a collar with pendants of gold pieces made for the lady's dog. He adorned their apartment with dozens of clocks which he had stolen, giving much attention to their arrangement and regulation. He remained unknown to the woman as a criminal and undetected by the police for months, but finally was caught in another state where he had also committed several burglaries.

Seen by a well-known psychiatrist, he was once more diagnosed as not having any mental disease. Altogether he has had several most careful examinations at the hands of competent neurologists, who have found no disease of the central nervous system. He has always been abstemious about alcohol and has never had deleterious habits of any kind.

The story of this young man, here not half told, thus involves ten or twelve incarcerations, numerous arrests, punitive as well as kindly treatment at the hands of many authorities, including, first of all, his own parents. He frankly remains a puzzle to himself as well as to others. He still is a healthy-appearing, generally cheerful individual, strangely optimistic about the possibilities of the future for him, hoping that someone can discover what is the matter with him so that he may alter his conduct tendencies.

This case, however strange it may seem, is only an extreme example of the dynamic power of irrational and unconscious motives which often have a permanent determining influence on behavior, even if this influence does not always appear in such spectacular and dramatic fashion.

The co-operation of the offenders in the psychoanalytic work was, on the whole, surprisingly good. With most of them it seemed as if they felt intensely the peculiar nature of their own problems, which they never heretofore had been able to verbalize; they appeared earnestly to seek relief in much the same spirit that psychoneurotics present themselves to the physician. There was no accrual to them of any external advantage; for the ones in prison there was no shortened sentence nor any benefit obtained by being transferred to another institution. The necessity that they felt for the solution of their problems was particularly exemplified by the appearance at the clinic of a young man, Henry Elton, who had not been seen there for years. He had heard through his family that an opportunity was being offered for further investigation of his problems and he had travelled some distance to find out about it. He had been living and working in another state where he was immune from being returned to a reformatory for breaking his parole. It seems that after release a year previously he had committed several thefts, and warrants were out for him in two states. He came inquiring about the kind of study that was to be undertaken, and said: "By God, if anybody could tell me why I do what I do, I would be willing to be called insane and go to a state institution to be studied, or anywhere else." As a matter of fact, he hoped so much to gain something for himself by psychoanalysis that in order to obtain it he gave himself up to serve an extra sentence of two years, inflicted because he had broken parole.

Five of the offenders were seen while in prison; two of these co-operated extremely well and went as far with the psychoanalytic procedure as was practicable. One, the same Henry Elton, was never more than half-hearted in willingness to face the true facts underlying his difficulties in spite of his consciously professed desire to be analyzed; another utterly refused to enter into analysis, although he had asked for the chance; and one came only to a very few sessions. Two of the group remained still under sentence at the end of our period of work; one who was earlier released came to the office regularly for a time to continue his analysis. The others were free at the time of analysis.

Differences found in working with these offenders, differences in their attitudes and in their circumstances, proved variables quite beyond our control. Some of them had considerable sentences yet to serve, and this, of course, made for discouragement and lessened the chance of accomplishing therapeutic results. Then transfer to a convenient penal institution proved to be not altogether an advantage because it created some undesirable attitudes in both the offenders and officials. The latter were not always helpful because of their skepticism and lack of appreciation of what was being attempted, and the offenders found themselves in a new situation that was not always as comfortable as the one which they had come from and that left them with an unfortunate amount of idle time.

But worst of all was the fact that those who were released during or after the analysis found themselves face to face with the terrifically discouraging economic depression, doubly discouraging to one who had just come without funds from an institution and with a criminal record. It seems possible to us that if this study had been carried out at a more favorable time, when employment could have been found and some of the cases placed under new living-conditions, the therapeutic results might have been far different. The fact is that these offenders were subjected to circumstances with which anyone with a good record would have found it extremely difficult to cope. However, the influence of the analysis is to be seen by our reports of the cases.

These studies represent no attempt to deny or even to discount in the least the important fact that in our day and generation, perhaps more than heretofore, there are many social and other environmental influences which tremendously tend to create delinquency and crime. The many invitations to antisocial conduct which are so plainly offered to children and young people, the many easy avenues open to them for delinquency, the social pressures on them by delinquent compan-

ionship, poor parental examples, and the lack of good upbringing make it clear why there is such a defective development
of any restraining conscience.

On the other hand, there is no greater mistake than to believe
that all human individuals are influenced by the same motives
or driven in their conduct tendencies by similar reactions to
what would appear to be similar experiences. True, the law,
based on its conception of justice, does take this view and judges
all men alike—that is wherein the law differs so widely from
psychological science. It appears perfectly clear to any careful
student of criminology that there are certain offenders not
classifiable in the usual psychiatric pigeon-holes, though they
may be neurotic personalities, who are most certainly driven
to engage in antisocial conduct by the dynamics of their unconscious mental life. It is mainly to a better understanding
of such personalities and such behavior tendencies that this
study has been directed.

## CHAPTER TWO

# *The Victim of Loyalty*

RICHARD VORLAND was brought by his mother to the Judge Baker Guidance Center when he was eight years old. She lived in an industrial center at some distance and came for advice concerning his problems because a social worker told her of the possibility of having him studied and placed in a better environment. He was twenty years old when the analysis was begun.

Richard, when six years old, just after his father died in an accident, came with his mother and brothers from their home in Virginia. His father, born in 1878 in the foothills of the Virginia mountains, lived in the South all his life. Richard's mother was also born in Virginia, in 1885, but came from a New England family with a strain of French blood. After her husband's death she came to Worcester, where relatives lived, and there worked in a bakery to support herself and her children. She was Catholic, her husband Protestant, and some of the children in their upbringing had been affiliated with the one church and some with the other.

Richard was the youngest of the five children. The oldest, a girl, remained with friends in Virginia and married there. John, eight years older than Richard, was already delinquent when in the South and had continued to be a difficult problem. The next child, a girl, went to live with maternal relatives in Ohio after the father's death. Then came Wilbur, two and a

half years older than Richard, reported by the mother to be
the boon companion of Richard. She particularly wanted Richard removed from his influence.

The mother presented Richard's problems as follows: He
was extremely truant from school and once stayed away from
home all night. For a year or more there had been much petty
stealing from home and from shops, and Richard recently had
secreted himself in the office of a factory and stolen a large sum
of money, part of which he gave to Wilbur. His mother was also
concerned because Richard took hazardous rides on trucks and
because he was so unmanageable and disobedient at home,
sometimes having severe temper tantrums.

Richard's father came of a family of good standing; he
himself was graduated from a Southern college, but in spite
of the fact that he was considered to have good intelligence
and was healthy he took a modest position, which he kept
without making any effort to advance himself. He was a
periodic alcoholic and when drunk was disagreeable and pro-
fane, deteriorating greatly in the last year of his life. He took
very little interest in his children and was very irresponsible
toward his family.

The mother is a small woman, often appearing haggard and
worn by anxieties and worries, but she has been a hard worker
and has always shown immense loyalties to her children. She
received rather meager education, married early, and was
frequently ill. She had little control over the children; working
to support them after her husband's death increased her difficulties. She was not fond of household work and preferred to
obtain outside employment rather than accept financial aid.
She frankly stated she had been able to manage the girls much
better than the boys. Though she came north to be near relatives, she was not on good terms with most of them.

The physical conditions of the home were poor. The family

lived in a congested district, the boys much on the street. The older brothers were never known at the Center. When Richard was first seen they had both recently been placed in charitable institutions.

The father began drinking heavily while the mother was pregnant with Richard. It was a very unhappy period for her. The birth-history was normal. He was not breast-fed at all; the mother reports that Wilbur was the only child that she was able to feed satisfactorily at the breast. There was much nutritional difficulty during infancy; Richard was a cranky baby and cried much till he was three years old. He was never seriously ill, however. None of the children had ever been very sick, and the mother attributes this to her care for their cleanliness and to keeping them away from others when they were very young children. She thinks that she kept Richard particularly close; he was with her all the time till he was six years old. She pitied him more than the others because he appeared so frail. To her he always seemed more like herself; he is as close-mouthed as she is, whereas his brothers resemble their father in being talkative. Though Richard from infancy had temper tantrums, which she did not know how to control, and sometimes seemed obstinately self-willed, she speaks of him as a lovely child until he was about seven. He was always fussy about eating and showed an almost abnormal craving for sweets. No other peculiar or deleterious habits were reported. She attributed his behavior difficulties to the fact that at seven he developed middle ear disease and to the fact that at this time he got in with a bad crowd, which included Wilbur. In later interviews the mother frequently emphasized how good the children always were to her, how loyal they have been to each other, how she has always taken their part; and she has added that none of the others has ever given her any "back talk." Richard, on the contrary, from the time he was six or seven, has sometimes become much enraged with her and complained bitterly about her admonishments.

The physical examination at eight years showed Richard's poor development and rather poor nutrition; many badly carious teeth; intermittent otorrhea, with moderately defective hearing; and a marked phimosis.

The psychological examination gave an intelligence quotient of 95. The boy had good language ability, but was only in the second grade, unable even to do good second-grade work, probably on account of his truancy. He was repressed and sensitive, with a thorough dislike of school.

In the earliest interviews Richard was easily won into making a frank statement of his life. He gave a vivid account of the ideas of stealing which he had derived from several companions, the ones that his mother had mentioned, and from his brother. He stated that his oldest brother had taught him and Wilbur much delinquency. Also this oldest brother indulged in sex habits which he exhibited in front of the younger boys. Obscenities and words of sexual significance, which he had heard inside and outside his own home, came up repeatedly in his own mind, although he hated them. (His mother said that in the year before her husband died he frequently accused his wife of immorality, and the children had heard this.) Richard was much concerned about these inner thoughts and demonstrated his practice of crossing his fingers in order to prevent ideas on sex subjects from coming up in his mind—a curious application of a children's game of denial. Several times he said that he often felt queer because of the words he had learned—his actual statement was: "Those things make me feel rotten and queer. It makes me think of getting into places and taking things, and then sometimes I dream at night of breaking in." He also went on to say that he wished that he could dream about playing ball.

Richard told much else, about the neighborhood gang who stole and "talked dirty" and engaged in masturbation, which he himself did not do very often, about movies that deal with stealing, and his fondness for his mother and brothers, at the same time alleging lack of remembrance of his father. (His mother had suspicions that his father had taken him as well as his brothers into saloons.) He played out on the streets sometimes until late at night. School did not interest him; he wanted to be a sailor and did not need education for that.

It was noted that the boy showed a slight facial tic, but his mother had not mentioned it.

It was naturally concluded that this was a case for long-time placement in a good environment, but it was also surmised that there were mental conflicts which might need exploration and that this possibly could be carried out through a sympathetic and intelligent woman visitor who had been very successful in such work with other boys. He was recommended for foster-home placement to a child-placing agency; attention to his physical needs and the furtherance of wholesome substitutive interests was stressed.

The above is the essence of what was known to the analyst when Richard agreed to analysis at twenty years of age and for this purpose was transferred from a county jail to temporary incarceration in Boston. Other details of much interest appear in the section that presents the confrontation of the psychoanalytic material with the extensive case record developed over the intervening years.

### RICHARD VORLAND'S PSYCHOANALYSIS

Richard Vorland was twenty years old when his analysis began in the prison to which for this purpose he had been transferred from a jail in another part of the state. The analysis lasted seven months, five of them conducted in the jail and the last two when he was free. He is a medium-sized, slender fellow, quiet and polite, speaking usually in a low, rather indistinct voice.

Richard assumed from the beginning a pleasant and co-operative attitude. He appeared punctually in the hospital section of the prison where his analysis took place, resented the guards' delay if they did not bring him up on time, and showed in general an engaging manner throughout his analysis.

He very soon grasped the sense of the whole procedure, associated freely, listened eagerly to the analyst's comments, and showed an unusual understanding of psychological connections.

In the two preliminary interviews he gave a sketch of his life-history. His father, who died when Richard was six, was always drunk. His next brother, Wilbur, and he were inseparable at this time and were almost entirely uncontrolled. At the age of seven he committed his first theft with his brother and a close companion of his brother. He took a hundred dollars from a factory office to buy candy. He did not know how much he stole—he took the banknotes and pushed the roll under his shirt.

After the father's death the home was soon broken up and the patient was referred to a child-placing agency. From the time he was taken by the child-placing agency his outstanding memories are all of work and work—which he hated. He was transferred from one foster-home to another. In one of the foster-homes where he came during Christmas holidays he had to work for the janitor during the vacation from school. He stole from the school. When he was twelve years old, he was very tough and tried to assault a girl. All this period in different foster-homes on farms he remembers as all work and no play. He finished grammar school while he was working on a small farm. Once in a rage he attacked his foster-father with a pitchfork.

He was about seventeen years old when he had his first job in the city, in a broker's office. It was a swindling company and they sold false stocks. He stole from the office continually. He earned ten dollars a week and stole twenty dollars or more each week. He was there five or six months and then signed up on a fruit boat, but on the morning he was to leave at five o'clock he had a nosebleed and his mother would not let him go. Then he worked as an elevator-boy and bell-hop in different hotels. In one hotel he stayed a year, liked the work there, and made good earnings, but after he lost this job he was without employment for a time. Then he was taken back again by the same hotel but was fired again, because he stalled instead of working. From another hotel he was fired because he chewed tobacco and spit out the juice. Then he worked in several other places. Once when he was drunk he stole a car. He was caught and after two months' imprisonment was paroled. Then again he had employment as elevator-boy or as bell-hop.

Once his brother, while driving in his car, with another fellow stole a suitcase. Richard assumed ownership of the car at his brother's request and was caught with it. He was arrested, but his brother bailed him out. His probation was extended for another year. One night while drunk he broke into a store and stole a radio. Someone "squealed" and he was "pinched."

During the analysis he completed this history of his delinquencies with innumerable data of minor and major stealings which never came to the attention of the police—breaking into stores, entering office buildings, and opening drawers with great technical skill, which apparently he learned from his brother. He showed some manifest pleasure in speaking about these tricks and about his criminal accomplishments, and also about his bravery, skill, and cynicism, but always stated that his brother was smarter than he.

In the very first interviews he frankly admits that he is dissatisfied with the kind of work he has been doing; he has no hope of achieving anything by it; the only thing he likes is driving a car, but he has lost his license. The only future for him is to become a successful crook. If his brother would go straight, maybe he would too, but he likes his brother too much to leave off; he wants to "work" with him. If it were not for his mother he would become a good crook, but his consideration for her inhibits him from being reckless and therefore he does not take great chances. He does not like to accept any help or be under any obligation; that is what he hates the most.

He likes excitement and "to pull a trick" on the police. He speaks for hours about his new criminal plans after he gets out of jail. He states that he has no conscience; the only thing which he resents is betrayal. He is loyal to his friends and expects the same loyalty from them.

The impression which Richard gives in the first two sessions is that he is boasting of his toughness, skill, and courage and denying any sentimentality and decency.

During the third interview he relates a dream which he had two years ago which immediately gives deep insight into his central problem and shows that we have to deal with a personality suffering from a pronounced neurotic conflict.

He dreamed he was walking in the air and fighting with a fellow over a girl. The fellow was after his girl. He was afraid of the fellow; nevertheless, he gave him a kick. He had a gun in his hand, but when he fired, the bullet fell out of the end of the gun onto the ground. Then he turned the gun upwards, thus, ⟋⟋ in order to achieve a further-reaching ballistic curve.

But even then it did not work. Then he threw the gun at the fellow because it was no good. The night before this session Richard had a "wet dream"; he dreamed his brother had sexual intercourse with somebody, but he had an ejaculation. Associating to these two dreams, he emphasizes that he never failed with a girl but once, and once had five emissions in one afternoon. The only time he failed he was drunk. For one and a half years he had a steady girl friend.

The first dream shows clearly that behind the surface attitude of emphasized courage there is a deep uncertainty linked with the feeling of sexual inadequacy and fear of impotence. The second dream shows the competitive sexual attitude toward his brother, whom he sees in the dream having sexual intercourse, but at the same time he, the patient, has an ejaculation. The assumption that in the first dream the fight with a fellow refers to his hostility to his brother, compared with whom he feels weak and sexually inadequate (the bullet does not shoot, but drops out of his gun), is confirmed by the patient at the same interview, in which he admits that although he loves his brother immensely, he has always been very jealous of him. His jealousy started when he was eight years old. Before that they always went together, stood by each other, played tricks together. But about that time his brother started to go out with other fellows, leaving him alone, and he felt terribly jealous. His brother was stronger than he. Saying this he corrects himself: "No, he was not stronger—at least I never admitted that." It is obvious that his competitive attitude covers his deeper dependent attitude towards the brother. This passive dependence upon his brother suggests a homosexual component in the dream in which he watches his brother's sexual intercourse.

He used to fight with his brother; he remembers episodes when his brother hit him. Once he broke the wheel of his brother's car. Then he stole five wheels from another car to replace it, but they did not fit. In the dream in which he fought with the fellow the scene was the same yard in which he lived when he was eight years old.

From this third interview on, for the most part, the patient dreams prolifically, almost every night. Seventy per cent of the interviews are filled with dream analyses which allow penetration of the deep layers of the unconscious.

In the fourth interview he brings a dream pair, one of which is again about guns, but this time about two guns. He wants to sell one of them to a gangster. The "two big pistols were wonderful" in the dream. The second dream is a sexual dream in which he enters the women's section of the prison and sleeps with one of the women there. In associating he speaks of liking guns, tells about many aggressive jokes which he played with guns, and asserts that he is a good shot. He knows the story of William Tell.

Evidently playing with guns and the joy of shooting are compensations for his deeply rooted inferiority feelings in relation to his brother. They also serve as a vent for the patient's aggressive tendencies. This is confirmed by the fact that immediately after speaking of his aggressions with guns (for example, shooting from the top of a building at the shovels of men who were working on an adjacent lot) the patient tells one of the most traumatic episodes of his life. He is sometimes terribly jealous of his mother. There is a boarder in the house who has relations with her. He has had several fights with this boarder and so has his brother. Once this boarder kicked out three of Richard's teeth. He shows the analyst the false teeth that replace the missing ones. Telling this episode he shows extreme emotion. "Why doesn't the boarder marry her?" If his mother did not love this man the patient would have killed him by now.

When the analyst questions whether he would not be just

as angry with the boarder if his mother did marry him, he answers: "Yes, I would hate him because he is no good, but I would not do anything to him." Then in a threatening tone he adds that if his mother stops caring for the boarder, the fellow will not live long.

In the next interview he tells of a dream in which he stole two automatic pistols and of his fear of the police because he carries pistols. Danger has a great attraction for him. He tells stories in which by smart tricks he committed extremely bold thefts. He likes to tease authorities. He knows this must be connected with his "inferiority complex" (the patient's own expression, which he never heard from the analyst). He understands his predilection for guns and shooting and the thrill of these foolhardy escapades which help him to overcome his sense of inferiority. Carrying shotguns gives him a feeling of strength and power. When asked to associate to the oblique position of the gun in the earlier dream, he associates with it erection of the penis, which takes the same direction as the shotgun in the dream.

He recognizes, also, that in his stealing there is an irrational element. He stole, for example, a wrist-watch from another prisoner which had no value, but might bring him into jeopardy. Yet he often returned money, for example ten dollars which he once found in a hotel.

His uncertainty about his masculinity becomes clearer and clearer. He associates to a dream in which he had some difficulties in getting a bathing-suit for swimming, his envy of men who are physically stronger in build than he, his envy of those who are better in sports, those who are richer or have beautiful cars. He recognizes that all his envy centers in his attitude toward his brother.

In a dream he was walking down the street with his girl. Three fellows attacked his girl and grabbed her. He told them to leave, but they did not go. Then he attacked all three of them. They threw him on the ground, but he succeeded in escaping, ran across the street, and then noticed that his girl was still on the other side of the street. He ran back and again attacked the men. He broke a bottle over the head of one of them who was red-haired. The other two then ran away. Immediately afterwards in an association, he tells that his brother has reddish hair. The sexual competition with his brother becomes quite conscious in connection with this dream.

Envious competition, however, is not the only attitude he has toward his brother. His passive dependence upon the stronger brother parallels the negative hostile tendency. In one of his dreams the brother is represented as a horse who leads him to the desired goal. One of his early dreams (eighth interview) reveals that in the deep analysis his aggression toward men centers in unconscious castrative tendencies. In this dream he rescued a girl who was imprisoned by a peculiar animal. The first obstacle in rescuing the girl was a tree standing before the door with the limbs alive with snakes. He cut the snakes off and rescued the girl, but then a peculiar animal stood in the way. He tried to cut it in two with his sword, but it grew again. The girl showed him how to cut the animal, which then took the shape of a bald-headed man. The girl pointed out that with the sword he could stab him in the middle of the back. Then the man changed into a brick walk. The girl stooped and took out the bricks from the same place she had indicated as the place to stab when the walk was a man. Taking out the bricks, she formed a path to facilitate walking. Then the scene changed and he was in a bookshop. It was owned by a fellow who kept magazines. He stole two magazines from the bottom of the pile.

This big animal was like a big snake without head or tail. Then it became a bald-headed man who had no features. This

bald-headed man reminds him of the penis. It is interesting to
see in this dream that in his fight against the man he takes the
aid of the woman, to whom he also attributed the phallic symbol: the girl has a sword as he has. At the end of the dream
he stole *two* magazines. The strong receptive attitude toward
women shows itself for the first time in this dream. The
woman helps him and paves his way." (She takes out the bricks
and forms a path to facilitate walking.)

It is also interesting how often in his dreams stealing is connected with the number two. In a former dream he had two
revolvers, in another he stole two revolvers, and also in his
later dreams the number two is found again in connection
with stealing. Knowing that number two in the deep layers of
the unconscious is associated with the two breasts this suggests
that at bottom his stealing tendency is built up on strong oral
aggressive tendencies (to take, to bite) directed toward the
female breast. (His strong oral trend was also indicated in
the pre-analytic studies by his extreme fondness for sweets as
a child.) In this last dream he wants to rescue a woman in
order to be helped by her, which corresponds to the conscious
wish to rescue his mother from the boarder for the purpose of
possessing her for himself in a receptive dependent way. This
strong dependent attachment toward the mother becomes
clearer and clearer during the course of the analysis. The receptive attitude toward the mother runs parallel with the passive dependent attitude toward the brother.

In the next sessions the guilt and shame reaction on account
of his parasitic wishes comes nearer the surface. He asks us to
do favors for his brother and then confesses that he has to do
compulsively whatever his brother asks him to do. If he is
reading a book and the brother wants it he gives it to him; or
if he has a necktie which the brother wants he gives that to
him.

In the next period of the analysis he expresses a very pessimistic outlook on life. He never will achieve anything; he could be an elevator-boy and slowly advance to a small job in a hotel or in a department store, but such a man has no pleasure in life, nothing but duties and children, no hope of advancement. He prefers to be a crook.

In the following interview, however, he indicates in a dream a more hopeful attitude, which he does not yet want to admit consciously and therefore has to express in a dream. He was going into an office building, as he often did—one of his old tricks. There were raincoats and hats. He took a hat and some stamps from a brief-case. The stamps were in strips, about sixteen three-and-one-half-cent stamps and some four-and-one-half-cent stamps. An old white-haired fellow who was working in the elevator shaft saw him through the glass door of the office. He thought he had better "beat it." He went out through another door, came to a lobby, and from there to the street.

He recognized in the old man looking from the elevator shaft the discouraging picture of his future if he goes straight. This is the kind of prematurely aged family man, an old man still an elevator-"boy," that he had in mind. Associating to the dream he says: "When this fellow looked at me in the dream I suddenly saw that there were many doors in the room and I took another door, not the one through which the man saw me when I came in." He discovers in the dream that it is not true that there are only two possibilities for him—to become an elevator-boy or a crook; in the dream he says maybe there is another way out. In this dream, also, there were two hats. One was too big and was somehow connected with his brother, he feels. It belonged to him. He took the other one, and this was waterproof. He explains this by saying: "Let my brother go his way, but I will become straight." It is interesting that in this dream, besides the cap, he steals stamps which have real

value, whereas the cap seems to have a symbolic meaning and
is related to his sexual competition with his brother. This suggests that in his burglary two factors are intermixed: (1) irrational motives, among them the envy of his brother and the
wish to be as efficient as the brother, and (2) a rational motive
for profit.

As the guilt feelings toward the brother, because of his combination of envy and dependence, express themselves in an exaggerated, masochistically tinged loyalty to the brother, so the
guilt feelings toward the mother on account of his dependent
parasitic attitude toward her lead to a masochistic attitude to
women. This is clearly expressed in the following dream: He
was in a bus riding back to the place of a former foster-home.
He was the only passenger in the bus. He had nice clothes on,
like a dude, and fifteen dollars in his pocket. He arrived in
Suxton; then he saw himself in a lunch-room, where he ordered coffee and a sandwich, which were very expensive.
Everything was twice as expensive as elsewhere. Three or four
people were there and he knew them all. He spoke to the
girl who owned the shop and said: "To hell with the prices
you charge here!" She slapped him in the face. He turned the
other cheek. She slapped him three or four times, but it did
not hurt. He did not feel any pain, it was rather a pleasure.
From there he went up-town on the main street. He figured
how much money it would cost him at the hotel and looked
the shops over in order to come back later and break into
them. He saw a rug-store and a Jew inside, and thought of
getting the Jew out of the store in order to open the cash register. He overheard him speaking through the telephone, probably to his wife, because he heard him saying: "Come down,
mother." He thought the Jew was addressing his wife as
"mother." The street was slippery, and when a girl came along
with many bundles, he offered to help her cross the street.

While helping her he dropped a package which he had in his pocket. A machine came along the street made of wooden boxes. He stopped the girl and waited until it passed and they went on. He looked at the girl and found her to be very good-looking. After he helped her across the street he went on. He came to a light sunny street (the other street had been dark and shabby) where girls and soldiers were walking in the sunshine. That is the street on which his high school was.

His associations to riding in a bus are: to be in style—big front—swell front. He always wanted to go back to Suxton; it is the only place he liked. He went there the last half of his second year at high school. He liked the man for whom he was working and also his wife; everything was nice there. He went away suddenly because he wanted to see his mother, but he went back again. He had to leave because he could not get along with the hired man who worked with him. This man wanted to boss him around and he had a fight with him. Then his employer sent him back to his home because he could not get along with the others. His employer told him once not to go with a certain girl because she was a bum.

His associations to being nicely clothed are: to have a swell front—to be a good crook. "Then you can get away with it better. You can't go into a man's store poorly dressed and expect to steal." His associations to the lunch-room which was expensive are: "Perhaps that is the price I pay for my crimes." The girl in the dream was taking much more money from him than was necessary.

His associations to being slapped are that some people like to be kicked around. The analyst asks him: "Are you one of those?" He replies: "No, I hate physical pain." He goes on to say that consciously he does not like to be beaten or dominated by girls.

"Yes, but in the dream you enjoyed it," says the analyst.

"Maybe there is such a tendency in you. Then, later you helped the other girl and dropped your own package, as if again you would have sacrificed your own property to help this girl. The first one took advantage of you, and you helped the second one and lost your package."

"Yes, but I found it again."

"If I understand correctly, in the dream you gave up the idea of robbing the Jew just when you heard him calling his wife on the telephone."

"Yes, but I could not have broken in if his wife came down and there were two of them."

"That sounds too rational to me. Perhaps there was an emotional motive also."

"Maybe I took pity on him because he was a married man. And then, he called his wife 'mother.' He was such a kindly man."

The patient goes on to say that he himself likes to give things to women, but also to men. "There is a big generous streak in me."

Here the analyst points out that he likes to take, but he also likes to give, thereby maintaining a balance. There is a chivalrous attitude toward women in his dream. He helps one girl, then spares the Jew on account of his wife, and from these chivalrous tendencies there is only a step to being exploited and dominated by a girl, as he was in the lunch-room. It seems that to be chivalrous toward women or to suffer for women is another means of getting rid of his guilt feelings, similar to the tendency to sacrifice himself for his brother.

"Then we don't learn anything new from this dream, because we knew that already."

"Yes, the new thing is that in this dream you get rid of your guilt feelings by being punished by a woman, or by helping a woman. So we see that this self-sacrificing tendency is directed not only toward your brother, but also toward women. But you are right; the same motive came up in the dream in which you killed the snake, which was a symbol of the male genital. There you had to kill the snake in order to rescue a girl."

The deep attachment to the mother interferes with developing a real affection for other women. In one of his dreams he was in bed with his girl friend and started sexual intercourse with her when his mother entered and he had to stop. He stood between his mother and the girl so that his mother would not see the girl, and sent her out of the room. In discussing this dream he confesses that he never will marry a girl as long as his mother is alive.

In the same session he speaks about his masturbation and the connected fears of becoming a half-wit if he did not stop. It is very interesting to observe that the same young man who speaks of his stealing with the greatest cynicism, confesses his difficulties about masturbation with the utmost reluctance, blushing and in a low voice. Undoubtedly, stealing takes the place of the forbidden sexual act, being subjectively felt as a lesser crime. Naturally this displacement can take place only because he is still fixed to the pregenital oral receptive form of the psychosexual relations. It is very instructive that after he confessed his masturbation, in the next interview he ostentatiously exhibits an extreme unscrupulous criminal attitude, speaks of his plans for more criminality in order to be able to loaf, tells a story of how he blackmailed a homosexual, but he would never blackmail a woman. In contrast to this cynical attitude toward crime he tells how a visitor friend of his wanted to gave him two dollars, but he took only one dollar because he doen't like to accept money from anyone. He cheated the same fellow, however, in playing cards with him. He wants the money, but does not want to be obligated. As he leaves this interview he says that he has only one plan after he comes out of prison—"bigger and better crimes." The tendency to emphasize the shameless attitude toward crime is obvious—it is as if he said: "If I am guilty at all, then it is only of crime, which I don't consider as bad, but not of masturbation"—the masturbation being closely related to the unconscious oral parasitic exploitation of the mother. Later in this same connection he reveals his dependent attitude toward his older sister, who helped him in the past, but consciously to accept help from women is connected with great conflict. One day he feels very irritable. His mother had visited him in the prison, and an aunt also came and brought him fruit. He thinks that makes him irritable. He has to be grateful.

A strong inner conflict arises in him as he becomes conscious of the strong passive dependent tendency and the self-deceiving way in which he wants to get rid of the shame because of his dependence by assuming an external appearance of chivalry, toughness, and aggressiveness.

The first dream in which he tried to kill his "crooked self," as he calls it, is followed later by a series of dreams in which the inner fight was represented by a fight between two individuals. The tendency to assume a passive attitude toward women explains a dream in which he sees a girl with a large penis. He attributed masculine qualities to women in order to be able to assume toward them the passive dependent attitude (sixteenth interview).

In the further course of the analysis dreams which contain veiled allusions to the wish to reform and to go straight occur from time to time, but consciously he does not wish to admit them yet, because going straight means for him to give in. In consciousness, as a rule, such dreams are paralleled by an emphasized criminal attitude and phantasies of raping the sister of the fellow who betrayed him to the police. He is always afraid of other people taking away his girl. He feared his brother in this respect, as is shown clearly in one of his dreams. (See dream of the three fellows who attacked his girl.) The idea of having intercourse with the sister of the man who betrayed him appears suddenly, seemingly without any connection, during the analysis. He can more easily express this wish toward somebody against whom he has justified reason for resentment. The next session after this confession he punishes himself in a dream in which he is put back in the prison to work after he has been released. The same night in another dream he gave his tobacco to a fellow-prisoner who is also being analyzed at the same time by the analyst. He also tries to relieve his guilt feelings for his rape phantasy by bitterly accusing the fellow who "squealed on" him and his brothers.

A period of depression follows now in which he does not eat, doubts the success of the analysis, and is full of self-accusations. At the same time he expresses a longing for his brother. He complains that the boarder forbade him to bring home his girls. The boarder hides behind his mother. He could kill him! He will not go home, but will go to live with his brother; but the brother brings home his girl friend to his lodgings and so they cannot talk together. "His damned girl is a nuisance." The passive feminine attachment to the brother comes nearer and nearer to consciousness.

At about this period in the analysis the patient's emotional relation to the analyst takes on more of the character of passive dependence. In one of his dreams he sees the psychoanalyst's picture. His feeling was that the analyst was gone, he no longer had any need for the analyst, because he could talk to his picture whenever he wanted to. This proved to be a compromise between the passive dependent attitude and its reverse. He wants the analytic hour, but the more he wants it, the more it hurts his pride. He has a deep longing for kindness and being loved on account of his hard childhood, being kicked from farm to farm. It was a wonderful feeling in the dream to talk to the picture—"and still I did not need you." He also understands now that he wants to steal because then he is obligated to no one. Stealing is a compromise similar to the one expressed in the dream: without work he can fulfill receptive and taking desires and still not be obligated to anyone. He does not receive, but he takes what he needs. He understands that he cannot accept help from his mother and sees that his criminality serves to make him appear "tough" and to hide the soft part of his nature. He cannot stand being helped by the brother, and still he wants to be helped. His loyalty springs from this attitude: if he is loyal to his brother and helps him in difficult situations he has the right to accept help in exchange.

In order to compensate for his strong passive receptive attitude toward the analyst at this period, the patient becomes rebellious in the prison. He refuses to obey the guards, compulsively argues with all the authorities in order to show his courage, but at the same time he expresses jealousy against the fellow-prisoner who is being analyzed also. He declares that he cannot accept help and never will; if he must learn to do that, he will never be cured by the analysis. He admits this feeling is based on hate and pride and therefore he cannot tolerate being treated well. As an example of this he tells of a paradoxical event in his life when he ran away from a farm where they treated him kindly. He ran away on the day before his birthday, when his foster-parents were preparing a party and presents for him. He went to his mother, as if to say: 'I prefer to be treated well and given presents by my mother and not by other people'; he rejects good treatment by running away.

That the gained analytic insight spoils the significance of his

criminality as a means of increasing his masculine vanity becomes clear in a dream in which his mirror (representing his
vanity) was broken. In the same dream he alluded to his vanity
in another way by picturing himself as a good-looking girl.
In the second part of this dream there was a big Christmas
dinner with chicken and ice cream in the kitchen of the jail.
After he gives up his vanity he can freely indulge his receptive
tendencies.

His wish to steal other men's wives is confessed more and
more directly; he confesses his interest in a friend's wife and
tells of relations with wives of several other men in the past.
Once when he was sixteen years old he had sexual relations
with a policeman's wife, thus "getting even with the police
force." He admits also that he is interested in his brother's
girl, not because the girl herself appeals to him sexually, but
out of a desire for prestige, to show that he is just as good as
his brother.

In this discussion he clearly describes two kinds of jealousy
which he always felt toward his brother. Even as a youngster
he envied him because the brother had adventures and girls,
but he was also envious of his brother's girls because they took
the brother away from him. He recognizes these two kinds of
feelings as the male and the female form of his jealousy.

The attitude of passive love changes now to aggressive feelings toward the analyst. In one dream he knocks down the
analyst's representative because he grabbed his finger and bent
back his fingernails. His fingernails symbolize his vanity,
because he takes great care of them and admits that his vanity
is centered in them.

In the following sessions his aggressive feelings toward the
analyst can be defined as envy. In the dream he steals a fountain-pen and writing-tablet which remind him of the analyst's
fountain-pen and writing-block which he uses during the

analytic hour. In the dream he drops the pen in his hurry and nervousness. His castrative attitude toward the analyst causes guilt feeling and he loses his booty, the pen. In this connection he remembers competing with his brother for the favor of a girl. The aggressive castrative tendency toward the analyst is a repetition of his feelings toward the brother.

In another dream, the mechanism of which parallels that of the fountain-pen dream, he is driving his brother's car to see his foster-mother. There is a big picnic, but he is not invited. He uses his brother's car to get to the mother, but he cannot enjoy the result. This dream also shows that behind his competition with the brother for the mother's favor there is not a masculine attitude but an infantile receptive wish to be fed by the mother. In this connection he remembers jealousy of the brother when the latter was taken by the father to the saloons; but his father took the patient also sometimes. He remembers once his father promised to take him to a saloon, but took the brother instead. After the father's death the mother took the father's position in the family, so the patient transferred back to the mother the receptive dependent attitude which he probably had begun to assume toward the father.

Another dream follows in which, riding in the subway, he is carrying some overcoats and bundles, but he dropped the bundles. In associating to the clothes he says that his brother is a "snappy dresser—looks like a millionaire." In the dream he lost the clothes for which he envies the brother.

Just at this period of the analysis when he began to show more signs of an aggressive attitude toward the analyst he was ill with the grippe for two weeks. During his sickness he had on consecutive nights two dreams in which he was going to be executed. During the first period of his sickness he felt very depressed, but his spirits improved as soon as his physical condition took a turn for the worse. The physical suffering relieved his sense of guilt and made the depression, the psychological form of torturing himself, unnecessary.

After the sickness he feels better. He has decided that he will not steal, at least as long as his probation lasts.

He has a dream in which he was hitting somebody who was attacking him with a hammer, but his blows were ineffective because the attacker did not feel them. The patient ran after him and got the hammer away from him. There were other persons, too, whom Richard then hit with the hammer. There was also a big elephant that he hit on the head with the same hammer. When asked what he thinks about the elephant, he says that it is probably his conscience, of which he cannot get rid. This inner conflict of whether to give up criminality or not is even more clearly expressed in the next section of the hour, in which he narrates the following dream:

He came to a clearing in the woods. There was a schoolhouse there and two or three other houses. He had a rifle and tried to shoot a fox, but the fox was too quick and he couldn't hit it. Then, suddenly, he heard a noise—steps on the ground. There were sheep coming up the road, stampeding. Someone shouted: "The Indians are coming." Then a fellow came running, an arrow stuck in his back. He tried to stop him and ask him about it, but he was in such a hurry that he could not talk to him. He was a "rat" who squealed. It became dark and the Indians were approaching. He tried to shoot one of the Indians, but he failed. Then he tried to "bean" him with the rifle. But he failed again, and the Indian grabbed him from behind and squeezed him. He was afraid that he would be scalped. At this moment, someone came out of the schoolhouse to help him and stuck a knife in the Indian's back. He felt the Indian drop.

The clearing in the woods and the few houses remind him

of places he saw in the country. The schoolhouse was the same kind he went to when he was a "kid." He returns to the scenes of his childhood in the dreams.

His associations to the fox are that it is hard to shoot, very smart. The fox expresses smartness—his smartness—his wish to master something, to be better than someone else. The analyst points out that it might be the criminal part of his personality, because that is the part he always connected with smartness, skill, and quickness.

To the sheep he associates destruction of property, disregard of others, stampeding down everything which belongs to others—"I don't give a damn if I steal!" Here the analyst explains that this is a pictorial representation of the same things as the fox, except that it expresses another quality of his criminal self—the ruthless, inconsiderate part of it.

In associating to the Indian the patient says: "Probably that means the same, but I can only overcome it with someone's help. You are the helper, coming out of the schoolhouse. That means knowledge. With a greater knowledge of myself I defeat the Indian." His associations to the squealing "rat" are: "A coward—that is F." (a fellow-prisoner who started an analysis, but did not wish to continue it). "He gave up the struggle and ran away from the cure."

The analyst agrees with this interpretation and adds: "Now the dream is clear. It represents your fight with your criminal tendencies. But it is interesting to compare the two dreams which you told me today. In one you fight with your conscience, and in the other you fight with the criminal part of your personality. It seems that you are not yet decided upon which part you should accept."

To this the patient replies: "I am really not decided, but I won't steal while I am on probation, and later I will steal only for gain, and not for fun. I don't want to get into the prison at M. But I have never been afraid of being caught, and it would be funny if now, suddenly, I should become afraid of it. I think the reason is that I don't want to accept your point of view and therefore I give another motive for my decision not to steal, and I say I won't steal because I don't want to be imprisoned, but not because I accept your point of view."

Analyst: "Yes, but what about this rational stealing?"

Patient: "Because going straight does not pay."

Analyst: "That is something which you don't yet know. Maybe you can be successful otherwise."

He admits that that is possible and that he is saying all this in order not to give in.

The analyst explains to him that in the dream there is another motive very clearly expressed, and that is his passive and female wishes to be overpowered. He understands that the Indian represents one part of himself and in the dream the Indian is stabbed from behind by the analyst. That shows that the patient has a peculiar passive wish to be overpowered, and just because this tendency is so strong, he never would give in to anything; that is why he is so sensitive to being influenced and being thought of as being helped. He has a very strong but inwardly rejected tendency to be passive, and that makes it so difficult for him to accept anything which reminds him of being passive. The analyst reminds him that they have already discovered why he wants to appear as a "tough" independent fellow when in reality he has a great longing to be helped; and that once the patient alluded to the possibility that he might have a strong longing to be helped and cared for because he felt that from early youth he was "kicked around." Probably this great passive longing is based upon the fact that as a child he did not get any gratification of the passive dependent tendencies of the child. These tendencies are still very strong within him and therefore he is ashamed of them and wants to repress them.

The patient admits that all that the analyst says he himself feels, now more clearly than ever.

The conflict about his criminality becomes the center of the next period of the analysis. He is afraid to tell his brother that he is going straight. He depends too much on his brother. Their stealing and criminality spite the world, however, and make him exert himself against the world, and this is a compensation for his dependence. Also, his helping his brother helps him to overcome his conflict. The root of everything is his feeling inferior toward his brother. He never will be able to overcome that. If he could not "lick a guy," his brother always helped him. His dependence reaches far back to his childhood. Once he tried to get away from his brother, but he could not. He thinks of giving up the analysis; he does not want to disappoint the analyst, but he will probably go back to crime; his fellow-prisoners make fun of him on account of his analysis. An Italian gangster knocked him out two weeks ago in an argument; the patient will take revenge—that is his duty—and his brother will help him. He wishes the analysis were over. He does not think it will do him any good.

He had another dream in which his sexual intercourse was interrupted. The woman in the dream was his friend's wife. The patient tells the dream in fragments, with signs of great resistance. He had another dream in which he had successful intercourse with his girl friend. In this dream at first the boarder opened the door as if by mistake and after a while his mother came in. The patient understands that the dream is a manifestation of spite toward the boarder and the mother. He admits irritatedly that he would like to have his mother for himself alone. On this occasion, for the first time, the

Œpidus situation is discussed with the patient, who has very few memories about his father.

In the following session he tells a dream which contains a very much veiled allusion to hostilities against his father. In the same hour he recalls an episode when his brother jokingly kissed the patient's girl and he felt great jealousy.

As a reaction to his becoming more and more conscious of his jealousy of the brother and mother, the resistance against the analysis increases. In one dream he represents the analysis as a poisonous gas against which he had to protect himself by stuffing rags into all the cracks around the door, an interesting representation of his resistance. But in another dream his brother's girl came to the jail to see him. During the analysis of this dream he becomes very irritated and belligerent. The analyst suggests that it is a wish-fulfilling dream—he wants his brother's girl to come to see him in the jail. The patient refuses this interpretation, saying he does not like her—"She talks your ear off. I don't like her chattering." Then his unconscious attitude betrays itself in a very dramatic way. He says he is always afraid when she comes that she will tell him bad news, that his brother is in jail.

Analyst: "I think this fear may be a reaction to your wish that it should happen."

Patient (very angry): "Don't be silly!" (This answer is entirely different from his former politeness.)

The analyst reminds the patient that he once confessed to him the flash of malicious pleasure he felt when he heard that his brother was "pinched." The patient then unwillingly admits that he is perfectly aware of his jealousy toward his brother, but not that he wants his girl. Finally, however, he agrees that he might be interested in his girl as a "common ground" for their "competition."

As a reaction, in the following interview, he is again full

of plans for further criminal activities and for assuming again the passive, receptive attitude toward his brother. He likes loafing, and his brother always gave him money. Memories of his childhood follow: he used to beat up all the children in the neighborhood with his brother's help. Ever since he can remember he has been stealing with his brother. He reveals amazing details of minor and major thieving in his childhood in this session. He also remembers running away from home when he was three years old.

One of his criminal plans for the future is to rob the library of a certain wealthy woman. He wants to help his mother and pay his brother's debts. At the same time he expresses much hostility against the guards of the prison, with phantasies of beating one of them to death. In these sessions he finds great pleasure in stubbornly adhering to his criminality. He admits that his ostentatious emphasis upon criminality during the analytic session means a protest against the passive dependence on the analyst.

He admits that he missed the sessions on days when he had no analysis, but he fights against this feeling and does not want to admit it to himself. In analyzing his dependent love for the analyst, which he wants to hide by spiteful talking about his criminal plans, we are able to understand his reaction as a repetition of his attitude toward his mother. Although consciously he maintains that the only thing which withholds him from criminality is his regard for his mother, we discover that unconsciously just the opposite is true. One important unconscious motive for his criminal behavior is spiting the mother as if he would say to the mother: "If you don't care for me and you have this boarder, then you will see what I will do; I won't become an honest man."

As a reaction to this insight he has the phantasy of donating money to the Judge Baker Guidance Center after succeeding in a big robbery. A sexual dream of an older, beautiful woman follows. Then another wet dream follows in which he fools the teacher and has sexual intercourse with a schoolgirl who is connected in his associations with the girl of one of his friends and with whom he once had a flirtation.

Other childhood memories emerge. When he was four years old, a child hit him on his head with a rock, and his mother dressed the wound.

In the following period of the analysis there is an interesting interplay of aggression against the psychoanalyst and consequent fear leading to a passive dependence, which, in turn, drives him again to rebellion and to the well-known overcompensatory mechanisms. So, for example, after the dream in which he slept with his friend's girl and fooled the teacher he has a dream in which he was captured by savages who were Negroes in Africa. They took all his clothes away and burned him, but first their chief, a man of large physique with hairy arms and chest, put oil on the patient, and this oil saved him from being burned. They burned all the hair off his body, the hair under his arms and his pubic hair. They did not want to burn him entirely—only to remove the hair from his body.

In associating to the hairy chief he remembers that his father had a heavy beard. Associating to the oil and burning the hair he connects it with the analysis. He says: "You are stripping me of all my masculine ideas—my stealing and my criminality. You are making me like a woman. The analysis makes me like a woman. Women have no hair on their bodies."

In direct connection then he suddenly confesses a phantasy of robbing the instrument-cabinet in the analytic room. Then a childhood memory of fighting other boys follows. In the following session he has a rather complicated dream of which only the main elements need be mentioned here. Two professors (the two authors of this book) are working for him. In this dream he turns the situation around so that he is the commander and the two psychoanalysts are working for him. The main point in the dream was that all parts of a radio must be placed behind a panel. He and another fellow went out with two ladies while the professors had to work, and he said that he would come back to see how the work was done. When he came back there was one condenser left outside. To this condenser he brought the following associations: "A variable condenser, to tune in to the different stations—to get different stations—to find different things in my personality. It was a bare room without walls or wall-paper—only boards—a typical radio station or repair-shop. The condenser was on the top of the panel. The condenser is the chief thing. Without that you cannot get any music—a method of getting information out of me. It is in the middle, the central part—my "belly-button" is in the middle. A technical way of getting information—a loop-hole—a key to the works behind it—the only loop-hole through which one can get information about how to run this radio."

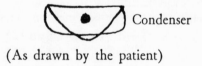 Condenser

(As drawn by the patient)

It is rather obvious from his associations that this condenser as a way to penetrate into his personality is a female symbol (belly-button, navel) and is a pictorial representation of his passive receptive rapport with the analyst. Everything must be brought behind the panel but the condenser is left outside. We see again the compromise: at the beginning of the dream he protests against his feminine attitude toward the analyst (the professors are working for him and under his directions), and yet at the end of the dream the symbol of his receptive attitude toward the analyst is "left outside the panel." It is interesting that he represents this passive (transference) attitude with an essential part of the radio, the part which makes the radio talk. His positive attachment to the analyst makes him talk and makes him reveal himself.

It is also most interesting that in the dream he makes the professors work; he assumes the superior role, going out with a girl while the professors have to work for him, and yet at the end the symbol of his feminine attachment remains outside the bulwark of repressions which the analysts have to build up in the dream, a situation just the opposite of the real situation, in which the analyst is working to eliminate repression.

As he becomes more and more conscious of his ambivalent attitude toward the analyst his hostility toward the brother comes openly to the surface. He dreams that his brother was shot by gangsters, and in a second dream he destroyed, through carelessness, the suit which his brother gave him. The dreams express hostility against the brother and then self-punishment.

At this period of the analysis he begins to see more and more clearly that his criminality is also a spite reaction against his mother. If his mother keeps after him, and "If she gets in my ears all the time," then he has no other choice but to go to work. With this he says that if the mother would pay more attention to him, maybe he would renounce his criminality. He adds laughingly: "I will tease my mother by telling her that she is responsible for her sons' being criminals." He thinks that this motive of spite was even more important with his brother than with himself.

As soon as he begins to see the spite reaction toward his mother he acts it out more violently in analysis. The interviews are again full of spiteful and cynical emphasis of his criminality and meanness. He has heard his girl got married. He hopes it is true, because then it will be more fun to be with her. "Her husband is there for the children."

He will stop analysis when he gets out of prison, he doesn't want to go straight. The analyst's theory is correct, but still it doesn't help him. "It is like killing a guy with a sponge."

Then he dreams that another doctor comes to see him instead of the analyst, and in the dream he argues with this doctor, whom he does not like. The dream means that he would like to express his hostile feelings toward the analyst even more directly, but he cannot, because he likes him. After this dream he again declares that he will go on stealing.

The following dream, which he tells during the same interview, shows with full clarity all his stubbornness, spite, and parasitic infantile attitude toward his mother. He was walking in a well-lighted corridor. A woman was sitting on the floor, the wife of his friend. There was a big pan on the floor, and some apple pies in it cut up in pieces. He thought there were seven pints of liquor round the corner, and that he would get them, drink, and afterwards have sexual intercourse with the woman. He went round the corner of the corridor, then turned round another corner, but the pints were not there. So he went to a bunch of "buggies" (Negroes) and started to give them a speech. He told them that in the village people were starving, in need of food and clothes, and that everybody should give something. The idea was that if he could collect two dollars he could buy some "booze." Everybody gave money. He went on talking to get some more. Then the woman came with the pies and passed around refreshments. He went on talking to get more money.

His associations to the corridor are that it was nice, clean, well-lighted, and laid out like straight corridors in a modern building. His associations to the woman are that she is another man's wife, she is dumb, she cannot talk good English, she is small.

Here the analyst asks who else is small. The patient replies that X.Y. (his best friend) is small and that his wife is small also. He speaks of another friend's wife who is small. He goes on to say that his father was a big man, and his mother is of medium height. The analyst asks who talks bad English.

"I talk bad English, the Wops and . . . I don't know."

Analyst: "I also am a foreigner. Maybe you allude to me."

Patient: "But you pronounce words well."

His associations to the pan containing the apple pies: "This is a luxury here in the jail. A good pie is a luxury in America. In the country you can get good ones. Mrs. A. [a foster-mother of his] made good apple pie and so did Mrs. B. [another foster-mother], Mrs. C.," etc. (He mentions all his foster-mothers.) "My mother used to give us good apple pie, but she bought it and warmed it up."

Associations to the seven pints: "Odd number; the number of pockets in my clothes; you can get drunk on seven pints."

Associations to the "bunch" of Negroes: "Ignorant people. You can swindle them."

Analyst: "Whom do you want to swindle?"

Patient: "Maybe I want to fool you. It is a dream in which I defy everybody. I do what I want just to be nasty."

Analyst: "And all that to have intercourse with this woman?"

Patient: "I didn't, though."

Here the patient tries to change the subject by telling another dream.

Analyst: "To go back to the other dream, I think it is a rather egotistic dream. You utilize this woman to get money. This woman with the pies is the symbol of the feeding woman, and that can't be anybody else but your mother."

The patient says that once a woman who weighed 185 pounds wanted to support him and have him live with her, but he did not like her.

Analyst: "In this dream there is eating, drinking, cheating, and sexual intercourse. Your infantile and criminal self manifests itself rather openly."

Patient: "I think it is just a protest against the analysis."

Analyst: "That is certain, but it is not against the analysis in general, but against what the analysis forces you to see, especially that you are so much attached to your mother, and that your behavior is a protest against her. But it also becomes clearer and clearer that this attachment is a rather infantile, receptive feeling, and in stealing you gratify this receptive, 'grabbing' attitude. If your mother does not satisfy your receptive tendencies, then you steal and drink."

After his criminal self is so fully unmasked he goes into an extreme of spite in which he identifies himself fully with his brother. In one of his dreams he was stealing with his brother, was chased by the police, and escaped. Then he tried to pick out his suit from his brother's closet and could not distinguish his clothes from his brother's.

He will go on stealing, but he will not be caught any more. He will have a big drunk with his friend when he gets out. He does not want to get married or have children or get more education when he gets out. As long as his brother steals he will steal. In this connection he remembers his wish to disobey his mother in his childhood and the wish to antagonize her by stealing dimes. If he cannot do what he wants at home on account of the boarder, he will not go home. His mother is responsible for the boarder's being still at home. He wants to make enough money to live away from home and give money to his mother.

A dream illustrative of the psychology of prisoners occurs in this period of the analysis. In this dream he overcomes the limitations of the prison life through a magic machine by which he can summon any person he wants to come to his room. A beautiful woman appeared on the bed in his room, but the dream ended before he had intercourse. Then a dream similar to one he had already had twice before occurs in which the boarder and his mother interfered with his intercourse with his girl. In this dream, unlike others, he could not finish the intercourse. This dream means that he does not want to become independent and have a successful sexual relation with a woman because he is too much attached to his mother. In his mind the two alternatives begin to crystallize: the one side is going straight and marriage; the other side is criminality and continuing the infantile attachment to the mother.

After gaining this insight the patient's attitude changes. For the first time he declares that he will become independent of his mother and that he does not care what she does, but still when he speaks of the boarder he becomes very emotional. He wants to continue the analysis after he gets out of prison. He begins to speak of a very gifted friend who could earn his living easily and yet is a criminal. He calls this case "pathological."

But this good attitude does not last long, and the deepest regression to the early receptive attachment to the mother thus far observed during the analysis follows as a reaction. In this period he is very much interested in eating. In one dream he stole cakes. In reality he steals onions and sugar from the prison kitchen. He dreams of cows and insists upon receiving milk in the prison.

He speaks of one jail where the prisoners live almost like guests in a hotel, ordering their meals, etc. Next time he will go there. He speaks of prisoners who commit some crime in order to have board and a place to sleep.

After two dreams in which he expresses the paradoxical regret that he will soon be released from the prison, one cannot help seeing that the prison life has some appeal to him, and the prison, in the depths of his unconscious, is for him a substitute for the feeding mother. This is clearly shown in the following dream:

He robbed a grain elevator with another fellow. It was in France. He was caught and brought before the court. "They sentenced me for life. We were studying in the jail. I had supper. There were numbers on the chairs where we sat. I was going to my cell after supper. The guards in this jail were women. I was going through a room which was like a room in a house and not in a jail and I asked a woman where my room was. I asked her very politely, saying: 'Pardon, madame.' She smiled at me and I smiled at her and she told me to come to her office. I went into another room up a flight of stairs and asked a prisoner where this woman's office was. The prisoner asked: 'You mean the motherly-looking woman?' I said: 'Yes.' He said it was next to the principal's office. I saw someone come out of the principal's office and walk by and go down to the corridor."

The patient's associations to the grain elevator were: "A senseless thing to rob. A surplus of food. Senseless to rob it, you can't steal it."

Analyst: "It evidently means something else. What do you think of in connection with a grain elevator?"

Patient: "Milk—Mr. F.—and [laughingly] you know."

Analyst: "I don't know what you are thinking of now."

Patient: "Mother. All the time at the back of my mind was mother."

Analyst: "Here you see clearly that your stealing goes back to some wish in connection with your mother. It is she who supplies food and you represent her in the dream as a grain elevator. There is the wish to be fed, loved, taken care of by your mother, and after this wish was thwarted, you did not give it up, but this wish changed into stealing. What you don't get you steal."

Patient: "You asked me the other day whether I enjoyed giving stolen money to my mother. I don't. Once mother asked me for fifty dollars. I had twenty-seven dollars, but I did not like to give it to her. I preferred to spend it for booze." Once he stole ninety pairs of silk stockings. He gave them away to girls, but not to his mother.

His associations to the French prison were: "A severe joint. They send people to Devil's Island. Supposed to be a tough spot. It also suggests learning—the French language. The French also makes me think of you. You are a foreigner. My mother is not French, but of French extraction."

Analyst: "That is a rather clever dream. You are sentenced in the dream to a French prison, an obvious reference to your mother, where the guards are women and you go to the office of a motherly-looking guard."

Patient: "Yes, it was a nice prison, and I spoke very respectfully to the woman, but I can't say that of my speaking to my mother. I am not as respectful as a son should be."

Analyst: "That is on account of the irritation you feel permanently toward your mother, and the reason for this irritation we already know well. But now, I think, even more than before, the prison is somehow associated in your unconscious with your mother. It is a place where you are taken care of and have no worries and no responsibilities."

Patient: "But in the dream it was a nice home, and only the name was prison."

Analyst: "If a jail were a nice home, that would be something perfect for you. You would be entirely satisfied, I assume, to be taken care of and have no responsibilities. That would re-establish this infantile wish to be fed and taken care of and be entirely passive."

Patient (laughs): "I would not miss taking advantage of getting into such a jail."

Analyst: "It is rather interesting that deep down the jail has some attraction for you, although consciously you don't like it at all, but this infantile longing for the mother is somehow satisfied in the prison, inasmuch as you don't have to care for yourself. That is already the third dream which shows your paradoxical regret that you will soon be released."

Another dream, in which he expresses the wish to stay in the jail and the fear of being released, is the following:

He dreamed he was in prison again, this time in M. for three months. He was with a famous thief. They sat down to supper. It was a pretty good supper. Afterwards they went to their cells. They were locked. They went into the next cell. There were no bars on the windows. They could see a fence quite near. One could easily jump over it. He saw a machine-gun on the fence at the corner of the house and therefore they did not try to escape, but, anyhow, he had no desire to leave. After they slept, they got up and had a very good breakfast.

But after this period of deep regression, which meant the abandoning of all aggressive masculine wishes, the giving up of all struggle in life and accepting the peace and security of the prison, a new reaction follows. He again expresses ambitions and aggressions in his dreams. He comes to analysis during these sessions with a big kitchen knife in his pocket; he had stolen it in the prison.

His spite reaction shows itself in a new light. In one dream he has sexual intercourse with a woman while schoolchildren are looking out of a window and observing. It was a wet dream. The dream, as was revealed by his associations, expresses the attitude that even if he doesn't go to school any more and had to leave school, he makes the schoolchildren see him having sexual intercourse. He is envious of the schoolchildren for their ability to become better educated, and he makes the schoolchildren envious, in turn, of his sexual freedom.

Then a dream follows in which the fact that his stealing is a substitute for his infantile attachment to his mother becomes entirely clear. He stole in an office building, which in the dream was connected with his mother. Then he was chased by a big man.

His aggressions against the analyst, the brother, and the boarder come to the surface more violently than ever before, with consequent fear and guilt and self-destructive tendencies. In one dream he hit himself so violently on the chin that he actually broke a tooth. Associating to this dream, he tells of a fight which he had the preceding day with one of his fellow-prisoners. Afterwards his brother came to the prison and had an argument with this fellow who had attacked the patient. He is very much ashamed to confess that his brother played his protector. He expresses again violent hostility to the brother.

In one other dream at this period he had a knife fight with a fellow in the dark. He had two knives, but the other man ripped him up and down his back. In analyzing this dream he becomes exceedingly irritated. When the analyst asks him who he thinks the man might be with whom he fought in the dream, pointing out that it must be someone against whom he has strong aggressions, but at the same time guilt feelings, because at the end of the dream the patient was hurt, he shouts: "That is not your business. Why do you want to know that? It is X.! I am not going to tell you." But by the end of the interview he accepts the interpretation that it is the analyst whom he attacked in his dream with a knife, which he actually carried in his pocket to every analytic session for about a week.

Soon after this dramatic session the dream of being interrupted during sexual intercourse with his girl friend at home is repeated, but it seems certainly to show a feature of progress. He dreamed that the girl was in his room at home. He tried sexual intercourse, but was repeatedly interrupted by his mother's knocking at the door. He became angry and put on his clothes to go away and find another room away from home; when they passed the boarder's room the door opened and he saw his brother and the boarder in there. His brother handed him some money. He walked out on the street and said he would find a room. The girl said they could find a place anywhere. He asked her whether she was working and she said no.

Patient: "A dream similar to the one I had before."

Analyst: "Yes, but there are rather great differences. We understand the beginning of it, that your mother is interfering with your sexual life and that you decide to go away, but in this dream you go away, which expresses your wish for independence, stimulated now through the analysis, especially the last session. What does it mean that the boarder and your brother are together in the same place?"

Patient: "That expresses that I have a similar feeling toward both of them."

Analyst: "But consciously you like your brother and hate the boarder."

Patient: "Both are keeping me down. Both are competitors. But in the dream my brother helps me. That expresses the fact that he is not the cause of my feeling that way toward him. He does not interfere with my life. He really helps me."

Analyst: "Yes, I think you understand that quite well."

Patient: "And my asking the girl whether she was working expresses the idea that now I have to support her."

Now the analyst explains to him the significance of the

dream. It is an effort to become independent and to assume responsibility, to give up the spiteful claims toward the mother and the parasitic tendencies which are also expressed in the kind of life he is living by stealing.

We see that he has a remarkable insight into the meaning of his dream, followed during the same interview by a similarly clear understanding of one of his chief motives for stealing. He admits the irrational element in it. He stole automobiles and after riding in them he brought them back. Once he stole a police car standing in front of a police station. Then he used this car for stealing. He broke into a cigar-store and took hundreds of cigars and cigarettes in boxes and then later he threw away the greater part of the cigars which he stole. Once he broke into a bakery and took three hundred pennies and then dropped them on the street one after another. Another time he took a slot-machine from the door of a toilet because it would not work. He adds: "It was mere revenge." He has no doubt that a great part of his stealing was done out of irrational emotional urges as a revenge for all the sterility of his life, for all the deprivations. He stole for the sake of stealing. This revengeful attitude did not always manifest itself in stealing. Once he cut the rope on which clothes were hanging before the front of a store and made all the clothes fall down, merely out of malicious motives. He would steal five cents' worth of candy—a kind which he does not like and did not eat—at a time when he had twenty-five dollars in his pocket.

At the beginning of this hour he drops out of his pocket a number of five- and ten-cent pieces, which then lie on the floor and which he does not want to pick up before the hour is finished. He leaves the interview in very good mood, apparently relieved after confessing all these (anal sadistic) malicious tendencies to do harm for its own sake.

The last four days in the prison he expresses alternately hope, discouragement, dread, and regret at leaving the prison. In one dream he gets back his license—driving is his favorite occupation. In the same interview, however, he expresses the opinion that everybody is dishonest, and speaks of corruption and graft in different jobs he has held. Speaking of leaving the prison he says: "Farewell to the good old shadow soup," alluding to the thin soup he gets in the prison.

On the last day of his imprisonment he expresses in a dream his accusation against his brother very clearly—that his brother is responsible for his being in prison—but, as usual, at the same time his guilt feelings toward the brother manifest themselves in the plan to smuggle one of his knives to his brother, who is in another prison at this time.

His reaction to freedom is at first quite paradoxical. He feels tired, cannot sleep, and is depressed; his dreams constantly express his longing to go back to the jail. In the first two months after his release from the jail he has seven dreams in which he clearly expresses his longing to be back in the jail. In the very first interview after he was free he tells of two dreams in which he was back in jail. In the first dream he was in jail waiting for the supper bell. In the second he was also in jail arguing with someone.

During the first few weeks of his freedom he indulges in some petty stealing. He steals a few magazines and six pairs of socks which he does not need. Another time he robs the cash register of a "hot-dog stand" of three dollars which he does not need, and gives half of it to a friend. Another time he robs an office of a somewhat larger sum. Immediately after this, on the following night, he has a dream that the police entered his house and took him to a police station—not the one to which he properly should go, but to one in which his brother once, when caught, impersonated him in order to get away.

The wish to steal now comes suddenly; he does not plan it

as before. In these first days of his freedom his former girl friend is preparing to be married. He is disappointed and thinks that is one reason why he steals.

A most depressing search for a job follows. He goes in and out of different employment agencies, spending the whole morning in futile waiting. The wish to go straight is visibly strengthening, but there is still evidence of great conflict. It is most instructive to observe how he represses the wish to go straight because it increases his conflict with his brother—both the guilt and the inferiority feelings. Thus we can observe the paradoxical psychological configuration that in his dreams the conflict between the wish to go straight and to remain criminal is unconsciously expressed. In one dream he was shooting at an animal, but the bullets did not hurt it. He interprets it himself as meaning that he cannot kill his criminal personality. In the same dream he told a girl that he was an interior decorator, which he himself explains by saying that he is an interior decorator because he decorates himself and gives himself the façade of freshness, boldness, and toughness as a reaction to his feeling of weakness.

Now in freedom he gives vent to his aggressive tendencies both in dreams and in reality. He dreams that his brother had a black eye, but associates to it immediately that the night before, he had a fight in a speakeasy which he enjoyed very much, and broke a beer-bottle on the head of another fellow. The situation at home is presented very vividly in his associations. Everyone is "broke" in the family; most of his friends and his brothers, both free again now, are engaged in criminal activity every day; they come and go, bringing home stolen articles; there is always excitement about the police; the mother leaves in the early morning for her job and returns in the late evening, only to go out again to a show with the boarder, while the patient has to dry the dishes. He has a desire to break a beer-bottle over the boarder's head. He cannot overcome his jealousy. It is only natural that in this environment he develops a malicious pleasure in seeing other people's misery, so that he will feel that he is not the only sufferer.

Dreams of a new type begin to appear which express the shy but gradually strengthening wish to go straight. He repeatedly dreams of a friend, Y., who works hard, goes to night school, and makes every effort to make progress in life. The following dream shows this attitude very convincingly:

He dreamed that he was in Maine with Y. They tried to "bum" their way home. There was "another guy" with them who jumped onto a freight train. A little car came along the road. It looked like a little cart. He stopped it and asked the driver to take them to Boston. They took a seat. He was steering and Y. pushed it with his feet, as children do their carts. He steered in a zigzag manner. Y. said: "You can do better than that." Then he ran it with a kind of lever like those of the handcars on the railroad track. They had to go up a big hill. It was hard work, but finally they reached the top.

His associations to Maine were that he used to live there years ago when he was thirteen. He went to school there and worked. It was "pretty cold there, sometimes twenty below zero." He did not like it there. He has driven there since with a fellow and two girls. They took their own booze. He went with Y. and his wife, arrived at eleven o'clock at night, and immediately drove back, but had flat tires and did not get back to Boston until eleven o'clock the next night. He tells of a famous road to Maine, the Newburyport Turnpike, an old road which has now been made over into a cement road, wide enough for four cars. There is a big hill on it.

Analyst: "Maybe you dream of Maine because it means to you the continuation of working, going straight, continuing where you stopped. The difficulties in driving the car mean, perhaps, your attitude toward the analysis now, which you continue partially under the influence of Y.'s example, but also on your own initiative. Reaching the top of the hill expresses your wish that it should succeed."

Patient: "Maybe so. I have no better explanation."

Analyst: "Was Maine a turning-point in your life?"

Patient: "Yes. There I took two grades at once, seventh and eighth, and graduated from a grammar school. I worked there as janitor of the school, but it was tough to go into the school to build a fire in the morning when it was twenty below zero. I was the oldest in the school. It was a small school, all in one room."

If anything went wrong in the schoolroom the teacher blamed him. He was the ringleader. He goes on to tell of different tricks they played in order not to have the school sessions. For example, they made smoke come into the schoolroom. Once in the summertime he was sent to a home near the ocean and went to school there. There were a couple of "guys" whom he couldn't lick or scare. He could not understand that in the beginning. He would not fight with them, but they would not fight with him either. Before that at home he and his brother licked everybody in the class, and also in the school that he went to later. He always had the feeling that if he could fight with these two he could lick them. They were the ringleaders. When he came to the school, he picked them out to lick, but he could not—especially one of them. That was the first defeat he had. Formerly if he could not lick a guy he tried to out-smart him or bluff him, but he thought in this case he was licked anyway. (Silence.) Then he says that he came to Boston with his oldest brother. They met a couple of thieves; his brother wanted him to go with them, but he did not. "It is tough to be broke."

Analyst: "Are you broke now?"

The patient replies that he is not exactly broke, but he might just as well be; he has about eighty cents or a "buck," which he borrowed from his mother or brother.

In this dream it is obvious that the journey in the handcar on the railway expresses hard work; his friend who is his example for going straight exhorts him: "You can do better than that," when he is steering the car in a zigzag manner. In his dream he returns to the occasion when he suffered his first defeat in a fight and had shied away from work; however, in the dream he overcomes the difficulty.

But the hopeful attitude expressed in the foregoing dream and associations alternates with a generally apathetic, depressed attitude. He does not steal any more, a fact which he cannot understand. He thinks the habit is definitely broken in him, but at the same time he is always ailing, has headaches and no appetite, cannot sleep at night, and stays in bed until noon. In one of his dreams he was sentenced to two years in prison, escaped, and then, however, was taken back again.

His attitude toward the analyst corresponds to his ambivalent attitude regarding criminality and respectability. In one dream he expresses the ambivalence toward the analyst in a very simple and direct way. He met a philosopher who was preaching. Later this philosopher was dead, but still later he was alive and the patient told him he was sorry he (the philosopher) was dead. The patient interprets the dream as the wish that the analyst should be dead, because he wants to go back to stealing. In the same night he also dreams that he was breaking the law and was captured.

From this time on, however, his mood definitely changes. He feels more hopeful and more decided to go straight. He goes into a store and buys something without having a desire to steal, a thing which has never happened since he can remember. He thinks the impulse to steal is gone.

His last ambivalent dream regarding working or stealing shows an interesting compromise: In the dream he was talking to his mother in the night. Y. came along with two "other guys," James and William. Y. had some beer with him. He did not want his mother to see the beer, but she saw it and laughed and offered to put it on ice. Y. gave her two bottles to put on ice, but he had one more bottle left, and after his mother went out with the two bottles, Y. gave the patient a drink. It was good, but there was a lot of yeast on the bottom. He gave some to the others. Y. got a lot of yeast in his mouth. The other two started to paint the eaves of the house with white paint. They dropped some. He does not know whether it got on his clothes or not.

His associations to James and William are: "Both these guys have worked all their lives. They are working stiffs. They carry pails, which signify that they work. Y. is more of a crook, but he works because he is married."

His associations to beer are that his mother always "squawked" when he drank, and then he made beer so that his mother should not "beef" so much.

Analyst: "What do you associate with your mother's unexpected acceptance of the drinking party?"

Patient: "I have no idea."

He continues with his associations to the yeast: "I don't like yeast. It is not good for you, like mud is not good. . . . It was home-made beer."

He associates to painting: working.

Analyst: "And the paint dropping on you?"

Patient: "That means to be colored by the same brand, spotted with the same brush; to belong to the same group."

In this dream he gets infected by the working spirit of his three working friends, James, William, and Y. Unquestionably it was not easy to pick out three honest friends in his criminal environment, and therefore it is especially significant that in his dream he manages to pick out these three "regular guys." The compromise consists, however, in the fact that his mother accepted the drinking party and even helped them. But at the same time his friends got the yeast of the beer in their mouths. In the dream he says: 'If I could have my mother help me and indulge me in my drinking, then I wouldn't mind becoming like James, William, and Y. and working.'

In the previous interview he had told a dream of again being captured by the police, but in the last interview the dream of the night before expresses again the wish to go straight:

He dreamed a "guy" was in a home. The fellow went out of the room and another just like him came in. The latter sat down in the same place which the first fellow had left. The fellow who went out was a good one and the fellow who came in was bad. Therefore, he should not have occupied the position which the good fellow left. The good fellow came back and ordered the bad one to get out. The bad one did not want to leave. A stout fellow came along then and the two—the good one and the stout one—grabbed the bad fellow and tore his heart out and killed him.

The patient said, "This does not need explanation, but it is funny."

Recently he had read a story called *The Duel*. A French officer in the secret service was supposed to impersonate a German spy and kill him while he slept, but the German officer who woke up and offered to tell the German secrets to the French officer. The French officer did not accept this proposal, however, and they had a duel, in which the French officer was killed. The German spy took his place, did his work, and continued his life. This story might have influenced his dream.

Patient: "But I used this story for my own purpose."

Analyst: "To express your own conflict, you mean?"

Patient: "Yes."

Analyst: "You and I tear out the heart of your bad half?"

Patient: "Yes, that is it."

Analyst: "The question is whether we have really already done it or whether it is a wish that it should be so."

Patient: "That remains to be seen, doesn't it?"

(End of Analysis)

### EPILOGUE

Two weeks after the last session Richard was again put in prison. The police became suspicious of his brother, made a search of the house, and found stolen money which belonged to his brother. The patient was at home and declared that the money belonged to him, because he thought that he could certainly prove that he was innocent. On the day on which the brother committed the crime for which the house was searched, Richard was sick in bed all day, having a broken jaw which he suffered during a street fight with a taxicab-driver. Therefore he thought that he could help his brother by making the false confession. He assured the analyst that he was quite innocent, and there is no reason to doubt him, as he had previously confessed to the analyst innumerable details of criminal acts of which he was guilty. He also fully realized that the analyst had no connection whatsoever with the police and was treating him only as a patient.

The day after his arrest the analyst saw him again in the prison and he said that his treatment had helped him. He said he saw how many people do things and then invent reasons for doing them which are very different from their real reasons. He also understood very well how people enjoy being in jail without admitting it; he pointed out that they had no worries and got fat; he was sure that they committed crimes in order to be imprisoned. He was hopeful that he would not be sentenced, because he was innocent and he had entirely decided to go to work; he wanted to become a moving-picture operator.

In a later interview when he was again out of prison he assured his analyst that he would be very happy to find a job on a farm and seemed to be very satisfied and hopeful.

A farm job was not readily forthcoming, and in the meantime there was a possibility offered to Richard of working in the country on one of the government projects. He did not care to accept this. A couple of months later information came that Richard and his brother Wilbur had gone to Ohio, and there, while camping out, one or both of them had engaged in the robbery of a jewelry-store. Because of Richard's state of mind after he finished his analysis, we have considerable doubt that Richard actively participated in this robbery. It is probable, however, that loyalty to his brother compelled him to give him at least some indirect help. As had happened so often in the past, Richard was the one who was arrested and Wilbur travelled back to Worcester. In a raid on the room of Wilbur's girl some of the jewelry taken was discovered. Richard was sentenced in Ohio. In the meantime Wilbur had been arrested for another offense and sentenced to a short term in Massachusetts. The eldest brother was already serving a longer sentence; so at the present writing all three of the brothers are serving time in prison.

SUMMARY

Richard's case is very revealing from many points of view. He is a criminal, externally similar to thousands and thousands of others. Since his eighth year he has been an inveterate thief, with no conscious conflict about stealing; he considered it as a means of living as well as a sign of his smartness, toughness, courage—briefly, as a virtue. The analytic investigation shows that his stealing is chiefly determined by irrational, emotional, and unconscious motives, and not so much by the rational motive of gain.

(1) His stealing is a reaction to a strong sense of inferiority, giving him a feeling of bravado and toughness. This sense of inferiority is itself a reaction to a strong dependent, receptive wish expressed in the attitude of obtaining things without working for them. In his receptive attitude the analyst could clearly differentiate between two sources: (a) a strong parasitic (oral receptive) attachment to the mother, and (b) an intense admiration and leaning on the stronger brother, which in the unconscious is built up on a distinctively passive female attitude toward the brother.

(2) His stealing also is a means of getting rid of guilt feelings which he has toward his brother. He helps his brother, exposes himself to danger for his sake, and even goes to jail for him, thereby relieving his guilt feelings.

(3) His stealing is also a spite reaction toward his mother, having the unconscious significance: "If you spend your interest and love on the brother and not on me, then I take revenge on you by disgracing you as a criminal, and at the same time if you don't give your love to me and don't support me as I want to be supported, then I will take by force and robbery what I need."

(4) Finally, deep down we see the paradoxical motive, expressed in numerous dreams, that criminality is also a means of getting into jail, where he can indulge in a carefree, vegetative existence, gratifying his infantile, parasitic wishes.

We can clearly distinguish these four unconscious motives behind his criminal acts:

1. Over-compensation for a sense of inferiority.
2. Attempt to relieve a sense of guilt.

3. Spite reaction toward his mother.

4. Direct gratification of dependent tendencies in a carefree existence in prison.

The analysis gave insight also into the psychogenesis of these tendencies and conflicts.

From his eighth year on, he was sent from one foster-home to another where, according to his accounts, he usually had to do hard work. Though Richard obviously exaggerated the hardships and deprivations in the foster-homes, unquestionably from his eighth year on he was undernourished in his receptive demands; his oral regression had its origin in the lack of those sublimated gratifications which other boys under better conditions enjoy in family life. The lack of real interest and love on the part of the environment threw him back to the original claims of being fed by the mother. This regression was indeed the manifestation of his thirst for being loved and cared for, which he had definitely to renounce from his eighth year on. But the atmosphere of his environment was not the best place to display any emotion which even remotely resembled sentimentality. Nothing had to be more concealed in this environment than softness and thirst for dependence. The display of exaggerated toughness and independence, courage, and generosity, loyalty to his comrades, was the result of the instinctual conflict between pregenital receptive and passive female longings on the one hand and masculine aggressiveness on the other. It was really a fascinating and unexpected result of the analysis to detect in the depths of this young bandit's personality the desperate little boy crying for his mother and seeking help from his older and stronger brother.

CONFRONTATION OF THE EARLY CASE RECORD WITH THE
PSYCHOANALYTIC MATERIAL

Confrontation of the psychoanalytic material with the extensive case record shows the analysis amazingly corresponding to the essential facts as known and giving an undoubtedly valid representation of the vastly important underlying issues in Richard's emotional life. Even discrepancies concerning the alleged deprivations in foster-homes proves the fact that deeper feelings about human relationships are much more important for character- and conduct-formation than are overt circumstances and reactions.

Richard was continued in foster-home placements until he was sixteen and had become well and strong and educated to the level of the second year of high school. The voluminous running account of his personality-development, of the foster-home conditions and his reactions to them, and of a good many other details constitutes an extremely interesting and reliable record for reference. Richard had to be re-placed a number of times because of his stealing and surliness, but in one home he remained longer than two years with an interim for a summer vacation in the mountains. In some of the homes the boy was regarded with much affection in spite of his behavior difficulties; he usually did well for a few months after entering a new home. One foster-mother regretted deeply having to give him up; she had grown so attached to him that she hoped she might retain him until he was grown up. Until Richard was about fourteen he was under the care of a very intelligent woman who was a social worker and whose duty it was to supervise needy families. She gave him a great deal of attention, really achieved much with him, and he was very fond of her. Even when he was eighteen, Richard in one of his letters to this visitor said that for all she had done for him he owed her a debt that he could never repay.

From the first, Richard was in homes of good standards, and especially because it was felt he had such a poor start in life, he was given all that a boy might seem to desire. His diet was carefully supervised and he was given extra supplies of milk and other nourishing food; on advice, he was amply provided with sweets. He was presented with nice toys and, after he became a great reader, he was given many good books. He had an allowance of money in order that he might not be tempted to steal. On account of his early poor progress in school a special tutor was employed and paid for by the agency. This enabled him speedily to catch up in school-work, and for the most part afterwards he received good marks. (At eleven years Richard's I.Q. was 109; at fourteen it had increased to 124. He then rated high in language and apperceptive abilities as well as on tests for mechanical ability.) He finished the eighth grade at fourteen and continued his education to the second year of high school.

The foster-homes were all in suburban and country districts where there was ample opportunity for outdoor life. Richard engaged moderately in boyish sports, but mainly developed himself by gymnastics. Notes from one home tell of his daring and great desire for climbing high trees; in another place he had opportunities for some hunting and practice with guns. Except for one or two events he seems to have done fairly well in social contacts with other children. Apparently he did not care much for animals.

Not until his last placement, where he agreed to work for his board, did Richard complain of being overworked. Earlier he had been regarded as a cheerful and willing worker at household chores, but this last was a farm job and he frankly said that he was utterly tired of farming and wanted to return to the city, and in this frame of mind he left. In letters or conversations with the visitor or in contacts with the clinic he never maintained that any cause for his unhappiness was conditions in any foster-home. Indeed, he changed foster-homes when it became necessary with expressions of regret and without any grudgeful attitudes toward the foster-parents.

Richard was early given good medical attention, and after a year or so of poor nutrition he developed quite normally; at sixteen he was a sparely built, well-formed, hardy young fellow. The ear disease which he first manifested at seven became much better, so that he no longer suffered from defective hearing, but there were flare-ups of the old trouble and at fourteen it was diagnosed as chronic mastoid inflammation, although no operation was advised. This trouble seems to have subsided during the ensuing years, and Richard has remained otherwise well.

When eight Richard was showing a slight facial tic. After placement this became much more severe, varying greatly from time to time, however. His visitor undertook his training through the development of self-control according to the principles of some common-sense psychotherapy. By the time he was twelve the habit spasm had practically disappeared and has not recurred.

From the first it was notable that Richard's bad temper, surly behavior, and stealing greatly increased or began again after visits to or from his mother or after having seen his brother. One of his worst periods occurred after his mother came to see him with her man friend, another after he went home for a few days. With intermissions, Richard's dishonest proclivities were shown in almost every foster-home. In spite of his good appetite for meals and a normal supply of sweet foods and candy, he spent much of the stolen money for buying candy, often generously giving some of it away. With these eating-habits in mind the visitor asked the examining pediatrician for advice, but he could find no physical cause for Richard's craving for sweets.

The record shows more strikingly than anything else the great variability in Richard's emotional attitudes and conduct trends. At times Richard was unquestionably happy and entered into family life and other social activities with normal zest, being sometimes a rosy-cheeked, responsive, well-behaved boy. At other times, without any obvious external cause, he appeared desperately unhappy, tense, miserable, pitiful. Earlier, after some of his misdeeds his features would be drawn and white as he was faced with them; it was only in the last year or two that he grew belligerently callous. Pictures of him at different periods show an immense variation of expression. His unhappiness was so pronounced for a time when he was about fourteen that it seemed to amount to a depression and the possibility of a developing psychosis was entertained, but after a few weeks of increased personal attention and encouragement these signs disappeared.

Richard's mother thoroughly approved of the foster-homes, showed no jealousy of the foster-mothers, and was always attentive to Richard in making him visits and sending him presents. In contradistinction to any attitude of rejection on her part, she has always shown the utmost loyalty to the boy, as indeed she has to her other two very difficult sons. The tie between mother and son, however, was mutual. The mother was repeatedly seen by Richard's visitor and was told plainly about his jealousy and his attitude toward her man friend. She in turn maintained that Richard's misbehavior had begun before she had this boarder and that she could not possibly maintain her home without his support; besides he was a periodic alcoholic and badly needed help.

In one home where the foster-father was a bit of a philosopher, Richard gave him some confidences concerning something which oppressed his spirit and which dated back to early childhood. Something had happened when he was five years of age; the boy was willing to reveal this general fact, but not the specific occurrence and just what it meant for him. Subsequent attempts to get him to reveal fully his feelings failed. By the time he came to adolescence Richard was in no mood to do otherwise than work out his destiny on a superficial and "hard-boiled" basis. It was the foster-father in the last home to whom he gave these half-confidences and with whom he quarrelled so desperately. It was after he left this place and returned home that Richard began his extremely surly and insulting behavior toward his mother, at the same time being willing for her to support him. And it was at this time that his mother confidentially related a recent violent scene to the woman visitor who had befriended Richard for so many years. The mother was much disturbed and disappointed by Richard's terrible language to her and his provoking conduct in the household. She informed him that she had stood it as long as she could and he must live elsewhere. He left, but after some hours came back, broke down completely, and wept for a couple of hours, bemoaning his own fancied homeliness and his position in the world. She attempted in every way to comfort him, while he responded by saying that she was the most beautiful, most wonderful mother in the world, ending by saying that he never wished this episode to be known to anybody. As bearing on this we note from the record that when foster-mothers attempted to make up to Richard in an affectionate way, he angrily repulsed them, and that when one of them suggested that he might like to have in his room a picture of his mother he replied that he did not need one because he always carried a picture of her in his heart.

There are other evidences in the case history, not only of Richard's attachment to his mother, but also of his spiteful behavior toward her—factors which became so clear during his analysis. Once when speaking of her admonitions he complained: "She is too much in my ear." More of his contradictory attitude toward his mother is corroborated by the following incident: When Richard was seventeen, and seemed terribly dissatisfied and unhappy in his home life, he was given an opportunity to get work at a distance, but he said that though he felt the pull to go and would have liked for once to get a thousand miles away, he also felt so deeply about his mother that he would not leave her. The record includes also an account of the fight with the man boarder when Richard's teeth were knocked out, and how the two afterwards made up and were willing to live together in the same household.

Much more about the relations between Richard and his brother Wilbur comes out in the analysis than in the record, and there is more revelation of their countless delinquencies. But in later interviews in the clinic it was clear that Richard had become greatly embittered about the world; he was more sophisticated and sarcastic. He spoke about the influence of criminal lawyers, of pull with the police and their relationship to the liquor traffic. His acquaintance already included, he said, "con men, dips, and bunks." There was graft everywhere. He told about waiting for Wilbur when a couple of girls passed and he wanted to accost them, but did not dare to do so because he saw a policeman behind them who gave him "a terrible look." Then Wilbur came along and asked him to tell where the officer on the beat was; Wilbur, finding him, was directed by the policeman to a "booze-shop" where he got a pint of liquor (this was during prohibition).

Richard's mother, too, has grown to know through experience that a criminal lawyer or others may exert influences that help greatly in mitigating the results of offenses. She has made many appeals for such help for her boys.

In spite of his tremendously recurrent exhibition of delinquent tendencies, Richard's personality-development is not without its contradictory sides. In early adolescence a diagnosis was made that Richard was an "introvert of the feeling type." At that period he certainly deplored his stealing, but stated that his surliness and bad temper were his worst faults. He was brought up as a Protestant, whereas Wilbur was considered a Catholic. After one of his rebellious spells when he was about twelve Richard proposed that he be baptized a Catholic and sent to the institution where Wilbur was in order that he might be cured. This was notwithstanding the fact that both boys were sent to an institution for a short time after the father's death, but soon ran away complaining bitterly about the place.

Other factual material from the record might be brought up as interestingly bearing upon the psychoanalytic material, such as Richard's notable admiration for strong, fine-looking men, and the great love of pistols and guns that he had shown in some foster-homes as well as in his own home. And then there is ample confirmation of Richard's equanimity, comfort, and almost feeling of satisfaction, as it were, at being in prison. Letters received from him and visits made to him during incarcerations prove the point.

Comparing the analytic material with the early contemporary records, it is certain that though the foster-homes were carefully selected and probably the best available, they did not substitute emotionally for the home which was broken up after the father's death when Richard was six years old. Richard's feelings about his placements from one home to another are unambiguous. He often spoke of how he was "kicked around" as a youngster from one home to another. It is of secondary importance and also futile to try to decide how much real affection and warmth he obtained in these different foster-homes; certainly he received less than enough to fill his subjective needs. There is little doubt that he exaggerated his earlier deprivations. His attachment to his mother was so strong at that time that nobody could take her place. There is much evidence that the mother had given a special amount of attention to this comparatively fragile boy, and their attachment was reciprocal. This may account for the failure of the foster-home treatment in spite of the fact that homes were selected with special care.

CHAPTER THREE

# The Undetected Shoplifter

WHEN Sigrid Amenson was twelve years old she was known to
the Judge Baker Guidance Center for a short time. She was the
fourth of six siblings and had been with her mother in Boston
for about a year. Before this the family had lived in a suburb
of New York City, and soon afterwards they returned there.
It was found that they were well known to several social agencies in New York, and these agencies corroborated Mrs. Amenson's story as far as it went, giving additional facts. The mother
was referred to the Guidance Center by a teacher who knew
something of Sigrid's difficulties, but thought she had great
possibilities.

The problem as advanced by the mother and partially confessed to by her daughter was that of extremely repeated stealing of money, bits of finery, and cheap jewelry, either from
home, neighbors, or shops. This had commenced when she was
perhaps seven or eight years old and had continued with great
frequency.

Sigrid was very tall for her age and presented a rather unusual
picture because of her good posture and notably regular strong
features and profile, her strikingly blond coloring, well-shaped
head, and intelligent, responsive expression. It is easy to see
why so many people thought her attractive. Physical examination revealed no abnormalities of any kind; with the exception
of being rather pale and having some carious teeth she seemed

to be in good condition. Her strength was decidedly good for her age.

On a considerable range of mental testing, Sigrid showed herself to have superior mental ability—I.Q. 114. Her reasoning and apperceptive powers were especially good. She had just finished the seventh grade, but did all the achievement tests for eighth grade. In the use of language she showed much facility. "A keen, alert mind," was noted. She showed impatience and some little nervous habits, but always demonstrated good persistence and self-criticism. She had been left-handed, but had learned to use her right hand well in school. During her earlier school-years she "talked backwards," as other children termed it. She used opposites with apparent sincerity, saying "light" for "dark," or "large" for "small," and expressed herself in words out of their normal order. For this contrariness and also on account of awkwardness with her hands she had been much teased. Some irritability was reported, but her dependability in housework was accented; her teachers were fond of her. She was popular with other children because of the remarkable facility with which she concocted long, interesting, imaginative stories.

Her health history was largely negative. A worried pregnancy was followed by a full-term, normal birth, the child weighing more than the average. She was nursed for two months; afterwards there was no nutritional trouble. She walked and talked early. There was no difficulty with establishment of sphincter habits. She was treated for vaginitis when she was about seven years old.

As for personality traits, Sigrid was reported as being active, affectionate, demonstrative, sociable, emotionally stable, very much of a little housewife finding enjoyment in doing things and being helpful to others, but it was said that she was very "deep." She was a great reader, very imaginative, fabricating

readily; some of the rougher girls on the street called her "prig-
gish." Those who saw her at the Guidance Center found it a
pleasure to talk with her because of her intelligence and seeming sincerity, liveliness, friendliness, and good manners.

The family history as obtained from the mother and from
one social agency who reported on the case included the fact
that Sigrid's father, born in 1883 in New Jersey, of Swedish
ancestry, during recent years had been immoral and alcoholic
and had developed into a chronic thief. He was then serving a
considerable sentence for larceny in a New York institution.
He came from an honest, hard-working family. The report on
the mother and her family was practically negative. Mrs.
Amenson, born in 1888 in New York of Scotch-Irish Protestant
stock, had worked before her marriage at sixteen; since then
she had suffered much from illnesses which necessitated several operations. She was infected with gonorrhea by her husband, probably after her children were born. Her troubles had
made her nervously upset, but the agency reported that she was
a good housekeeper, well thought of in the neighborhood, and
that the children were carefully brought up.

Sigrid's siblings were reported as being often underweight,
but aside from this, hospital examination showed them to be in
average health. Two of her three older brothers had nervous
habits. Following Sigrid came Alma, one year younger, an attractive child who had been a "prize baby," and then a boy
four years younger. All of them were said by the mother to have
normal personality and behavior tendencies. One agency visitor
recorded them as nice, mannerly children, doing well in school.

Home conditions for six or seven years had been especially
bad on account of the behavior of the father. He often failed
to support his family and was abusive when he drank; the family moved frequently and were always in poor neighborhoods.
The father seemed to have much influence over the mother and

she refused to prosecute him, but when, after he went to prison, there was dire poverty and the children had to be placed in foster-homes at times, she started divorce proceedings. The family received much aid from organizations, and by them Mrs. Amenson was considered to be reliable and rather efficient.

Through Sigrid and her mother it was learned that when Sigrid was about eight she had a minor sex experience with a man, and that for a couple of years she had lived next door to a group of thoroughly delinquent girls who were immoral and stole. The mother stated that Sigrid had told her that she had a tremendous temptation to steal when she was in shops, but generally could resist it.

In some psychiatric interviews Sigrid told freely of her long make-believe stories which were related to her interested siblings or to others, of her fondness for acrobatic stunts, of her love of clothes, and her delight in making clothes for herself and her dolls, about her extensive reading, her desire for schooling, and so on. Her avowed ambition was to be an author or a nurse. She spoke of her painful experiences during her local treatment. Sex knowledge had been acquired from the girls next door; they told her of the good time they had with boys in a barn; but then her mother had given her some instruction about those matters. The man had never really done anything with her sexually, but her family had made much of it. She hated and avoided boys. (Her mother stated that this attitude toward boys was only a recent development—formerly she engaged in much active play with them.) Her dreams were vivid, especially one about a wild bull chasing her and cornering her; she woke up just when he was ready to run his horns into her. Very repeated stealing and frequent temptation to steal were readily confessed to by Sigrid. She long had known her father to be a thief, and supposes she was born just like him. He had punished her severely for stealing—"It was all right for him to take things, but he didn't want us to." He had never said or done anything bad to her; indeed, he was "pretty good" to her. He often came and slept with her and her sister when the household was crowded and they had wonderful times playing together.

Advice was offered to the mother and the teacher concerning the management of Sigrid, and it was reported in a few months that the girl had been doing much better. Then contacts ceased because the family moved back to New York.

Nine years later Sigrid again appeared, asking for help to overcome her terrific temptations to steal. She was once more living in Boston, this time by herself, and held a fairly good position as an assistant secretary in a large advertising concern. She was very attractive-appearing, tall, blonde, slim, upright, with straight, strong features and high coloring. She was dressed very well. She referred the Guidance Center to her employer and it was found that he took much interest in her; indeed, he consulted the Center about her possibilities, without, however, knowing her essential problem. She did satisfactory work for him.

Her mother had long ago been divorced and was remarried and Sigrid had been caring for herself for five years, living either at a working girls' club or with friends. Sigrid said that at one period she had gone for help to a woman psychiatrist in New York. When the Guidance Center proposed the possibility of an analysis she was very willing to enter into it. She already through her reading knew something of psychoanalysis and, indeed, it had been suggested by the psychiatrist. It was arranged for Sigrid to have evening sessions in the analyst's private office.

When the psychiatrist in New York was corresponded with, she very kindly turned over her records of the case, including much information about the family that had been obtainable in New York through welfare agencies. Sigrid had confessed to the psychiatrist an immense amount of stealing during the intervening years, especially much clever shoplifting, always without detection. She had broken with her mother five years earlier, and since that time the latter knew very little about her daughter. The analyst did not see the case record or the New York psychiatrist's study until after six months of the analysis.

### PSYCHOANALYSIS OF SIGRID AMENSON

It is sheerly impossible here to give more than a sketch of the exceedingly interesting material which was obtained during one hundred and twenty analytic sessions with this highly intelligent young woman, Sigrid Amenson, who presents such complex personality characteristics. A bare transcript of the interviews would require hundreds of pages. Aside from her stealing-proclivities, she presents other problems that belong in the realms of characterial, emotional, and social adjustment, and even her physical functions are involved. It is beyond the scope of this publication to deal with all these and we must confine ourselves to consideration of the bases of her delinquent career, although it must be confessed that these other problems formed part of the structure underlying her behavior tendencies.

Her stealing is like a chronic disease, she says; she has been stealing nearly all of her life. It is only because she has been so clever about it and has the appearance of refinement and integrity that she has been able so far to elude arrest and appearance in court. But she feels that this might come about at any time and almost wishes that it would. She plays the game with boldness and assumed assurance that belies her real fear of being apprehended. She would hardly like to total the value of things taken, amounting to thousands of dollars, but at times she has kept a secret record of days on which she has stolen and the things taken. Once she says that everything she has on, clothes and jewelry, has been stolen at various times. When either with or without funds, she cannot resist the impulse. Although she has never actually done anything of the sort, she has imagined and planned forgeries and big robberies, even of banks. Recounting what comes into her mind in various situations, she relates, for example, of being at a teller's window and quickly making all the plans for loosening some bars and seizing a package of bills as the teller turned away to telephone— the while smiling pleasantly at him and wondering if he suspected what was going through her mind.

Before she started to school and afterwards, Sigrid indulged in childish, but often very clever pilfering of eatables at home and from neighbors when the family were in deprived circumstances. When she went to kindergarten, she took pencils and crayons. She was sent home for this, and remembers that her mother said: "Even in school she steals." Soon she was taking trinkets and little fineries and accumulated quite a collection of silk and lace things which were discovered and returned. Of course, she was punished for all this, sometimes by whippings given by her father. At an early age she had a hiding-place for articles taken and used to delight in looking over the things there.

During recent years, when Sigrid can remember the accompanying feelings, she is sure that her stealing is very often preceded by an intense craving to take something. Sometimes it is a general feeling of desire to steal, "a bursting desire which makes me sick," and sometimes the desire is definitely attached to some particular article of woman's apparel or accessories which she has seen on display. The urge may last for a couple of days and gradually fade out or only disappear after she has stolen. There was a period of a couple of years when she was practically free from this obsessive desire, and at other times she has had some success, particularly during the analysis, in fighting it off. The stealing itself is undertaken with cool determination, accompanied by an underlying feeling of excitement which ends with trembling and other physical manifestations, finally followed by a great sense of relief. When the stealing has represented an especially dangerous episode, Sigrid, thinking that she was being watched or followed, has been almost uncanny in her shrewdness in rapidly thinking up ways of escaping detection, always with increasing excitement and an aftermath of feeling exhausted and being obliged to seek rest somewhere.

The objects stolen cover a range of articles which she could utilize or take pleasure in possessing or which she might give away. Mainly they have consisted of all sorts of clothing and jewelry, but she has also taken other useful things, and even toys for children. To one family she poses as the fairy godmother; they call her this because she has been such a good friend to them in their poverty, believing that she has sacrificed herself to get many things for them. To be sure, she has sometimes deprived herself for these people, but the story of other occasions is illustrated by the following: A hot-water bag was needed for the sick baby; Sigrid intended to buy it with her lunch money, but when she went into the shop, a feeling of excitement came over her and she adeptly purloined it. On rarer occasions, in a sort of frenzy she has scooped up a lot of articles, then has been seized by remorse, and has replaced them with a cunning equal to that of her stealing.

It comes out that for one type of article Sigrid has a special penchant, namely, for handbags and pocketbooks. She has accumulated a large collection of these, keeping some of them neatly put away unused, taking special pleasure in thinking of them. Worn, dirty pocketbooks are abhorrent to her. Her collection enables her to have a new and clean one whenever she desires and special ones for different costumes and occasions. She has thought for days of some special one that she has seen in a shop and has maneuvered for long with a great sense of excitement until she has been able to take it.

Beginning at the time when she was a shopgirl for several months, when fourteen years old, most of Sigrid's stealing has been done from shops, but she also has taken a good deal of money from many different sources. When a little Sunday-school girl, she managed to abstract some from her teacher's pocketbook and she speaks particularly of the intense desire which she has had to open pocketbooks and take money when she sees them lying around, as in an office or in a women's dressing-room at a party. One great fight that she had with herself during the analysis was in such a dressing-room where there were many pocketbooks, and her mixed feelings of disgust at the uncleanliness of some of these as she opened them and her urge to take the money, which she resisted, made a curious story.

Very much more than this and many of the details of her stealing were revealed during the analysis. Sigrid feels that for one thing, she has an ingrained habit of stealing. "All my life I have been stealing." When she is in need of money or clothes, the idea of stealing to supply her needs comes to mind very readily, especially when she perceives easy opportunities. But Sigrid never alleged that her stealing was caused by pecuniary disadvantages; indeed, she stole much when she was holding good positions and less sometimes when she was at a low ebb financially. A second factor is pride in her own accomplishment; by successful stealing she has many times proved to herself her own cleverness; in some way at least, she has some superiority. Thirdly, when she is stealing, some force seems to be drawing her on to accomplish something. Sometimes she feels as if she can stop, then she has a panicky feeling, as if she were afraid that she would not steal; if she were not a thief she would miss something and would not be the same person at all. In a dream which she relates it seems to her that she has almost a duty to steal from pocketbooks. At one time while rapidly reviewing in soliloquy the affectional relationships of her life, particularly of her recent years, and her ambitions, she ends by saying: "Nothing in my life that I have ever cared for have I been able to get, and that's why I feel like stealing."

Then in many sessions it comes out that there is a definite dynamic association between Sigrid's sexual urge and her stealing. She vividly remembers that when she was five or six she engaged in autoerotic practices directly after stealing. She felt that the former were much more sinful and in the ensuing years begged in her prayers to have strength to overcome that temptation many times more than she did to be relieved of her desire for stealing. Now, as she analyzes her recent sensations when she is stealing, she recognizes them as being analogous to or actually accompanied by sexual sensations. During the earlier part of the analysis she had an access of both urges which brought the association clearly to consciousness. When this was going on, she went to a club entertainment and, she says, was much disturbed by a flute solo. She left the crowd and went into the refectory, where preparations for a supper were assembled. She was seized with autoerotic desires, to which she partially gave in, and then she suddenly grabbed spoons, knives, forks, napkins, threw them into a box, and walked out with them. When she reached her room, she started reading and continued for a couple of hours with entire forgetfulness of the incident. Coming to herself then, she threw the box into an outside ash-barrel, with a continuance of the feeling of relief and accomplishment that she had when she first took the things, and no sense of regret about it. "Something stronger than my will made me gather those things together." But it was clearer to her than ever that the two urges were associated. Then later, when she had a little confidence in herself, she tells of going into several shops to see what her reactions would be, having kept away from stores for a period. "It was strange; I soon had a great desire to have something; I felt that I had to get out of the store. I had a strong sexual urge and got panicky. I asked myself before I went in if I had any strong inclinations in either direction, and I would have said no." Then Sigrid goes on to tell about the strange fascination which pocketbooks have for her—"In a flash I think I could take one; in a split second the thought comes into my head, as yesterday when taking lunch with a friend I saw a woman put down a pocketbook and leave it there for a little while."

These immediately underlying or associated phenomena of Sigrid's compulsion to steal came out clearly early in the analysis, but how did they develop, either separately or as forming a behavior pattern? This was the problem to solve.

The analysis proceeded in much the usual fashion when such a neurotic personality and such neurotic behavior trends are faced. Sigrid with her high intelligence and gift of expression was always interesting. She came no doubt to the analysis with full conscious intent to be cured. But there was an underlying ambivalence about this; it was as if deep down she did not want to alter herself. She confessed an amazing amount, none of which from any corroborating facts we had any reason to doubt, but she never told quite all, as we later discovered, and she never seemed thoroughly and entirely to have the deep-lying wish to stop stealing. Her expressed feeling that she would not be the same person if she did not steal gives some indication of the obstruction. Sigrid talked well, she associated freely, her insight was remarkable, she was clever in the interpretation of her many dreams. She also showed the usual resistances of a difficult case, she occasionally uttered hardly a word during the hour. Emotional upsets were common, with tense physical reactions; more than once she jumped up and left the room, and several times she did not appear for some days.

The "analytic situation" developed by a mild first transference followed by a hatred of the analyst, and then a strong positive transference, with many dreams about the analyst and much feeling of dependence upon him. The latter phase continued until the summer vacation, with the analyst mainly in a father rôle, as was shown by partial identification of the two in dreams.

Sigrid's feeling about the psychoanalysis is most interesting; to her it was amazing, she said, in what it brought out. At times she felt depressed if she couldn't come, she was jealous if anything interfered with the hour. She was greatly encouraged as well as sometimes discouraged by the procedure. She was downcast because vacation was coming on. If she couldn't continue she would go on stealing. "Just as soon as I decide not to tell you anything it comes out in my dreams. I have resolved to come and prove to myself that I would not tell something and then I do. Now I think of you as I thought of my mother, I always resolved not to tell her things."

Sigrid was relieved of some physical symptoms which distressed her and attributed the relief, probably correctly, to the analysis. "It is nothing short of a miracle," she said. But often she was in a turmoil, not only about her inner conflicts and behavior difficulties, but also about her life situation, the question of where and how to live with her slender means. This complication of her inner and outer needs was extremely difficult, and ominous for complete recovery.

An account of Sigrid's dream life would make a volume by itself. The scenes most frequently represented in her dreams were related to her own stealing, running away from someone who was about to attack her, being in precarious situations, as "on a fence" from which she might fall, and sexual episodes. Her father and mother appear under many conditions, often hateful, but not always, as when she is with her mother, "or it may not have been my mother," at a window looking out into a hideously black sky and suddenly the sun bursts forth beautifully and comforts her—a wonderful dream, Sigrid asserts during a session when she expresses much gratitude to the analyst because she then seems free of her impulses to steal. There are dreams in which she is of noble birth—her father is King of Scotland, and her mother "Mary, Queen of Scots," or she is the daughter of St. Francis of Assisi, who tells her that on a certain day if a dog bites her, she will be proclaimed "Queen Dowager." Sometimes she is seeking in some way to be made over and appears in various disguises. One dream was of the end of the world, with tempests and earthquakes all about her, while with a girl companion she was lost in a wilderness. But at the same time miracles were happening; wonderfully beautiful, tall, straight trees were springing up. Sigrid tells her friend: "We are not destroyed, there is a God," and feels that amid this scene of combined destruction and re-creation she has to accomplish something before she dies.

Sigrid's associations to her dreams were equally rich and very frequently opened up matters that were deep issues for her, as when she dreamed that the analyst and one of his colleagues were undressing her and discovered her dirtiness underneath, with especially filthy feet, the colleague shaking her head and saying she never would have imagined it. From the dreams and associations come out many of her pleasant and unpleasant childhood experiences, many of her earlier and later loves and hates. Mrs. X. in the office where she works she thoroughly dislikes; she dreams about her as somehow resembling her mother in her stern attitudes. Then comes the confession of what Sigrid had previously indignantly denied, but which had been suspected at the office—namely, that she had stolen money from this woman's pocketbook.

The picture of Sigrid's earliest life that we can construct from the analytic material is that of a normal, happy little girl, three or four years of age, learning sewing, household duties, and good manners from her mother, whom she then regarded with very normal affection. This part of her life was never brought up until the latter part of the analysis when Sigrid dreamed that she belonged to an aristocratic family and her mother asked her if she wanted to go on some pleasant trip; in the scene there was a man whose name she heard. In her associations to this dream it appears that the man bore her mother's middle name; mentioning this brings a flood of emotion and Sigrid says that the feeling-tone of the dream represents just the feeling she had for her mother when she was very little.

After her fifth year came the long period when the family was in dire straits because her father had become dissipated and irregular in his working habits. Coveted food was hidden from the children, and soon Sigrid found herself cleverer than the others in getting at the cupboard, and enjoyed the distinction, often sharing her spoils. They lived in a miserable neighborhood, with poor companions for the children. Her little sister was a pretty child, "a prize baby," made much of by the mother and other members of the family. Feelings of inferiority developed. Sigrid was left-handed, awkward, and for two or three years had trouble in learning to read; she was nicknamed "Clumsy" and "Stupid," while her sister was called "Lover." Sigrid had peculiar autoerotic habits and felt herself sinful, believing that other girls never did such things. The local treatments which she had at the hospital seemed a punishment for wickedness; she wondered if she would grow up to be the same as other girls, she questioned whether she had lost her virginity. Then Sigrid grew fast and was lanky. She thought she had a big nose, big ears and feet, and people said: "How did you happen to be a girl?" She was very sensitive about the poor clothes that she had to wear to school; in many ways she felt different from other girls. Chided once for being like her father with respect to stealing, she first realized that her father was dishonest; her likeness to him was mentioned many times afterwards. "I felt like dying when I was called a thief."

Before Sigrid had gained the ability to do well at her studies, she played much with the idea of saying incorrect or non-sensical words in the place of those that she did know as they occurred in sentences or in poetry, or she said sentences backwards. She achieved some notoriety for this. Then she had her own secret words for tunes, and when others sang she quietly used her own version of the song. There was compensation and superiority in the thought that she was fooling people—she remembers it in just that way.

Other early atempted compensations came through Sigrid's finding herself able successfully to compete with boys in many of their sports; indeed, she won prizes in competition; and too, she felt self-aggrandizement through her immense development of phantasy life, which led her to be a favorite teller of stories to other children in the family and to outsiders. An interested teacher aided her to conquer her reading disability, and a woman in another part of town for whom she tended a baby introduced her to good reading. She speedily became an omnivorous reader, at first of romances which gave her another avenue of access to superiority because she was able to let it be known in her poor surroundings that she was acquainted with good literature. For this and for the aristocratic manners which she adopted she was persistently nicknamed "High Hat" throughout the neighborhood. About this time one of her phantasies and play activities was to pretend that she was a blind girl; it was a sort of escape from the sordidness of her life, it seemed to blot out miserable things which she had seen.

So one of the first steps toward high ambition and desire for a really good education was taken early. Achievement of superiority has for her always been to become educated. Above everything else she always wants to be able to meet intellectual people on an equal footing. It is a sore point with her that her mother had so little appreciation of her that Sigrid was taken out of school at fourteen to go to work. But through all these years Sigrid has read an immense assortment of books, including the best classical literature and many modern novels, wasting no time on newspapers or ordinary periodicals. She delights in studies of character and has delved into abnormal psychology with a great feeling of wanting to know everything about human nature. She particularly enjoys tragedies and accounts of suffering; she fairly lives in the characters that are portrayed. Her favorite book is Dostoievsky's *Crime and Punishment*. The story of her own life she thinks more than equals some of the things she has read.

Until she was about nineteen, Sigrid, wherever she lived, was a regular attendant at church, Sunday school, and young people's church meetings. For years she never missed a Sunday, either as a pupil or as a Sunday-school teacher. In early adolescence she often engaged in ardent prayer to be beautiful, to be pure, to overcome her temptations, particularly to conquer her stealing tendencies, but yet she stole money from her Sunday-school teacher's pocketbook and probably other things from the church. While immersing herself in church activities, she often felt guilty because she was not what others thought her to be. After she quarrelled with her mother and left home at sixteen, for a couple of years she was more active in church than ever; she felt as if she were not "living with God" and during that period she assures us that she did not steal. Her ambitions still remained high, and a man who wanted to marry her during this period was rejected because he seemed altogether too ordinary. A tremendous recurrence of her old temptations began when she had a light love-affair and sexual stimulation from it She began to feel depressed because she was becoming a hypocrite, but still felt some security in personal help that she received from the church.

Sigrid has tried other ways of helping herself, by reasoning with herself, by chiding herself, and by confessing to herself her various sins as they were recently committed. She seems to have gone to the psychiatrist in New York with the idea that if she told to someone else all of her stealing she would be confronting herself with her delinquent career in such a way that it must inevitably change. Spurred on by the inquiries of the psychiatrist, she kept a record of scores of things taken and of their cost. She says that she took a fiendish delight in making the calculations; it represented a form of self-punishment like that indulged in by Marmeladov in *Crime and Punishment.*

Through the attitudes and feelings revealed in the analysis one can easily discern a continuing feeling of inferiority entirely hidden to outsiders. Sigrid's motto is: "Never show the world that you're down and out." In her blackest moments and most destitute circumstances she assumes a front of vivacity, cheerfulness, and good-fellowship. Yet she reveals that she frequently says to herself: "Poor girl, you have a curse upon you," and often thinks that she is doomed by her miserable origins; she is an Amenson.

Sigrid no longer has to compensate for many things; she has grown to be rather distinguished-looking, having an enviable figure, a pleasant voice, an excellent choice of language, and poise and manners which enable her easily to make cultured friends. She has been careful about her habits, rejecting smoking and drinking and even the use of cosmetics. Despite lack of formal education, she has a well-stocked mind through continuous reading of good literature, and intellectual men find her a good comrade. Through being so accepted, she is able superficially to cover up the sense of guilt which is often with her, and the feeling of being "different." But after all, she says: "It is rather interesting to be different. Life is a struggle! I should have missed many things if I had had money and hadn't stolen and so had lots of experiences. It gets me why I should think so much of myself; I was really common and ordinary, all except in my phantasy life. But I have felt I was too good for anybody."

There seems to be no doubt that Sigrid really has had great ambitions, which were in marked contrast to and perhaps were reactions to her miserable early environment and her family status. She says that often she feels that she will be a great success and accomplish much. She makes great efforts at times, enjoying spurts of work, but then come the frustrations of thwarting impulses. When wanting to do her best she sometimes does her worst.

Sigrid's inordinate interest in and desire for clothes has rather deep implications. Much as she has always wanted to be a boy, yet she has also the urge to be one of the most feminine of creatures. Many times in the analysis she dwells on the significance of clothes for her. Her happiest moments when she was a child were when her mother made up something new for her to wear, muslin dresses and bows; she hated the patched dress in which she had to go to school. Already at seven or eight it made her proud to hear other girls approvingly comment on something that she wore. Her father insisted on her putting on her best when she went to walk with him. Nowadays she has the greatest longing for many changes of costume, a different one every day. She says: "It makes me feel a new person," or: "It gives me new confidence," and once: "I would have five thousand dresses if I could," but after a pause: "Why should I have them when Mrs. A. hasn't a single new one for Easter." (Mrs. A. and her family are the people to whom Sigrid plays the fairy godmother.)

Sometimes when she has a wild desire to steal, the only thing that seems really to fit in with the desire is a new dress, from the wearing of which she gets poise and self-satisfaction and the feeling of being a different person. She can't wear the same dress long before hating it, and she wants more expensive ones than the girls in her position ordinarily have. She has spent a good deal more upon dresses than she should have done; she thinks too much about clothes. Wearing good clothes makes her feel superior, better than she is. In her dreams of nobility and other dreams of wearing jewels it is what she wears that gives her distinction.

The theme of desiring to be a different person appears frequently in the analysis. Sigrid has dreams of being disguised, even of going through an elaborate fiery process to change the color of her skin so that she cannot be recognized. There is a torture element in this dream, and to it she associates her ideas of the Inquisition. "Yes, perhaps the analysis will change me." (Is there any significance in the fact that this dream—only in its vividness, she says—leads her to recall the dream, when she was about twelve, of the bull chasing her? Twice during the analysis she spoke of this old dream without remembering that she had spoken of it nine years earlier.) Sigrid frequently brings up the fact that she wants to change her name.

Contrasted to Sigrid's great interest in feminine adornment is her continued delight in wearing men's clothes when occasion permits. Even though she loves soft pretty things and has the urge to collect them, she wants to be a man, just as when she was a little girl she wanted to be a boy. Then, tall and active beyond the ordinary, Sigrid not only enjoyed hugely the fact

that often she could do better in sports than boys could themselves, but she liked to dress in boy's clothes, occasionally daring
to wander out in the street in the evening thus attired. During
adolescence she took male parts in church plays, several times
acting the groom in a wedding scene. Her young phantasies
included much of the type of adventure that boys delight in.

One dream is of escape from assault through using a deep
bass voice. This dream involves her father, who was going to
assault her; she tried to bite off his finger. She indulges in some
autoerotic practices—associating to it leads Sigrid to say that she
has a masculinity complex; that her mother was wont to say
that she had a crude voice and laugh; that as a child she had
much interest in male sex organs. An elaborate dream is about
fighting men with a sword in her hand. Another one is of being chased and threatened with a knife by a repulsive man
who somehow seems to be her father; she gets the knife away
from him, and a girl is murdered. Relating this dream brings
up the memory of her father entering with her into the game
of dressing up; he would put on his wife's garments while she
dressed in her brother's clothes. And when his wife was at the
hospital he often did the cooking, wearing house-dresses.

Sigrid's mother dwelt much on the hardships of womanhood, and when the little girl went to the hospital for local
treatments she not only experienced much discomfort, but was
deeply impressed by what she saw of the sufferings of other
females. Before she was eight she had heard the cries of a woman
in childbirth next door. A girl showed her disgusting evidences
of menstruation. She recalled these and it is clear that they
were very traumatic experiences for her, making the lot of
womanhood seem most undesirable. Over and over she asserts
that she always wanted to be a boy, and: "Even now I hate
being a girl."

The fact is, Sigrid repeatedly tells us, that in nearly every respect she is two persons in one. She likes and yet hates men; she has had for long two close female friends, one a married woman and the other a girl of about her own age, but male companionships and friendships predominate. She welcomes any opportunity for social relationships with young men, but doubts if she can get any sex satisfaction from them. "I can't let men put themselves out to give me anything." With some men she feels that she takes a feminine attitude, with others she is a masculine good fellow.

This dual attitude Sigrid discovers permeating much of her mental life and behavior tendencies. She has a lot of good in her and yet she keeps on stealing. She hates her father and is disgusted by him; at the same time she realizes now that she is tied to him more than she has ever let herself think; she has a guilty feeling about her overfondness for him still. She dreams she met her father, who had had all of his money taken by a woman vampire; in the dream she pitied him and was stirred by him. Much resistance is shown to the associations of this dream, and Sigrid says with high emotion that she absolutely must go out and steal things for an entire new costume. In another dream, in which a house was entered by her and she felt guilty, she was two persons and the people finally chased out her "other self." Once with great force Sigrid says that she is not only two persons in one, but the most changeable person on earth and has been "the greatest liar in the world."

Sigrid has had ideas of suicide, but they have been fleeting, as when she thought of throwing herself from a ferry-boat in New York when, under the stimulus received from the psychiatrist there, she made a resolve to begin a new life and threw overboard a suitcase containing hundreds of dollars worth of stolen clothes. The joy of living which she feels in her buoyant moments prevents any real moves toward self-destruction. Depressed from unemployment, she has considered various methods of suicide, but says to herself finally: "Why should I throw away such good material?"

No evidence has appeared of any hatred toward the beautiful and beloved "prize baby" sister. Naturally there must have been jealousies, but always Sigrid has been much brighter and more mature, and her emotional attitudes toward her younger sister were earlier somewhat those of pride, while in recent years she has been almost maternal in her desire to help this girl, who herself has had to cope with great difficulties in love-affairs and through poverty. Sigrid's attitudes in this seem to be normal rather than to represent any over-reaction.

That the mother-child relationships in Sigrid's case have been very important in the development of her personality is shown by their frequent appearance in the analytical material. For the very little girl the mother played a very different rôle from what she did later. Sigrid was passively dependent on her and thought of her as a beautiful and good mother. Since Sigrid was five or six years old there has always been some barrier between them. The mother, married when only an adolescent, soon found herself with several children to care for and a husband who rapidly became more and more shiftless and erratic. She was very alive to the attraction between father and daughter, and Sigrid has vivid memories of being blamed for this when she was not much more than six years old, the mother evidently sensing the arousal of sex life in her daughter. For Sigrid it soon became something of a competition with her mother for her father's affection, and evidently her mother exhibited some feeling of jealousy about the matter, telling Sigrid not to sit on her father's lap, not to show her legs, and so on. At any rate, the mother succeeded in making Sigrid very alive to the response between father and daughter.

Beginning at that time, there was a definite lack of satisfactory affectional relationships with her mother, which Sigrid has always craved. It comes to her frequently, and always with emotion, that she was the naughty child who was not to be loved, she was not even kissed; not that her mother was as harsh in whipping her as was her father, but there was no bond between them. Sigrid felt not wanted by her mother, who even said: "I wish I had never seen you." Her mother was fair enough with the children, she wanted them to do what was right, she had them say their prayers regularly, but Sigrid exclaims: "If my mother had ever taken me in her arms and loved me, I should have been a different girl, I should have melted." The dream of being with her mother when the sun broke through betokens Sigrid's underlying desire for the old existence when there were comfortable relationships between her and her mother.

Sigrid developed aggressive tendencies toward her mother; she stole from her, but never from her father. Recountal of a dream of a fight with lions is followed first by resistance to associations and then acknowledgment that it is related to a picture of lions which hung on the wall when she was a little girl. She has not thought of it for many years. Sigrid would look at the picture and imagine the lion jumping on her mother; then if her mother were dead and in a casket, how pretty she would look! At night she cried herself to sleep thinking about it, and with her facility for story-telling she described the phantasy to the other children and they all cried. This came out early in the analysis, Sigrid adding: "It goes to show how much we did care for her. We never cared for father like that." Then there was another picture of waves dashing high over a rock, and Sigrid placed her mother struggling and drowning in the water. Later in the analysis it was shown that the child really wanted her father just for herself; the way to obtain this in phantasy was to get rid of her mother, while a due amount of sorrow might be expressed for her phantasied decease. During the analysis Sigrid goes to see *Mourning Becomes Electra,* which to her seems a very natural account of family relationships. She could have murdered her own mother.

Sigrid's father's image and her memories of him are set deep in the foundations of her emotional life. Ever since she has been separated from him, when she was ten or twelve years old, her phantasies and dreams have been largely influenced by his image. He was kindly and joking and playful when she was very little. There was rough and tumble in bed with him and if there was company he slept with the two little girls. Then came the time when there were drinking and card-playing men in the house of whom the mother disapproved. The little girl was afraid of them. Her father was sometimes sick and disgusting after these bouts and could not be disturbed in the morning, although Sigrid and her sister continued to have some jollity with him. Sigrid has vivid memories of sitting on his knee and liking him, admiring his cleanliness and the nice way in which he kept his hands, enjoying the smell of the toilet preparations that he used. She combed his hair and had strange new feelings when she sat on his lap. To be sure, he was sometimes irritable and his hand was heavy and hard when he punished her, but somehow she never minded that, really.

Associations to various dreams in which her father appears lead her to say that she has long felt that he aroused her, stirred her in some way; she has even wondered if he chloroformed her because "I suspected that he had done something to me; for years I have wondered about it." She cannot explain her feelings toward him. They are partly guilt feelings; in spite of all her disgust for his later behavior, she has a guilt sense related to a feeling of overfondness for him. During the analysis she once goes to visit him, sees him degraded, and feels somehow contaminated, yet at the same time she has a sense of jealousy because he seems familiar with some woman in the household where he lives. She feels afterwards that she must have had some peculiar relationships with him.

Sigrid's sympathies were often with her father; she feels that when her mother berated him as depicable she was "the only one in the family that had the guts to stand up for him." Punishments meted out to her by her mother for stealing made Sigrid still more sympathetic with her father after she knew that he stole. In one of her continued phantasies her father would be gone and she would often be searching the world over for him, perhaps expectantly standing on some wharf awaiting his return. Actually once on a Christmas day, with almost nothing to eat in the house, she led the other children down to the local jail to peek through the window and see him there—they all cried bitterly outside. Though in late years she has seen her father only twice and found him so short, untidy, and dissolute, Sigrid nevertheless in her phantasy life and in her current dreams reverts to her earlier image of him and to her earlier feelings about him—in this way he remains for her the tall, immaculate, debonair figure that he seemed to her when she was a little child.

Sigrid finds it intellectually interesting in the analysis that certain physical characteristics which she picks out in the young men that she meets, characteristics which attract her, are unconsciously often just those which she so admired in her father, such as tallness, particularly well-kept hands, color of the hair, carefulness to wear a clean shirt. But in all this she cannot separate actuality from her early phantasied image of him.

Sigrid's mother often said: "You are just like him," and sometimes added that Sigrid was surely an Amenson. Before this, Sigrid had recognized resemblances, she thinks; they were both left-handed, they had the same color of hair, "he could look you in the face and say things that were not true, and so could I." He liked many of the nice things that she liked, and he, too, was conceited. Above all things, they both stole; Sigrid cries out: "I am him all over again." Sometimes she has attempted to explain to herself her own behavior tendencies by heredity, but then again she says that physical structure cannot account for it since one of her brothers also closely resembled her father and he did not steal. There must be something more to it than that, she thinks.

Sigrid knows that she was closer to her father than to her mother, she was never afraid to tell him that she had stolen, and if he whipped her ("It seems strange that I didn't mind his whippings"), whereas she would always deny everything to her mother. She was supposed to dislike him, but she really didn't. Sometimes her mother held forth on the better qualities of her own family, and Sigrid has hoped that she might have inherited some of these, but when she confronts herself consciously with her own behavior difficulties, she always reverts to the formula: "I am an Amenson." During the analysis, following dreams of noble lineage, she endeavors to construct a genealogical chart, writing to her mother for information, obviously with the desire of proving to herself that there was a better than ordinary strain in the family blood, some of which might be hers by inheritance.

When Sigrid thinks of her father's miserable progress downhill, she hates the thought of being like him or bearing his name, and she believes that he did injury to her, but yet at the same time she realizes that underlying this is some strange feeling of sympathy and kinship with him; thoughts of him still arouse in her some sexual feeling. She is sure she loved him more than her mother did and it is partly her mother's fault that he is what he is.

Of all the material that flowed into her mind by associational channels during Sigrid's analytic hours, she resisted telling her early phantasies perhaps more than anything else. Recounting her delinquencies is much easier than revealing this content of her early mental life; the latter seems much more shocking. When she was very young, Sigrid found that through her vivid imagination she could work up stories and situations that would startle herself. She would put her head under the bedclothes and phantasy with such a feeling of reality that she would become frightened and jump up in order to stop it. Before she could read well, she made up long-continued stories to herself, and then for years she entertained her brothers and sister in bed at night, having a calendar arrangement by which on certain nights in the week there were continuations of the stories which belonged to that particular night. But what she hesitated to reveal in her analysis were the phantasies which she kept to herself. In these she would be kidnapped and overpowered and undressed in an automobile, and there would be sex attacks upon her, the nature of which were very vague to her at that time. Various men were the perpetrators; to them she gave names, and since this was at about seven years, when she had pretty poor ideas of men, they often appeared in phantasy as beautiful and almost like women. Or she lived and slept with these men and she had a phantasy about being the only girl in a boys' school, not being allowed to go until she kissed every boy in the school, half of them while she was dressed, and half of them while she was completely undressed—the boys being undressed too. She could have escaped if she had broken her word, but she had to see how much she could stand without breaking her promise. She does not remember what the promise was. Then the phantasy about this kissing would get dull and boys would lie on top of her; then she got tired of this. She was always lying on her stomach when she told these stories to herself.

In another group of phantasies, which ran on for months,

Sigrid possessed the secret of life. There was a company of enemies who wanted to get this secret away from her and she was tortured by them, but there was a commander on her side to whom she reported and there was a hiding-place to which she could go, so she always evaded revealing the secret. She ran away with a man to a Western canyon; they blocked the entrance and built a cabin and had a wonderful time there. These phantasies all had their sexual components, and Sigrid says that the exciting episodes in them resembled her stealing affairs because when the phantasy was over she would be horrified and "feel all in."

There were other phantasies of being whipped with a strap, strung up by the thumbs, being burned, having heavy labor to perform, living in a garret in rags, starved, but always she pictured herself as having a beautiful face and the possibility of a great future. These phantasies began very early; Sigrid thinks that the ones with the sexual import began when she was about five and gradually increased in extent and variety. She was just beginning to learn to read and her favorite stories were those of Cinderella and other tales of suffering; she wept over them. She pictured herself as suffering, unwanted, as being hated and eating off the floor. There was no punishment of others; she had no slaves, she was always the sufferer, but it comes to her mind that a number of times she had an intense desire to hurt somebody; once she thought of suffocating a baby. Once in recent years she had the opportunity in a game of tying up a boy; she whipped him with savage delight and ran away and left him. In one of her childhood phantasies she peopled with children a room where she was able sometimes to be alone, giving them names which she remembers well. They were well-behaved and innocent; she would not have them otherwise.

With a continuing deep sense of shame about many of her

phantasies, she resolved at about ten years of age that all this must be stopped. To help herself she made a great effort to read good books and think of better things. It was then that she first began praying that she might be pure. She became so ashamed of her phantasies that she repressed the memory of them, and the details have never been recalled, she says, until now in the analysis.

It is interesting that the revelation of this vivid phantasy life, so forgotten, began after a dream about the analyst in which she started some familiarities with him and he exclaimed: "Remember who I am," adding: "The poor girl has a curse." Then Sigrid, associating, says that her phantasy was her real curse. After starting to tell about it, she failed to appear for several days. When she came back, she said that she had dreamed every night about the analyst in vaguely remembered ways. Just prior to this time she had been suffering a good deal from headaches and said that she felt that there was something she ought to "get off her chest." After she had revealed the character of her phantasy life, she was immensely relieved of these physical troubles.

Quite apart from interpretation of the stealing compulsion, which is introduced later, this tremendous development of phantasy life and its special content demand explanation. More than the ordinary compensatory phantasies of childhood life was involved; it was all related to and accentuated by Sigrid's early psychosexual traumata. Evidently when Sigrid was very young her phantasies dealt much with the idea of rape and suffering. The masochistic phantasies had sexual import; they were connected with early sexual stirrings, and whippings by her father served to bring the two easily into association. Her secret-of-life phantasy very probably for her had the significance of parental intercourse. And it would take no great stretch of the imagination to believe that her safe hiding-place in the earth, in mother earth, had unconsciously the meaningfulness of rest and safety in the mother's womb.

Only the aspects of Sigrid's sexual experiences that seem related to her stealing compulsion need mention here. Some of her traumatic experiences have been mentioned; there were others. When she was about eight, a man several times took her to walk and induced her to put her hand in his trousers pocket; she says she feels there was more to that than her family ever knew. To be sure, her father tried to find the man for the purpose of arresting him, but as Sigrid looks back on the affair her memory of the man seems confused with that of her father; she used to investigate his pockets for small change. It was probably earlier when she awakened one night and was greatly frightened by one of her father's drinking companions standing in the bedroom doorway; she was afraid he was going to do something to her. Sigrid remembers that at about the same time, and lasting for years, she had some queer visual sensations "of things getting larger and larger." At about the same age she and her sister wondered whether they should or should not look into a window where they could see an undressed man. Sigrid herself when alone was fascinated, as she expresses it, by observing the sex organs of a man undressing next door. She listened with much curiosity when she heard her mother warn her brothers about masturbation.

When Sigrid was ten or eleven she associated with some girls who often stole and who told her sex stories. They were playing about a barn, and one of her vivid memories is that she had an immense desire afterwards to set fire to the barn. The girls said they had sex affairs in the place. Sigrid states that she had much interest in fires during her girlhood, and the sight of them or thought of them always excited her. One of the greatest fights of her life has been against autoerotic practices, which have been more or less continued except for the interval of two years or so when she did not steal. She occasionally has dreams of naked men, and during the analysis she had two very vivid dreams of men without a penis. Frustration in a love-affair just before she saw the New York psychiatrist was followed by an orgy of stealing.

Within the past three years Sigrid twice has developed remarkable phantasies of being pregnant. Once she carried the idea so far that she began to imagine that she felt some symptoms of pregnancy and denied herself enjoyable activities as if she really were pregnant. She even told others that she was going to have a baby.

During the analysis Sigrid felt vastly encouraged at times, but during other periods her old urge to steal came over her. She likened the analytic experience to plunging into a river and swimming about in order to be thoroughly washed. Once she said it was much as if she were going regularly to church again in order to feel clean inside. Toward the last she had a dream about her father and after exhibiting resistances to telling of it, she said: "I am supposed to see now what I didn't see before, why I stole, but what would happen if I stopped the analysis; what would I have for outlets except what I cannot have?" It was at the same session that Sigrid emphatically asserted that analysis was a most amazing experience; what it had done for her was nothing short of marvellous. But at a still later session she exclaimed: "Everybody must be crazy to think that this much analysis can cure me."

For a period of months Sigrid undoubtedly was free enough from her compulsions to steal so that she did not give way to them, but then came a time when she found herself involved again in very difficult economic and social situations. She was tremendously upset emotionally and said that she now needed sermons more than anything else. She had a dream of the analyst rescuing her from assault. It was during this period that, as we later had reason to know, Sigrid stole on numerous occasions, not now specializing so much on articles of clothing or adornment, but rather helping herself to small sums of money, books, and trinkets belonging to those with whom she was associated. She even stole a key and at night entered the office building where she worked during the earlier part of her analysis; there, besides money, she elected to take some other things of no great value. She also appropriated a few of the analyst's possessions.

Very much related to the recurrence of Sigrid's compulsion is the fact that in the last month or so of the analysis she was very far from being entirely frank, either about what was going on within herself or about her external situation.

In the one of the last hours Sigrid had the following dream: She was on a rocky ocean shore, leaning over, trying to catch with her hands some queer-looking fish. A man came along and said to her: "Don't you know those fish are poison? If you will read a book it will tell you all about them." She inquired and was told that the name of the book was *Up from the Egg*. She thanked the man, let the fish alone, and started along a path on the edge of the cliffs, which were high and rugged. She saw a big house, apparently of white marble, that had three fine pillars in front. She knew that it was the analyst's house; it was like a beautiful temple there on the rocks. She wanted to go to it, but saw how hard the path was. Crowds of people came along headed in the same direction and asked her what the place was. She told them and they followed her at first like a parade, but then she found herself alone and got lost. She slipped on the rocks, fell into the ocean, was nearly drowned, and felt terribly unhappy because she couldn't seem to make her way to the place. Then she met the analyst, who told her she was going the wrong way. He said she had to go up over the cliffs. She started a difficult rocky climb, but fell down, hurt herself, and became frightfully discouraged because she felt that she never could reach the desired destination.

### INTERPRETATION

In this case, which so abundantly proves the driving force of unconscious mental life, our presentation of the analytic material is necessarily very incomplete; much more could be offered from it to buttress the structure of interpretation. On the other hand, while not everything was elucidated, yet the main foundations of Sigrid's difficulties were uncovered.

Our special challenge is the specific and unconscious meaning of the stealing, which has been so extraordinary, so repeated, so tied up with compulsions. Sigrid feels herself driven to steal; she does not know whence the drive arises. Evidently she wants something which is somehow represented either by the act of stealing or by the objects stolen or by a combination of both. The question for us is why she has this special compulsion which places her in jeopardy and brings so much subsequent inner disturbance and self-recrimination.

For the sake of getting at deeper issues we can leave out of account Sigrid's childish pilfering of eatables, and we can pass over the effects of habit-formation and that small proportion of her later stealing which was directly allied to her urgent needs. (Possibly the stealing of money from pocketbooks more recently in New York was largely attributable to dire necessity.)

As one major finding it is perfectly evident that the act of stealing is for Sigrid closely analogous to the sexual act. She often has a prior feeling of terrific urge, and in the face of opportunity she is cool, and determined somehow to relieve her inner tension. Then, while actually stealing there is tremendous excitation, followed directly afterwards by a definite exhaustion. Sigrid recounts her childhood combination of erotic practices with stealing; even in recent years she has sometimes given way to the two activities at almost the same time. During the analysis she observed herself closely enough on some occasions to be certain that she was conscious of definite sexual feeling when there was the temptation to steal.

It is clearly to be seen that the desire is to do something dangerous and forbidden which may bring emotional and somatic relief. Sigrid specifically feels that she wants something that for her is not obtainable otherwise than by stealing. Sexual activity and stealing exist for her in strong dynamic associations—sexual affairs represent the worst offense; with much less pricking of conscience can she steal. Denied what she craves, she gets what she can.

But evidently there is also significance in some of the objects taken, since Sigrid shows an especial penchant for them. She steals an inordinate number of articles for female adornment, a fact which we deal with later. Her remarkable acquirement and collecting of pocketbooks is evidently based upon the symbolic meaning of these articles—pocketbooks and purses may readily symbolize the female genital organs. This interpretation is very near the surface in some analytic sessions—Sigrid felt damaged by the local treatments and doubted if she remained as well equipped as are girls normally, and what she was deprived of she unconsciously wants to regain. She emphasizes the pleasure that she has in the secret possession of these articles and lays particular stress on the meaning for her of their inside cleanliness.

Naturally the analysis was concerned with more than revealing these associated phenomena; the basic factors of the compulsion to steal were in question. Of course, there might have been something in constitution or innate predisposition as the soil upon which the compulsion grew, or at least which aided its growth. Her bodily structure in mid-childhood played a part in the development of her personality tendencies. Later on, it is largely by virtue of her unusual appearance that she is readily able to avoid detection or suspicion, as well as to appear attractive to people in much better circles than those in which her family moved. Also her left-handedness and her disability for reading were important for her personality-development at the time when her creative imagination and phantasy-formation and her facility for verbal description were strongly active.

That Sigrid is so essentially narcissistic hardly proves any constitutional factor; rather it bespeaks a peculiarity in emotional growth. However, she never appears to have presented a specially inflated ego. Her self-regard must have been severely wounded by her mother's harsh disparagements, although she reacted to his with a compensatory show of pride and the establishment of high ambitions. Perhaps this capacity for rebound somehow represents something constitutional.

There seems no indication that the early development of the little girl was anything but favorable and normal. Up to five years or thereabouts she apparently exhibited very satisfactory behavior tendencies. She was normally dependent on her mother, she is reported to have been a little housewife with especially good manners. From her mother at that time she apparently had ample opportunity to develop a good ego-ideal, and from her mother's instruction came her conscience or super-ego. It comes out in the analysis that Sigrid senses unconsciously those years as being the most satisfactory of her life. As shown by dreams and emotional attitudes, she misses the old relationship with her mother; underneath her hatreds, aversions, and conscious strivings for independence she yearns for that old state of affectional dependency.

Next in Sigrid's development we note that at about five years she showed unusually strong sexual interests and impulses, at the same time wishing to be a boy. Following this we have little or no indication of a latency period, unless it might have been for a short time just prior to puberty, when she became so acutely conscious of her dangers. With the advent of adolescence came another sexual awakening and then began the continuance of outbreaks of sexual urge which in one form or another have characterized her later career, except for the interval of relative freedom during a couple of years when Sigrid made a strong endeavor to sublimate.

The family romance, the Œdipus situation, is immensely accentuated in Sigrid's case and has many bearings on the evolution of her personality. Indeed, we see that for her the Œdipus love never has been resolved. Now, it is well known that for a little girl this love is largely resolved through emotional relationships to the mother, through intensified mother-identification. In this instance such a normal identification seems to have been almost entirely thwarted. There were several reasons for this. The child who started out so well in her attitudes toward her mother and to family life soon found that her mother was fonder of the younger, prettier child. This and the mother's exhibition of hostility to Sigrid when the mother became jealous at the discovery of the Œdipus situation, led Sigrid to feel emotionally undernourished and to sense the existence of a barrier between her and her mother. The resultant injury left a deep scar that is presented to view again and again in the analysis.

Other factors stood in the way of healthy mother-identification: From early years Sigrid had gained such an impression of the hardships of the feminine rôle that to her it seemed highly undesirable. Secondly, her competition with her mother for her father was so strong that she was openly blamed for it and had a great sense of guilt in regard to it. The activity of the super-ego now steps in; she continued to want her father greatly and developed so much phantasy life about relationships with him that her conscience could not allow mother-identification; she could not feel strongly for her mother and at the same time be her guilty competitor. Thirdly, her likenesses to her father, physically and in behavior characteristics, were often held up before her and she inwardly dwelt on the resemblances. In the family life she felt herself somewhat in *his* position and grew to have great sympathy (empathy) for him, even coming to believe that perhaps her mother was partly to blame for his conduct. With all these forces militating against emotional rapport, how could Sigrid identify herself with her mother? Indeed, in the analysis, notwithstanding the conscious acknowledgment of her mother's fairness and early love for her, Sigrid's strong feeling against her mother's attitudes is perfectly evident. Yet there was some longing for femininity, as is shown by the early purloining of finery and by the fact that her phantasy life included many feminine experiences, though frequently accompanied by masochistic elements.

Sigrid's identification with her father often comes to the surface in the analysis, standing though it does in essential opposition to her libidinal impulses as a girl, a member of the opposite sex, toward him. Both unconscious emotional attitudes, plus their inherent contradiction, have played an important part in the genesis of Sigrid's difficulties. Retaining her father much in her phantasy life as a love-object, in actuality she was deprived of him and, not being able to grasp at mother-identification for her redemption, a solution was for her to turn to the masculine rôle. Then the fact that she not only found herself readily able to pattern after boys in some respects, but also regarded herself in particular as a replica of her father influenced her still more toward assuming masculine attitudes.

We can also easily see that the desire to be a man, or, rather, to have a penis and be a boy, was all along at least partially a reaction to the masochistic phantasies which made mother-identification so difficult and womanhood so unacceptable.

And the earliest masochistic coloring of the female rôle is a result of the pronounced ambivalence toward the mother. The unconscious wish that the father should be cruel to the mother, as indicated in the lion dream, means suffering for the female. If this is her picture of femininity, then she, with her guilt feeling about the phantasy of her mother's maltreatment, must suffer if she remains a female. Very naturally in phantasy, in the wishing life, comes the flight to masculinity.

But thwartings again arose: Just as she could not as a girl possess her father, so she could not completely be a boy or thoroughly identify herself with her father—she lacked something, the physical structure, the penis. Besides this we may note that the ego-ideal derived from her mother stood in the way of this identification. With all her practice in the arts of delinquency, Sigrid has never been able to duplicate her father's unmoral, criminalistic attitudes. Something within her has forced her to maintain some sense of dignity and considerable ambition. Sigrid has experienced terrific ambivalence toward her father; side by side with her strong affectional urges she had hatred and fear of him. She certainly felt that she was ill-treated by him, though with her masochistic tendencies she apparently accepted without resentment his heavy punishing hand—perhaps, indeed, his whippings fed her libidinal desires, according to the formula of this well-known phenomenon.

We see how these factors in simultaneous contradictory activity could form the foundation for Sigrid's extremely poorly integrated personality. Her continuing oscillatory love-hatred, feminine-masculine conflicts are deep sources of her troubles. Even now she has underlying desires to love where she hates and hate where she loves; she wants to be utterly feminine and yet reaches out for the masculine rôle. Such an essentially unintegrated personality is almost necessarily predisposed to compulsions.

Something of the nature of Sigrid's conflict is represented in her repeated dreams in which she flits from one room to another, or hops from window to window, or is precariously balanced on a fence, or is trying to get somewhere and feels herself unable to move. As a matter of fact, it is while associating to these dreams that she is led most strongly to reveal her unconscious strange hatred of being a girl and the force of her desire to be a boy.

Related to the problem of her personality integration is the fact that for years it has seemed to Sigrid impossible to think of herself as having normal sexual satisfactions. From her dream life and free associations we can readily interpret that love experiences with men mean for her some revival of the old father-daughter situation. Her love-object choices, as we see in the details of her attraction to various men, partially recapitulate the unresolved Œdipus. The guilt and conflict about this preclude her from having normal emotional attitudes toward men. However, she can effectively suppress the sense of guilt when her sexual tensions are active by allowing her stealing ideas and impulses to be the most urgent elements in conscious mental life.

So what there is remaining of the Œdipus and of the feminine-masculine conflicts causes Sigrid, with her vague but insistent feelings of incompleteness, to think of herself as unable completely to enjoy a man or completely to satisfy one. Her veering unconscious impulses have been greatly perturbing to her psychosexual development. Very specifically we find that recently her stealing compulsion has been coincident with her going from man to man, in a sense as a feminine Don Juan, never completely satisfied with her relationship to any man.

Sigrid's inferiority feelings have been overtly based on her early personal handicaps, her unfortunate life situation, and

the autoeroticism which she condemns. These have been sufficiently mentioned in the analytic material, and some indication has been given of her attempted compensations in actuality
and in phantasy. But the sense of inferiority involves deeper
issues. Unconsciously she feels that there is something wanting
in the structure of her personality. This is made very plain in
the analysis of her compulsion, which shows that her excessive
stealing of clothes cannot be passed over lightly as merely
indicating that the finery taken was for the purpose of making
herself appear attractive or that she might exhibit her good
taste in dress. The deeper picture is of her desire above all
things to be another person, "a new person," successfully feminine. And new clothes always seem to offer the possible chance
of achieving the feeling of being such another person. She
grows terribly tired of herself in the same costume for more
than two or three days at a time. She is dissatisfied with herself
as she is and continually seeks changes of dress for some un-
attainable satisfaction, some completion of her personality.
Clothes for Sigrid are symbols of complete femininity.

Sigrid cannot accept anything other than an extremely successful female rôle. Her stealing of new clothes expresses this
desire. Some of the stealing, however, represents the wish to be
a man rather than a suffering woman. She wishes to be a perfect woman or to be a man, but not the woman she is. Or
perhaps the unconscious wish is to be a woman and at the
same time to have a penis. In any case the stealing seems to
have a bisexual determination: Sigrid is not altogether content to be only a man or only a woman. She wants to be both.

It is sensible to believe that Sigrid's compulsions may have
had still other determinants. We might readily deduce that
the early stealing of little fineries which she hid and gloated
over may for her have represented avengement and recom-
pense for her wounded self-regard. It is to be observed in

many a narcissistic child that unconscious desires for vengeance come to light in the form of misbehavior. As an injured, disparaged, but aggressive child, it was quite natural for Sigrid to do more than phantasy compensatory superiority; her ego needs could be fed by acquiring distinctive possessions. Then, since others had done wrong to her, why should she care if she did wrong to others? This childhood attitude has been maintained, for never a shred of feeling about the sheer wrongfulness of taking property belonging to other people ever appeared in the analysis. And other signs of the spirit of revenge are exhibited: Sigrid has shown vindictiveness to her mother and to those who unconsciously remind her of her mother—she steals from them. Or when she finds that she cannot remain in a state of dependency on her analyst, a relationship similar to that which unconsciously she would have liked to have had continue with her mother, she turns on him. After the vacation she attempts partly to explain her misconduct toward him by saying: "I knew you were going to desert me." We may reasonably suspect that the entire picture of her stealing has at least some of the coloring of vengeance, of getting even with the world.

Why does Sigrid continue stealing when by it she punishes herself so much? We know that she does suffer inwardly; her tenseness, physical disturbances, and haggard features at times testify to the fact. She really injures her own ego. To herself she is not only the offender, but also the judge. Does her behavior in stealing express an impulse toward self-punishment that may relieve guilt about her phantasies and unconscious desires? She once said: "Stealing seems to relieve my sense of guilt." Running through her life certainly there is a strong element of masochism, summed up in her statement: "I thoroughly enjoy making myself miserable." Even the recklessness with which her compulsion places her in jeopardy seems to indicate some unconscious urge for punishment—although we see that her conscious ego never lets it go too far; in a dangerous situation the conscious response is a remarkable exhibition of shrewd cleverness in evading detection and external punishment.

We have sketched the sharper outlines of the picture. We see a very incompletely integrated personality whose compulsions to steal represent a drive to relieve inner tensions which are caused by unfulfilled unconscious wishes. Through not recognizing the nature and source and interplay of her feelings of dissatisfaction and incompleteness, she never does and never can by the act of stealing make up for what she unconsciously feels she lacks. Underneath, she continues to relieve childhood situations and to behave according to patterns established in childhood. One feels that if Sigrid, with her obvious potentialities, can grow further in insight and can emotionally break down her hindrances, she may be able to re-educate herself so that she can meet the secondary, mainly social, difficulties which confront her, and lead a satisfactory feminine life.

### EPILOGUE

Comparison of what through the psychoanalytic procedure was gained for the understanding of Sigrid's personality- and character-development with what was learned by a short clinical study of her at twelve years of age shows that much more might have been suspected then of the possible genetic factor. But no opportunity presented itself for continuing work with her.

Much more interesting is the comparison with the psychiatric interviews of two or three months in the year preceding the analysis, but it is only fair to state that the psychiatrist who so earnestly endeavored to help Sigrid felt that deeper issues were not being uncovered and herself advised analysis. This psychiatrist in New York kept a good transcript of the interviews, and from this record we gather the following: Sigrid revealed perhaps fully enough the disturbing influence of her recent love-affairs, many facts about her stealing, the antagonism to her mother and at the same time her craving for her mother's affection, and something of her early inferiority feelings. She told at length of a childish dread of her father because of much whipping by him and acknowledged that he had probably handled her sexually. She stated definitely that when seen in Boston at the age of twelve, she did not at all tell the truth about her mother and father because she was afraid that if she did her mother would "put her away," nor did her mother give the real facts about the family situation. Although she led "a clean life," her mother often accused her of immorality and continually upbraided her for her early stealing. To the psychiatrist she denied autoerotic practices and centered the statement of her problem on her stealing impulse and the difficulties of her relationships with young men. Sigrid proclaimed it a miracle when she threw overboard her suitcase of stolen things, and appeared very grateful to the psychiatrist for what had been done for her.

Evidently not much else was brought out in the interviews with this competent psychiatrist; Sigrid apparently was not conscious of the deeper psychology involved in her career or else she was not then willing to face it.

Since the uncompleted analysis Sigrid's career has been checkered. She felt bitterly her own disappointment in herself through breaking down again with such virulent misconduct while still being analyzed and after some months of doing comparatively well. It had been easy to see and it was fully realized by Sigrid that in her social milieu, which she had largely created for herself, she was living on the top of a volcano. Not only on account of her inner tensions, but also through external circumstances, there was almost bound to be an outbreak of trouble. But with her ambitions, her great craving for occasional social excitement, her financial straits, and her unwillingness to live on a very moderate level, she refused every suggestion to place herself in circumstances which would naturally have seemed to be the first requisite of therapy. Her friends tried to help her, but were met by Sigrid's obstinate attitude of desire for independence. Then came absolute unemployment and Sigrid went back to New York.

After several months the analyst heard that Sigrid was in court in New York, having been apprehended for numerous thefts from pocketbooks in a public building. Sigrid gave the probation officer the name of the analyst, and a lengthy correspondence between them ensued. After meeting Sigrid, the probation officer, a social worker of good training, became much interested in the girl. It was found that Sigrid had been almost entirely without funds, that she was associating with a group of cosmopolitan intellectuals, many of them people of good university standing, with whom she was putting up her usual good front. Sigrid was placed on probation because this was her first court appearance, although she confessed to the judge that she had been stealing for years.

Sigrid stated that it was entirely a good thing for her that she had been caught; she appeared very contrite and said that she wanted to make every effort to cure herself of stealing, and that she was very willing to go on with analysis. Contact was made with her mother, who appeared vindictive and refused to give Sigrid any chance with her. This undoubtedly made the people associated with the court somewhat sympathetic with Sigrid, so evidently a homeless girl. The psychiatrist who earlier had tried to help Sigrid very generously came on the scene and had a long interview with the mother. (The interest in this is that the report of the interview tends to corroborate a great deal of what appeared in the analytic material concerning early family attitudes and relationships.) A skilled analyst in New York was willing to accept Sigrid as a patient, since analysis still seemed to offer the best chance of success. Sigrid, continuing to face many external difficulties, began with him, but after a couple of months he reported indifferent results. Sigrid had shown great resistances, her transference to the first analyst was a difficulty to be encountered, and she apparently had never developed a deep enough unconscious desire to get well. Sigrid was irregular in attendance at the analytic sessions, sometimes not appearing for a week or two; she had very little employment and lived from hand to mouth; she felt a great lack of security in her social contacts, particularly because of some newspaper notoriety. Her stealing impulses were not conquered, though there were, if any, but minor outbreaks of these.

A year later the New York analyst kindly gave an account of what transpired during this period. Sigrid regrets not having continued the analysis after two months of irregular sessions with him; she believes that so far she has been immensely helped by psychoanalysis and proposes some day to pursue it to really satisfactory conclusions. To his original statement he adds his conception that one trouble in the analysis with him was that Sigrid continued her childish drives to exploit the therapeutic interest of psychiatrists and the many others who had tried to help her. In this she found realization of her capacity to win love and to compensate for her intense inferiority feelings. The free associations of this period confirmed the fact of Sigrid's essential bisexuality and her sense of being deprived of the satisfactions of either womanhood or manhood.

During the year, finding that her reputation prevented her obtaining employment, she established a small independent business in close proximity to the home of some people of good standing who, knowing something of her troubles, still believed in her and befriended her. She has done very well, so much so that she has had to have assistants in her business, and has been able to pay off most of the debts she earlier incurred. The fine probation officer who has attempted to do thoroughly constructive work with Sigrid writes confirming this, saying that of course, with such a clever girl, she cannot be absolutely certain, but she thoroughly believes Sigrid to have changed immensely for the better.

As the analyst has occasionally seen her, Sigrid very noticeably has appeared at times more masculine, at other times normally feminine. Through her assumption of a famous New York society name for her business venture she reveals her old desires to be aristocratic, beautiful, and dominant.

One outstanding feature of this later analysis during two months was Sigrid's strong opposition to commenting on the first analyst except by reference to his generosity and her indignation at his discontinuing treatment (at the vacation period). Dreams occurred which represented both men—for example, a lunch-counter dream in which there was a man who handed her food, and a cashier who took her money. (The New York analyst properly insisted on charging her a very small fee in order that she might have a better attitude toward her treatment.) Her associations showed that by refusing to say much about the first analyst she was concealing her transference attitudes toward the second. In later contacts she insisted that, with one exception, she had committed no more thefts. However, she often phantasied stealing, but evidently only of taking feminine objects. In contrast to these phantasies of adding to her femininity, her relationships to men were of an unsatisfactory nature; she has only sought men who were not masculine and who offered her the pleasure of domination.

Still later, adding another six months, we hear again from the probation officer and the analyst. The term of probation expired some months ago, but before it ended there were suspicions that Sigrid was not doing so well. In certain ways she was indulging in extravagances that did not seem justified by her earnings, and she was associating with young men and their families in a social circle which undoubtedly necessitated misrepresentation on her part. There was nothing to be done about this because she was not detected in any delinquencies. The analyst writes that he has had almost no contact with Sigrid during this period, but recently she has reappeared. This may be taken as indication, he thinks, of the fact that she apprehends the danger she is in through reawakening of old impulses and from the attempt to float in a social situation which, with her background, is precarious for her. She presents herself again for further analysis, seeking to be cured.

# CHAPTER FOUR

## *The Day-Dreamer*

DAVID DIEDRICH was thirteen years old when he was brought by his mother to the Guidance Center. His parents were fairly well-educated English Jewish people whose forebears had emigrated to London from Germany. They had both been in America since they were young. The father, forty-five, was a shopkeeper, hard-working, kind and devoted to his family. The mother, forty-three, has impressed everybody by her courage in the face of many difficulties, her intelligence, and her self-sacrificing spirit toward her family; she is a splendid character. There are three sons: Harry, two years older than David, and Alfred, three years younger. The whole family has been brought up in the liberal or Reformed Jewish faith.

David had never been in the juvenile court, but had been considerably delinquent through stealing, running away from home, and earlier telling fictitious tales while begging for money. Within a few months after he first came to the Guidance Center, David ran away three times, once remaining two weeks. On one occasion he went to New York and obtained a job with a brokerage concern; there he forged a check and while endeavoring to cash it was arrested and sent back to Boston. A month later, when he was still less than fourteen years old, he disappeared and was gone for a year and a half. During this time he occasionally wrote to his parents from various parts of the country, telling them not to worry about him and saying that he was enjoying his travels. Suddenly he reappeared, apparently glad to be home again, but a week later he was gone once more, this time for nearly a year.

Returning home at sixteen, he maintained that he had satis-fied his "wanderlust" and wished to return to school. A scholar-ship was obtained for him in a tutoring school and he began his studies with apparent enthusiasm. He also had a part-time job. A short time later he stole a small sum of money from his employer and once more ran off, this time, however, return-ing in a few days. Having forfeited his job and his scholarship, he seemed much discouraged and it was not long after this that the psychoanalytic study began.

In spite of his earlier minor escapades and his pitiful tales to strangers about being mistreated or an orphan, until he was about twelve he had seemed very respectful to his parents. It was then that he became impertinent and reacted to reprovings by a tremendous show of temper, screaming out that he wished all the family were dead. He had become a good deal of a braggart, telling how he would earn vast sums of money and would enjoy himself. When he ran away he took moderate amounts from his family with which to begin his journeys.

David had been brought up in a well-cared-for, modest home where the mother had demanded little from the children be-cause she thought that they were deprived of much that she would like them to have. Her great trouble had been with the two other boys, who had in young childhood suffered from an insidious form of tuberculosis and who continued to need much care. The oldest boy was an unusually thoughtful lad, an exceedingly good student, who proposed to become a law-yer. Already at fifteen he was partially self-supporting and his parents were very proud of him. The youngest was also a quiet boy, who, except for his health, presented no particular problem. However, it was David who had always seemed the most attractive of the three, since he was the liveliest and had the keenest sense of humor.

At thirteen David was normal in height, but considerably obese, with suggestions of endocrine dysfunction. His developmental history seemed absolutely negative, he had always been very healthy. At sixteen he had grown to be tall and well-proportioned and now was slightly underweight.

The psychological tests proved very interesting as throwing light upon David's facility for impressing others with his energetic personality. He rated as having superior general ability, I.Q. 118, with exceedingly good powers of memory and language ability. At sixteen, though he had not finished the eighth grade, his vocabulary was equal to that of college freshmen, and a year or so later, when he had done more reading, similar tests scored at the level of college graduates. One would hardly say that he is glib in conversation, but rather that in the use of language he is remarkably facile. Besides this he has a well-modulated voice and always appears very rational and persuasive.

In his interviews David was always friendly and greatly interested in discussing himself and his career. Earlier he maintained that he liked his father rather better than his mother because the latter did the punishing. His older brother, who was always the "shining example," he hated. He frankly stated that his earlier tales of woe to strangers had been to gain sympathy and attention as well as money and candy. He delights in day-dreams of great success. He went to New York to become a big business man, as he had read in books of others doing. It is not conscience that makes him return home—"I'm more afraid of consequence than of conscience. I haven't any."

After his first long absence David appeared very self-confident and well-poised. He claimed to have been to Europe, the West Indies, and China, and seemed very precocious in physical and mental development. He boasted of sex exploits and of prominent people he had met. He had run away for the sake of romance, but now thinks he would make a good business man or a successful writer. He insists that on his trips he has never been dishonest, nor has he had any criminalistic phantasies. He imagines much how he may become rich and have many enjoyments, which include giving pleasure to others. He would like to provide for his parents in their old age, and particularly do a great deal for his mother, because he is really very fond of her. She was probably too good to him.

The psychiatric interviews were all on a superficial level and little treatment was ever undertaken—the boy was at home for only short periods and during these times behaved quite well. His parents never considered taking him to court or sending him to a disciplinary school.

### PSYCHOANALYSIS OF DAVID DIEDRICH

David Diedrich was seventeen years old when his analysis started. The treatment continued for five and one half months. His father has been able until recently to support his family decently. In the last year, however, there have been great financial difficulties.

David was not yet twelve years old when he first ran away from home. He took ten dollars from his father's cash box and went with it to New York. The next morning he was picked up by a policeman, whom he told that he was kidnapped, whereupon he was returned to his parents. Two years later he had another running-away episode. One day he found a pocketbook containing a dollar and small change. He kept the dollar and returned the rest in order not to be suspected. The theft was discovered, however. At that time he was taking music lessons. A week after he found the pocketbook, instead of going to his music lesson, he took his trombone, pawned it, and ran away.

Between his thirteenth and sixteenth years he ran away several times, usually after having stolen some money. He stole from his mother and also from his employers. Once he embezzled one hundred dollars when he had a job in New York. It was after this that he remained away from home for a long period. In 1930, when he was sixteen years old, he was given a scholarship on account of his special intelligence, through the influence of the Judge Baker Guidance Center, but very shortly after that he ran away again. In spite of having a job where he earned rather well, he left home again without giving any reason.

David is a rather good-looking, tall, slender boy who converses fluently. He gives the impression of being informed about everything. He has an easy worldly manner, which, however, gives place sometimes to immaturity, shown by his asking rather childish questions. Very soon one has the feeling of a certain unreliability regarding what he says about himself. He is almost arrogant in his boasting. He has a quick mind, understands the point at once, and can talk in a very interesting and dramatic way. He has some insight into the fact that something must be wrong with him and says that he cannot concentrate on anything. He has a very strong and conscious feeling of inadequacy, which he tries to cover up before others. He feels that his wish to run away from home is something irrational, which he cannot explain exactly, although he tries to give some rational reasons for it. There is a rather general discontentedness with himself, and also the wish to change. About stealing and dishonesty he has a similar feeling—that it is an impulsive trend which is in him and which he cannot always control.

He understands the technique and purpose of the analysis very quickly and is eager to start. The very first sessions reveal an extremely strong sense of inferiority and paranoid ideas of being laughed at and rejected by the environment. He very soon brings up both his paranoid fears and his sense of inferiority in relation to the analysis. Why was just he picked out for the analysis? He is, after all, not the worst. He considers it as a kind of punishment or the sign of being very inferior. Parallel with these inferiority feelings and paranoid tendencies, his envy and aggressiveness come to the surface. He has the impulse to steal something from the analytic room, and this wish is closely associated with the desire to start an affair with the secretary of the analyst. The wish to steal and his plans with the secretary repeatedly appear closely together in the free associations without any intermediary links. Another manifestation of his envy and wish to bring himself up to the level of the authority reveals itself in a compulsive reading of psychopathological literature and the wish to know about books present in the treatment room. To justify and to cover up these envious feelings, he has the tendency to connect the analytic session with suffering, to blame the analysis for increasing his sense of inferiority and for depreciating him.

His emotional reactions toward the analyst very soon and easily can be traced back to the family situation. He feels himself as the most inferior and least appreciated member of the family, he has pronounced envy of both his brothers, but especially of the older one, who is the college student and for whom the parents are willing to make every kind of sacrifice; whereas he feels neglected. He wants to explain his tendencies to run away as resulting from this situation. He maintains that both mother and father, but particularly his mother, prefer his older and also his younger brother to him.

He describes with great detail how everybody in the family, including his cousins, ridicules him. He shows great hatred for them. He would like to "choke" them, to humiliate them. Already when he was eight years old, he remembers, his brother was preferred. The brother had ice cream every day, but he had "lickings." While he brings up this material, he repeatedly comes back to the question: "Why was I picked out to be analyzed? I am not the worst." He obviously wants to see in the analytic situation a kind of humiliation and reproduces in it the family situation. Parallel with this strong manifestation of his sense of inferiority, there are all kinds of reaction-formations. He has very vivid phantasy, and daydreaming occupies a great part of his time. He phantasies that he is the son of Rockefeller or compares himself with Spinoza. These phantasies, however, are constantly followed by strong feelings of envy. He envies everybody on the street who is well dressed. Apparently the day-dreams and the phantasies of success and of being superior do not help him to overcome the sense of inferiority and envy. He is continually oscillating between these ambitious phantasies and an extreme sense of inferiority. He very soon understands the connection between his inferiority feelings and these phantasies. He soon gets insight into this method of getting rid of his sense of guilt, which derives from his aggressive envious tendencies: he tends to put the blame on others. He remembers that each time he ran away from home, he tried to justify it afterwards. "If my father treated me better, I never would have done it." In running away he has the wish to become free, devoid of every obligation to others, to become successful without the help of anybody and then return as a rich man and show people what a fellow he is.

Another method of getting rid of his sense of inferiority is assuming an over-critical, deprecatory attitude toward authority. This method became manifest when Edison died. He was annoyed by the fuss that was made about Edison's death. "After all, he is only a human being like others."

In his day-dreams the phantasies of being adopted played a very important part. He wants to belong to another family. When a small boy of five or six, he lied to a fruit-peddler, saying that his father and mother were dead. In this way he induced the peddler to give him apples. Later the phantasies of being adopted by a wealthy man became predominant. He phantasies also that he will be taken to Germany by the analyst after his cure is effected, and that the analyst will give him his automobile when he leaves the country. These receptive phantasies, however, lead regularly to an inner conflict; on the one side there is the sense of inferiority, and then he swings to the opposite extreme, phantasying independence and success or picturing his situation as that of extreme suffering. He blames his parents for expecting returns from their children. He wants to justify himself in having such demands.

Very soon, pronounced identification wishes with the analyst begin to show themselves. He wants to read Freud and does read Havelock Ellis. Very typical is his compulsive wish, which recurrently repeated itself for weeks, to look at the titles of three books on the shelf and to fix the clock which has stopped. The three books symbolize the analyst's knowledge, probably determined in a deeper layer through the phallic significance of the number three. He wants to know everything the analyst does. He wants to help the analyst fix the clock. In connection with these compulsive ideas, death wishes against the analyst enter his phantasy. If the analyst were dead or at least would leave the country, then he could go out with the analyst's secretary and get the analyst's car. The session after he disclosed these phantasies starts again with his admiration of the analyst's English and his clothes, and he returns to the phantasy of receiving the analyst's automobile.

These associations lead then to a confession of his periodic impotence and to homosexual phantasies, but heterosexual wishes predominate. If he runs away, his first thought is to go to a woman. Immediately after these confessions he again begins to brag about his knowledge of philosophy, Schopenhauer, Plato, Nietzsche. His knowledge is very scanty, however, and he confuses the philosophers. Right after this there is a real orgy of inferiority feelings. He wonders whether he is a moron. This kind of material predominates in the first two weeks of the analysis. There is a sequence of inferiority feelings, excessively ambitious phantasies, envious hostile feelings toward authority, receptive passive attitudes toward authority, again a sense of inferiority, and reactive hostility.

In the third week of the analysis he tells a dream. On the corner of a street where his family formerly lived, the landlord came and gave him two hundred dollars. Suddenly his uncle appeared and grabbed it out of his hand. The uncle ran away with the money and he chased him. The uncle ran down a long, dark street and then he felt himself falling down. He suddenly caught himself and woke up. The associations very soon revealed that the uncle, who died a long time ago, was the representative of his father. He explains that his father robs him in reality. (David had an agreement with Dr. H. to receive five dollars weekly for his carfares and little expenses because, on account of his analysis, it was difficult for him to find a job. This five dollars played a great rôle later in the analysis, but even at the beginning he felt uncomfortable about it. He had great difficulty at the beginning of the week going to Dr. H. and asking for the five dollars. He gave this money to his father, who handled it for him.) To being robbed by the uncle he promptly associated the father, who takes care of his money. The dream was an obvious attempt to project his own aggressive tendencies against his father; it corresponds to his general method of putting the blame for his own aggressive tendencies on others—not that he wants to rob his father, but his father is robbing him. The two hundred dollars he associated to an advertisement of a car which could be bought for one hundred and forty-five dollars. He figured that he would need two hundred dollars to buy and run the car. The car again is connected with his wish to own or to receive the psychoanalyst's automobile. In the dream the aggressive grabbing tendencies toward the father are fused with those toward the psychoanalyst.

The dream ends in a nightmare, the reaction of his conscience, which seemingly cannot be quieted by the projection mechanism. To this terrifying end of the dream, falling down in a dark street, he associates nightmares of his childhood. They were often connected with blood. He would see a man lying in blood, or animals fighting and biting one another, or a man who cut his own throat and drank his blood. Once on the occasion of such a nightmare he fell out of bed and cut his head. His mother sometimes scared him with stories of the bogy man. He thinks that was the cause of his nightmares. Once, when he was nine years old, he dreamed that something terrible was going to happen to him. The next day he went swimming with his mother and then he noticed that he had a hernia. Then suddenly he asks whether the analyst thinks that on account of his hostile feelings toward his father he feels so guilty that he ran away from home. While associating to his relation to his father, he suddenly has the phantasy of being in Hollywood and having a good time with movie stars. He begins to realize that what he wants to steal and to have is money and sexual gratification, which are connected with each other. The analyst previously called his attention to the fact that his associations to steal something from the analytic room were suddenly followed by the wish to take out the analyst's secretary. He comes back to this remark and admits that there is some connection between his wishes to steal and to have sexual gratification. During this session he comes very near recognizing that his aggression toward his father and toward his brothers is connected with the wish to possess the mother for himself.

After the session in which he told about the dream of the uncle, he has four consecutive revealing analytic sessions. In the first of these, he tells two dreams. *Dream 1:* He was in a synagogue. He was an old man with a long beard, standing before the altar and just about to say the prayer for the dead. Then he saw his grandfather coming out of the altar in a long white robe. His grandfather talked to him in Hebrew. He said: "You made a mess of your life and I will take you with me." He was frightened and woke up. He had to urinate and afterwards had some trouble falling asleep; he was afraid of death. *Dream 2:* His mother, his father, and he went to a show. They sat in the front row. A big fellow, the master of ceremonies, suddenly asked him to step upon the stage and sing. He had some stage fright, but started singing. Everybody was shouting and applauding. He bowed and woke up.

The first dream, as his associations showed, was motivated by his guilt feelings, which had been stirred up in the last hour, in which his Œpidus phantasies came near to consciousness. The second dream is one of success and gratification which can take place through the mechanism of dream pairs.[1] His conscience being relieved by the first punishment dream, in the second dream he gratifies his ambitions to become a successful singer in the presence of his parents. The further associations to singing, however, lead to sentimental memories of a Jewish folk-song—a kind of lullaby which his mother sang to him when he was going to bed.

[1] F. Alexander: "Dreams in Pairs and Series," *International Journal of Psycho-Analysis*, Vol. VI (1925), pp. 446–52.

He confesses in connection with this dream that he has been day-dreaming during the last few days more than ever. His day-dreams are mostly centered on the analysis. For example, he sees himself with Dr. H., Dr. B., and the analyst in the analytic room. The analyst declares that the analysis was a great success and that he is cured. Dr. H. shakes his hand and gives him an assignment for a job. Then he thinks of having a roadster and plenty of money. Telling these phantasies, he sits up on the couch and points to a hotel de luxe across the street. "Some day I will arrive there in a big car with a chauffeur in livery."

The next session is full of resistance and extreme negative feelings against the analyst. He criticizes the analysis, which prevents him from getting a job. How can the analysis help him? He admits that his antagonistic feeling comes from the fact that the analysis forces him to see his hostile, antagonistic, and envious feelings and disturbs the excuses with which he tries to justify them. "Nobody likes to know that he is no good. It is true that you did not tell me exactly that, but that is what I make out of what you tell me. I magnify everything afterwards. I wonder why I in particular was picked out." He continues in a complaining tone: "I did not do any serious harm to anybody." He tries now in an entirely transparent way to make out of the analysis a kind of punishment. He is extremely depressed and wishes that he never were born, but during the same session this embitterment and martyr attitude gradually change to aggressiveness. Why shouldn't he steal? All his friends have nicer clothes than he. The analysis makes him feel more conscious of his inferiority. Before that, he enjoyed life. He does not care to understand these things. He simply wants to have good food and clothes and go to shows. He has not spent even a quarter on movies for weeks, while his brother goes every week like a clock. Everyone else is envious, why shouldn't he be? He wants to enjoy the moment and does not want to think of tomorrow.

In the following session the hostile feelings against his family reach a peak and now enter his consciousness without distortion. He had a nightmare which he tells with the remark: "If I go on dreaming like that, I would rather give up the analysis." *Dream 1:* He was just coming home from the analysis. He saw a man on the car-track killed, bloody. At home he started a violent quarrel with his father and mother; then with a bread-knife he attacked his father and killed him. His mother started to struggle with him. He shouted: "Stop! Otherwise I will kill you too!" And then he killed his mother.

He awoke with a strong erection and was quite wet. His younger brother heard him talking in his sleep. He could not fall asleep again until toward morning. Then he dreamed another dream, in which he killed himself. *Dream 2:* He went to hell, but the devil told him that he did not belong there. He then went to heaven and was told that he was justified in killing his parents because they "picked on" him during his life.

After telling these dreams, he is excited and starts to blame the analysis for causing such dreams. Associating to the first dream, he admits that he often thought of suicide and also often wished in anger that the whole family were dead, but he never wished it seriously. When he came home last night, his mother tried to persuade him not to give up his friendship with a certain decent girl. He became angry with his mother and told her not to meddle in his affairs. Before going to bed, he ate a pomegranate and thought how similar the color was to blood. I explain the hostility towards his mother expressed in the dream as a reaction to the thwarting of his wish to possess the mother. He confirms this by saying that his mother very often said: "I don't care what people think, I like Harry better."

After a short period of resistance he becomes entirely conscious of his attachment to his mother and his feelings of jealousy toward the other members of the family on account of this attachment. The hostile feelings toward both brothers become gradually conscious in their real nature. At the same time he expresses with increasing frankness his hostile feelings toward the analyst. He also reveals his attitude toward money, which he considers as the only means of becoming independent and overcoming his inferiority feelings.

Subsequently the oral receptive nature of his attachment to his mother becomes very transparent, especially in the following dream: He saw a parade of women fully dressed with old-fashioned, low-necked dresses, the breasts being exposed. He pulled one woman aside and asked her what the idea of this parade was. She said that they were the women he looked at today in the pictures. He woke up with an erection.

To this dream he associates lullabies his mother sang to him. "They are the most beautiful melodies you ever heard in your life." The next associations are to Jewish restaurants to which he always went when he was in a foreign place. He thinks of Christmas, of giving gifts to the analyst, to Dr. H. and Dr. B., which is apparently only a covering up of his wishes to be given presents. Continuing the associations, he complains that he was not invited to a dinner given by his cousins, although he helped one of them find work. This association shows exactly that the preceding association about giving presents to the analyst, Dr. H. and Dr. B. was motivated by his wish to get in return presents from them, as if he would say: "I want to give you doctors presents. Do not be like my cousin whom I helped, but who now does not invite me to a dinner party." Then he wants to stop the analysis because he is hungry. He thinks that if he could live one year in luxury, do anything he desired, have at his command all the money he wanted, he would be satisfied. He finishes this session by expressing his astonishment at the fact that such people as the analyst can enjoy life working so much.

In the next session he complains of a pain on his right side and thinks it may be appendicitis. Then follows a period of the analysis in which he frankly brings forward his oral receptive tendencies. He does not want to be changed, he only wants money, and he expresses rather manifestly the wish to stop the analysis, which disturbs these tendencies. Once he says: "You will be glad to be back in Germany," which of course really means: "I would be glad if you were back in Germany." In the same period of the analysis he develops a symptom which had occasionally appeared before—namely, he becomes impatient toward the end of the session and scarcely can wait to finish the hour. Parallel with this symptom his conflicts on account of receiving the five dollars from Dr. H. become more and more intense. Sudden compulsive suicidal phantasies occur during the hour, but at the same time these receptive wishes and claims become more and more manifest. He asks Dr. B. to employ him as an office-boy. He again has a dream revealing his oral tendencies: He saw many women with exposed breasts as in the other dream. He went to bed with one of them. The others were walking around the bed. He asked them what they were waiting for and one of them answered: "We are next."

In this dream he has quite a company of women all at his disposal to satisfy his oral receptive sucking tendencies. In the same interview he confesses a very conscious envy of Dr. H. in whose bill-fold, when he gave him the money, he saw a

ticket for the Harvard-Yale game. During this period he frequently expresses the wish to receive a new overcoat for the
winter to take the place of his old one.

Then his analysis was interrupted by a dramatic episode. A
pocketbook was stolen at the Foundation and he or a girl was
suspected of having taken it. While this affair was being investigated, it came out that he went to the house of one of the
office-girls and made approaches to her. The girl, however,
refused his proposal. He admitted the episode with the girl,
but denied the theft. Later it was definitely established that he
was not guilty of the theft. As a reaction to the refusal of the
girl, he had a comforting dream: He was at a party. He was
the only man. All of the others were women. He wanted to go
away, but the women would not allow him to go. They
grabbed him. He was fighting them and then he suddenly
felt himself falling and he was out of bed when he awoke.

He himself immediately interprets the dream by saying: "I
think I dreamed it because of the controversy with Miss X.
I compensate for my sense of inferiority. In the dream the
women do not let me go—just the opposite of what happened
in reality." He associates to this dream a nightmare of his
childhood: He was sleeping with his mother and a big powerful man tore him away from her and tortured him. He woke
up screaming. Without any connecting link he continues: One
teacher told his mother that he has a wonderful imagination
and that if he would use it well, he would become a great
author, but if he used it poorly, he would become the greatest
crook. Then the idea of running away to New York suddenly
appears in his consciousness. He sees the foolishness of this
idea, but it comes compulsively. Following the train of his
association he has a memory of childhood. When he was a
child, he once saw his mother on the other side of the street.

He started to run across and was struck by a truck. He was taken to a doctor and he had to stay home a week, but he was merely shaken up a bit.

The memory of this accident is one of a series of associations which were all induced by the failure of the episode with the office-girl, which had quite a traumatic influence on him, since it might expose him to everybody in the Center. This episode, the nightmare of being torn away from his mother, and the memory of the accident are all emotionally connected; all express the wish for sexual gratification interrupted by a painful experience. The attempt to seduce one of the office-girls belonging to the Foundation to which the analyst belongs reactivated these older memories of his attachment to his mother, which were connected with fear and guilt.

A period of repeating the same material follows. Envy of the analyst, phantasy of running away, strong resistance, together with blaming the analysis, emphasis on his martyrdom at home, hopelessness about obtaining a job, phantasies of becoming rich, with subsequent suicidal phantasies, fill up the hours.

Then he has a dream in which he killed the analyst: It happened at the other office, on C. Street. He came into the treatment room, drew a knife, and killed the analyst. He went to the police and gave himself up. Then all night, while he was sleeping, he saw the analyst's face. Every place he turned, the face appeared. Toward morning he urinated and then got some quiet sleep.

This dream marks a turning-point in the analysis. The envy and hostility toward the analyst and Dr. H. become entirely conscious.

In another dream he was standing outside the door and Dr. H. gave him the five dollars which he receives weekly. Then a horse jumped on top of him and stamped on him with its hoofs. His interpretation of the dream is that the powerful horse took revenge on him because he accepted the money from Dr. H. whom he envies so much. He would now like more than ever to stop taking the money because he has found a temporary job, in a restaurant, but he needs an overcoat and would like to continue receiving aid until he has enough saved for the coat. In the same hour an interesting attempt at self-justification takes place when he speaks about anti-Semitism. He discusses persecution of the Jews and ends these trains of thought by enumerating all the important Jews like Einstein, Mischa Elman, Heifetz, Spinoza, and Mendelssohn, all of whom helped make the earth a better place to live in, and yet they were outcasts.

At a later session he reported six dreams. *Dream 1:* He was seating people in a restaurant and one big fellow came down the stairs and choked him. It was a real nightmare. *Dream 2:* He was working in a restaurant and the general manager came to him and told him that he was to be advanced and become the manager. He sees himself ordering people around and becoming a person of authority. After this dream he woke up, but then went to sleep again. *Dream 3:* He was riding on a horse and fell off. He woke up again. *Dreams 4 and 5:* The fourth and fifth dreams were very hazy. All he remembers is that they represented different scenes in a department store where he was working. In the store there was an episode similar to the one at the Center when a pocketbook was stolen, but different people were involved. There is a faint idea of a woman in it. *Dream 6:* This was very vivid. He was working in a department store beside a girl who was tying bundles. The general manager of the store came over and said: "You both go down to the store detective. I think you took it." He knew a watch had been stolen. He woke up with a violent desire to urinate.

After associating to the dreams, he himself comes close to their solution. In the first dream he describes his success in his present job in the restaurant, but ends by being choked by a big fellow. The second dream is again one of clear-cut gratification. He becomes the manager of the store. He can enjoy this success, as the claims of his conscience are satisfied in the first dream. The third dream is again a dream of failure. In the following three dreams he is accused of having stolen with a girl who, the associations prove, is the one in the Center to whom he made the approaches. It is apparent that the purpose of these last three dreams is to replace the sexual guilt with stealing. This interpretation he himself gives by asking the analyst whether the sixth dream could not mean that he wanted to have intercourse with the girl and felt guilty for that and therefore in the dream he was accused of another bad deed—theft instead of sexual intercourse.

In the following session the deepest layers of his unconscious came to the surface in the form of an orgy of pregenital phantasies. The hour was introduced by the reporting of a wet dream of the previous night. In his dream he was with a girl whom he picked up on the street; he went to her room. Before and during the intercourse he felt as if he were wallowing around and lying upon something wet and soft. He often has this feeling in sexual dreams. His associations lead to the confession of his cannibalistic tendencies during intercourse. He feels like biting the flesh of the girl and seeing the blood run. These oral sadistic phantasies are evidently associated with the infantile anal pleasure to which the dream has a clear reference —"lying upon something wet and soft." He associates with the dream a nightmare which he had when he was six years old: He saw a big woman with a horrible face who took him from his bed and drowned him.

This particular dream has recurred again and again. It is

obvious that this terrible woman is his mother, and very probably this dream originates from the fear sensations of his childhood during the training for cleanliness. The punishments for
soiling and wetting the bed must be the background of this
dream. Probably it refers to the infantile experience that after
he soiled himself, his mother washed and spanked him. The
fact that this childhood nightmare is emotionally associated
with the above dream shows that the wallowing around and
lying upon something wet and soft is the representation of
infantile sensations of soiling himself; and in the nightmare
of the terrible woman who drowned him, the punishment was
drowning, corresponding to being washed by the mother, who
probably at the time scolded or spanked him. Once before, he
had a dream that a girl put a knife in him during intercourse
and he was wallowing in his own blood. These associations
and dreams very clearly brought to the surface his sado-maso-
chistic tendencies in connection with his own anal and oral
sadistic gratifications. In one dream he bit the woman and
had sexual pleasure, and in another dream the woman hurt
him. These alternating sadistic and masochistic gratifications
are present also in the sequence of his self-punishing dreams
followed by dreams of success and power. At the end of this
session when he gets up from the couch he feels great pain in
the right side of his abdomen. These pains continue in the next
hour, together with a headache.

The second session after he confessed these pregenital tendencies, he talked about his travels in Germany and everywhere
in Europe. In the preliminary interviews, he told the analyst,
as he had already told many others, about his travels around
the world undertaken as a sailor or steward. He maintained
that he had been in India and China, had seen London, Paris,
Hamburg, and Berlin, and he spoke in detail of his interesting
experiences in these different parts of the world. It never had

been established that his stories were invented, although some of the psychiatrists who knew him earlier had doubts about them. The vivid way in which he spoke about his experiences, however, and the many plausible details he gave partly dissipated the skepticism of the hearer. Since the beginning of the analysis he never reverted to them until three months had elapsed. Like his impulsive stealing and truancy, these phantastic lies were also closely related to his feelings of inferiority.

Finally in two dramatic analytic sessions he confesses that these stories about his travelling to foreign places were all invented. After this confession he has a dream: He saw the analyst on the boat leaving America. The analyst left him his car and he was riding in it. Suddenly there was a big accident and he awoke. His interpretation of the dream is that he is punished for envying the analyst the car.

In the next session he tells of a sexual affair which he had with a prostitute and at the next moment the picture of his mother flashes through his mind. This was the session in which he confessed that he never had been in China—his experiences there being the one travel story he had been heretofore unwilling to relinquish. After making this confession, he asks for the first time during the whole analysis for permission to leave the analytic room to go to the toilet. In the next session he remembers that when he first ran off he threw away the two dollars which he stole from his father, dropping it behind the radiator in the police station for fear that his theft would be known.

In the following session he reports two dreams which express his full Œdipus complex. *Dream 1:* He was going to leave the restaurant and was having his meal there before leaving. The manager came to him and told him that he regretted it very much, but he must let him go. At this moment a machine fell on him and started pounding him with sledge-hammers. *Dream 2:* He had intercourse with—"I am ashamed to say it— with my mother."

In connection with these dreams he remembers that as a child he listened to parental intercourse. After a few associations in which he pictures himself in a new derby and spats, he becomes exceedingly restless. "After I told you the dream, I became terribly restless. Every minute was like an hour." In this dream pair the mechanism of receiving through punishment the justification for forbidden gratification is most impressive. In the first dream a father image, the manager, dismisses him and he is struck by sledge-hammers, and in the second dream he has sexual intercourse with his mother. It is of great theoretic interest that this clear-cut incest dream followed a few days after he had made his confession about his phantastic lies. It seems that this unconscious confession was facilitated by the fact that he told the analyst his greatest conscious secret—namely, the falsity of his travel stories, the emotional source of which was the same as the incest dream— the satisfaction of his masculine ambitions.

In the session following the discussion of the incest dream he confesses having had homosexual experiences with a man who helped him out with money. The restlessness at the end of the hour from now on becomes stronger and stronger. At the same time his attitude toward his family changes. He day-dreams less. Seemingly all his neurotic manifestations are concentrated in this restlessness, which usually occurs in the second half of the sessions. In associating to this restlessness, repeatedly the idea of cunnilingus comes up. In one of the sessions the following sequence of associations occurred: He reported a dream: He was an artist on Beacon Hill. He painted women who wore wonderfully draped skirts, but their breasts were bare—just the same as in the other dream a few weeks ago. He went from one model to another and sucked their breasts.

Patient: "Now I have the desire to stop, and feel very strongly that I should like to leave. This is the feeling which I always have. I get tired of everything."

Analyst: "It is interesting that this feeling now comes in the same connection as yesterday. Yesterday when I asked you to associate to this feeling, you came to the idea of sucking— cunnilingus. And now, today, after you tell me the dream in which you suck on the breasts of the models, you have the idea of stopping the analytic session."

Patient: "Perhaps when I was a baby my mother forced her breast on me and I wanted to stop. But that cannot be so, because I was a bottle baby. But then, perhaps my mother forced the bottle on me. Is that possible?"

Analyst: "I do not know that, but we will see whether we can find out something more."

Then he continues; when he was a young boy, he slept in the same bed with his older brother. His brother wet the bed often and he ran to his mother and said that it was not he who wet the bed. He did it to protect his reputation, not to "squeal on" his brother. He thinks that at the time, if he had any feeling about the matter, it was superiority toward his brother because his brother wet the bed and he did not. "Or do you think that I felt inferior even at that time and that it was only a defense mechanism? But I now really have the feeling that I have told you everything and that I want to go." Then he again complains about pains in his chest and in the right side of his abdomen.

Returning to the dreams, the analyst asks him to associate his dream idea of being an artist. "I hoped to create something, to paint, or to be musical. I always associate any creative work with homosexuality." (As later became evident, for David homosexuality and cunnilingus were identical. He confused both words and used the expression "homosexuality" not only for intercourse with men, but for using the mouth in sexual relations, no matter whether with a man or with a woman.) "Maybe there is a connection. I always thought that homosexuals are more inclined to do artistic work." He sits up and the following conversation ensues:

Analyst: "Please lie down. Have you something else to say about painting?"

Patient: "Right after painting in the dream I dreamed of sucking. I always secretly wanted to paint. I admire painters. Tell me, is cunnilingus very common?"

Analyst: "Rather common."

Patient: "I thought only homosexual women do that, not men. Can one outgrow it?"

Analyst: "Certainly one can."

Patient: "I find it very hard to tell you anything now, especially today. I want to go home and show my mother the ties." (He had bought ties for his father's birthday.)

These associations show that David's wish to leave is connected with certain guilt feelings, which again are reactions to the gratification of his oral aggressive wishes. During the whole analysis David had the greatest conflict in accepting the weekly five dollars from Dr. H., but at the same time, he wanted to have it and it was of special significance to him to get the money. To get, to receive as the expression of his oral fixation, is connected with extreme guilt feelings, as became evident on several occasions, for example, during the session in which his oral sadistic and extreme masochistic phantasies and dreams followed each other in close connection. He wants to possess the mother alone, to be the favorite, but at the same time this wish is connected with the strongest guilt feelings against father and brothers. His restlessness during the hour is evidently repetition in the transference of the same feelings which induced him to run away from home. He ran away when he became involved in his guilt feelings and sense of inferiority; envy of other members of the family became so intense that he could not stand it any longer.

In this phase of the analysis it was impossible to decide what was the real basis of these emotions in the family situation. There is no question that David had the tendency to put himself in a martyr rôle in order to relieve his guilt feelings, and he tried to make the analyst and himself believe that the mother preferred his older brother. He behaved in the same way toward the analyst. Although he knew that being picked out for the analysis was a certain distinction and good fortune, he tried to turn the situation around and consider the analysis a kind of punishment. He went into a real orgy of inferiority feelings and self-accusations as a reaction to Dr. H.'s assertion that the analysis was a distinction and might be of great benefit to him. Therefore from the beginning the analyst assumed that the picture of the family situation which he gave was distorted, but there was no reason to assume that he not only exaggerated but entirely falsified it. When he said that his mother preferred the two other brothers, this sounded rather probable because these two boys were very good boys and the hope of the parents for the future, whereas David was actually the black sheep.

According to our methodological procedure the analyst during the analysis was not acquainted with the data which were collected about David from other sources. This material was seen only after the analysis was finished. According to these data the mother's real favorite was David. This fact is probably the nucleus of his maladjustment. Being the successful competitor in the family, he developed extreme guilt feelings regarding the gratification of his receptive and possessive tendencies. At the same time he remained orally fixated to the mother. He wanted to possess the mother for himself, and just because he really was the favorite his sense of guilt toward the rest of the masculine members of the family became so intense.

At the end of his analysis the analyst informed him of this assumption. He confirmed it by saying that he felt this to be true all the time, but could not express it so clearly, but he knows that he really always ran away after he stole or received something. When he ran away the first time after having stolen the ten dollars, he had more money all at once than ever before in his life. Again he ran away after he found money. Another time he ran away after he found a good job and was earning well, and still another time after he was given the fellowship through the aid of the Center. During the analysis he ran away a day after his mother had given him a fountain-pen, and an old friend of his, a musician, had given him a ring, all of which he reported in the analysis prior to running away. After the same session in which he told of these gifts, Dr. H. gave him the five dollars, but informed him that it was the last time he would receive it. He felt terribly ashamed that he himself had not suggested that the allowance be discontinued before being told that it would stop. This fact aroused shame and guilt of an extreme intensity. His running away was always a reaction to guilt feelings after gratification of his receptive tendencies, no matter whether he was given things or stole them. Now the data collected from other sources make it possible to throw light on the analytic material and show the methodological value of the confrontation of both kinds of material, that gained from the patient himself and that from external sources, concerning others toward whom the patient's reactions are directed.

The fact that he was the favorite of his mother gives a very striking explanation for the peculiar sequence of his associations after the dream of being a painter, when his restlessness became so intense. He had the idea that his mother pressed her breast upon him or forced the bottle and afterwards, seemingly rather without connection, the memory of his brother's bed-wetting and his reporting the brother to the mother in connection with superiority feelings toward the brother, who was older and still wet the bed. It is evident that this series of associations in connection with his restlessness means: "I want to run away from you who want to help me, the same way as I want to run away from home, from my mother, who preferred me to my brothers. She overwhelmed me with love, forced upon me her love (bottle or breast), and yet I was so mean that I reported my brother's bed-wetting. I cannot stand receiving love, because I was so mean to my brother."

Although the associations to painting are not sufficient to explain why, in the oral dream in which he sucked the breasts of the models, he represents himself as a painter, we are still able to make a probable assumption. To painting he associates productivity, and his wish is to become a painter or a musician —to produce something. We know from analytic material that in painting very often the anal tendencies are sublimated. The first productivity of the child is his anal product, and the relation between painting and soiling is well known. Probably in the dream he balances his passive receptive wish, sucking the breast, with the productive anal ejective function—painting. He is not merely a suckling baby at the breasts of the models, because he paints. Probably the emotional nucleus of this dream is the situation of the baby at the mother's breast sucking and at the same time defecating. This is the most primitive manifestation of passive receptive and active ejective tendencies—the first realization of the emotional balance between receiving and giving.

To return to the course of the analysis: In the interview following the one in which he brought up the thought of being a baby, and his mother forcing her breast on him, he again reported suicidal phantasies and a dream of being dead. The next day he came to the session, but it could not be undertaken on account of his violent pains in the right abdomen. The first complaint about the abdominal pains (twenty-fourth interview) followed the hour in which his oral receptive tendencies came undisguised to the surface for the first time and were discussed in the analysis. That was the interview in which he reported the first dream about women with exposed breasts. In the same session he spoke about his mother's lullabies, going to the Jewish restaurants, the phantasy of giving Christmas presents to the doctors in the Center, and the wish to go home to eat. The first time after his analysis began that he had abdominal pains, but not during a session, was, however, three days before that, right after he discussed his conflicting feelings at getting the five dollars. He had a phantasy of collecting this money and saving it until the spring and buying a car with it. In this session he realized that getting five dollars from Dr. H. had, besides the real value of the five dollars, an especially emotional significance for him. He wanted to be the favorite of Dr. H., and that was a proof of it. His receptive attitude toward the analyst he also discussed in this session very elaborately after he asked for ten cents for carfare because he had spent more than he had expected and had no money.

Now, however, he had very severe pain. The analyst's examination made him suspicious of appendicitis and David was sent home. A few days later he was operated on for appendicitis and an appendix with very slight pathological changes was removed. It is difficult to exclude a psychogenic factor in the development of this disease. There seems to be some connection between his guilt feelings and the pathological conditions which gave him pain. During the six dreams which he reported in his thirty-eighth interview, he felt very intense abdominal pain during dreams four, five, and six. During the analysis of the restlessness which led to the oral phantasy toward the mother, he had similar pains which came suddenly while discussing the phantasy. During interview thirty-nine, when he reported about his cannibalistic phantasies, he had recurrence of the pain on standing up. During interview forty he had a very strong emotional reaction to Dr. H.'s offer to continue giving him the five dollars in spite of the fact that he was earning money. Directly after speaking about this he had cramps on his right side. He complained of pains almost always in connection with the gratification of oral receptive tendencies. The appendicitis developed two days after he had the sudden idea that his mother forced her breast on him and when the restlessness during the hour became the greatest. One cannot entirely discard the assumption that those physiological processes which led to appendicitis were influenced by his sense of guilt on account of the gratification of oral receptive tendencies. Unfortunately there is no possible way of exactly proving the causal connection between these concurrences. One can only hope that very thorough parallel investigations of simultaneous physiological and psychological phenomena may at some time give more reliable clues for the solution of such problems. These remarks consequently should be regarded only as reporting a noteworthy, possibly very significant, coincidence between the appearance of certain psychological and certain physiological phenomena.

His operation and the convalescence in the hospital interrupted the analysis for twenty days. In the first session after his analysis was resumed he described his reactions to the operation as a state of acute excitement which he called a psychosis.

He thought that he was going to die and then he wanted to kill himself, to choke himself, "to cheat death," to commit suicide instead of dying. He really started to choke himself, but the nurse prevented it. He was given a hypodermic and under the influence of it he had the following dream: He was playing with a dog. The dog turned into a woman. They were wallowing in mud and he had difficulty in inserting his penis. Then David asked: "Is that wallowing in feces?"

Then he had a second attack which he called "psychotic." He asked the nurse to buy him a knife so that he could kill himself. He wanted to jump out of bed and kill himself. He fought with the nurse. After that he quieted down and his convalescence was uneventful. He had some temperature all the time. He had no pain during the last days. He lost sixteen pounds, but he feels physically well and mentally he is very well. The only thing is that now he cannot complain about his pains, and that is what he misses. This remark sufficiently shows that he tried to exploit his pains for relieving his guilty conscience. The validity of this statement is independent of any possible causal connection between the pathology of the appendix and his guilt feelings.

His attitude toward the family has changed. He feels very much improved. In the next hours, he describes the family situation with great sympathy. The restlessness at the end of the hour turns up again. In the next session he has a dream about his brother's death: The family was called to the hospital where his brother was. When they arrived, he was already dead. His mother scolded him as if he were responsible for his brother's death, and told him that he must now become a much better boy than he had been.

At that time his younger brother was actually ill and in the hospital with pneumonia. In this session he confesses that he has death wishes toward members of his family all the time.

He wants to be the only son. Today he saw his mother putting on a pair of stockings. "I forgot that she is mother and had the same feelings toward her as toward another woman sexually. That I can tell you this astonishes me. I never would have thought that I could tell that to anybody." Although he already had had an incestuous dream, this is the first time in which the sexual attachment toward his mother becomes conscious in the waking state. At the end of the session his restlessness becomes extreme. He wants to go, to stop the analysis. Then a long pause sets in, during which he falls into a dreamlike state and phantasies that he murdered somebody, but he could not see who it was. He was to be electrocuted, but he killed himself by injecting cyanide with a needle. To the question: "Whom do you think you want to kill?" he answers: "To be frank, you, Dr. A., because you keep me here."

In the following sessions, after his appendectomy, but before his last running away, which is discussed above, the restlessness at the end of the hour appears regularly with great intensity. A new wave of the wish to run away from home occurs. The conflict at taking the five dollars from Dr. H. becomes more and more intense, he phantasies the death of Dr. H., who leaves him money. However, outside of the analytic sessions he feels better adjusted. All his neurotic manifestations are concentrated in the analytic hour. He again has phantasies of great success, giving large donations to the Center.

In one of these sessions he tells this dream: He was going to a house of ill fame. When he got there, the Madame sent him into a room. Then his mother came in. She was a prostitute. He told her to get her clothes and then he took her home. In connection with this dream he remembers a series of sexual affairs. One was with a thirty-five-year-old prostitute who picked him up on the street in New York and supported him for three weeks.

The phantasies to run away return in every session. In another dream he killed the analyst and Dr. H. and robbed them of their money. He connects these hostile tendencies with the fact that in the previous session the possibility of his taking up some studies was discussed. He felt that he was being coerced into doing work which he did not want to do. After this dream he woke up, but later in the night he dreamed that he attempted suicide with gas; his mother came in, opened the window, and saved his life.

In this session he again becomes restless toward the end of the hour and he recognizes this feeling as entirely the same as his urge to run away. In this hour we are able to work out that the restlessness comes from an extreme sense of guilt which he feels toward the male members of the family. He wants to get rid of father and brothers, to possess his mother in the oral receptive way. Killing the analyst and Dr. H. and robbing them is a substitute for his patricidal wishes. In this session he gets complete insight into these facts, but in the following hour the reaction to this insight shows itself in a dramatic way. He decides to stop being psychoanalyzed. He was reading a book containing articles on psychoanalysis. The author said it was very rare that psychoanalysis could completely cure a patient. And then he continues: "Let us be frank, Dr. A. I am not coming any more because I think the whole of psychoanalysis is bunk and my faith in it is shaken. The six months are wasted. Maybe I think that because I have been reading books on psychoanalysis and listening to people speak about it." A young doctor in the hospital told him that psychoanalysis has no basis. He thinks that this doctor was right. Then he goes on speaking about Hitler and anti-Semitism, begins to criticize the analyst and his English, but then, suddenly, without any connection, his attitude changes. He has a phantasy. He is a successful man and he reads his case in a magazine. "Now I am putting analysis on a pedestal again, and a minute ago I deprecated it. Which feelings are right?" Then he develops a phantasy of himself becoming a psychoanalyst. He again has the idea of taking out the analyst's secretary. The father conflict, attacking the father, depreciating him in the person of the analyst, is followed by a complete identification with him, putting himself in his rôle.

A few sessions later he has this dream: He killed his whole family and then himself by gas. He had to go to hell. At this period his conscious attitude toward the family has largely changed. He has great sympathy with his parents whose situation is getting increasingly worse. But at the end of the session he becomes much embittered on account of lack of money and emphasizes the fact that in spite of all his efforts he cannot find a job; he behaves aggressively and with irritation toward the analyst.

The next session is again full of phantasy of success and the next one again an hour of depression with the phantasy of committing a hold-up. In the same session he blames the analysis for harming him. In the following session he again wants to stop the analysis. He had a dream which he does not want to tell. After long hesitation he tells this dream: He had a love-affair with the analyst's wife, whom he has never seen. This brings up a memory of sexual relations with a school-teacher in New York.

The next hour is a direct continuation of expressing his tendencies of father-identification and possessing the mother (the analyst's wife). He wants to work in the Center to write a book, and after the hour asks Dr. H. for a room in which to write. The complete identification with the analyst is apparent in these associations. In the same interview he complains of a sore throat, of feeling hot and dizzy. He reports a dream: He was on board of a ship. Many rats jumped on him and were eating him up. Then he was in a brothel and had intercourse with a prostitute. He pulled out a knife and killed her and cut out her heart. He could not get rid of the blood which was dripping from him. Associations to the rats: *Arrowsmith*. The story centers on the battle of science against the bubonic plague. There is a scene of rats running away from a burning building.

Analyst: "The rats are eating you up in the dream. Associate to that."

Patient: "I can't. I wonder whether it could be idleness devouring me."

Analyst: "I think in the dream the rats represent your own grabbing, envious tendencies with which you have to fight here in the analysis."

The association, the fight of science against the bubonic plague, shows that the dream refers to the analysis, which is battling against the rats—that is, his oral aggressive tendencies expressed in his envy and jealousy.

Analyst: "Associate to the second part of the dream."

Patient: "My great interest in women."

Analyst: "But why the killing and the removing of the heart?"

Patient: "I did not want intercourse with her—to do away with all prostitutes. This lady did sign the note." (This is a reference to a lady whom the family asked to endorse a statement guaranteeing a loan to the father.)

Analyst: "I think this dream expresses again your devouring tendencies—to cut something out of a woman. Your association that you got money from the lady is in the same direction—to get something out of a lady. Similar are your gigolo phantasies. The tendency is to get, to take, to receive, and not to work, not to make an effort, not to give something from yourself. That is the early infantile attitude toward the mother. That is what you are fighting against. The rats symbolize all these parasitic, robbing tendencies."

Patient: "Yes, the rats really steal something and run away secretly and that is what I do."

In the same session he says that he thinks he should have an operation. He has some gland under his cheek which troubles him. His mother was sick today. She has a sore throat and fever. (David complained at the beginning of the hour of a sore throat and feeling hot and dizzy.) In the sequence of his associations it becomes quite obvious that after the extreme identification wish with the father image (the analyst), driven by guilt feelings he identifies himself with the suffering mother and wants to be operated on.

Analyst: "I think you are imitating your mother's disease. These 'rat' tendencies against your mother cause guilt and then you identify yourself with her in her disease."

The patient sits up and says: "Sometimes during the wrestling bouts, if one of the wrestlers starts to bleed, I get excited and afterwards I picture myself bleeding."

Analyst: "Yes, that is the same emotional reaction. At first you enjoy the cruelty and then you yourself suffer."

It was after this session that David actually went to Dr. H. and asked his opinion about writing a book. Dr. H. apparently discouraged him and he came into the next session in a very depressed mood. He blamed the analysis for destroying all his phantasies. He definitely wanted to stop the analysis, but at the next appointment he appeared. He met a wealthy friend who gave him a ring; his mother gave him a fountain-pen. He has the phantasy to go to a prostitute with the five dollars which he will get from Dr. H. He plans to go out with a girl whom he respects and adores. His restlessness again is much in evidence. He speaks about a relative who is a well-known music-teacher. He hopes to get a job. He scarcely can wait until he can see his girl friend.

After this hour Dr. H. told him that he would not receive any more allowance, but he gave him five dollars in order to pay an employment agency to find him a job. The next day his mother telephoned to say that David had disappeared. A few days later the family received a note from him sent from New York.

Six weeks later he comes and reports that he found a job in New York and is living with relatives. He is well dressed, smiling, and cheerful, but shows signs of embarrassment. He feels very well. He is working and saving money, sending some to his parents. He feels much more settled than ever before. His phantasies have gone. He has much less sense of inferiority. The only trouble is that he still cares more for clothes than he should because he can't afford to buy clothes yet, especially since his parents need help. But he feels friendly toward other people, he does not compare himself with them all the time. He takes himself in a matter-of-fact way and has much more interest in other people. His attitude, especially toward his parents, has changed. He is himself astonished that he does not brag any more. He enjoys life; he has been to the opera. He reads. He has not given up his plans to study and improve his chances in life, but he waits for a better opportunity. Intellectually he realizes that the analysis helped him much, although occasionally he hates the memory of it. He never felt better than he does now.

He explains that he ran away because he felt terribly ashamed that he waited until Dr. H. cancelled his allowance. Dr. H. gave him the five dollars for an employment-agency fee, but he did not get the job and so did not pay the fee. He spent that evening with his girl friend, went to the movies with her, and afterwards he told her he was going to New

York. The impulse came over him suddenly, just as on former occasions. He felt very badly that he did not return the money obtained for the employment office and therefore left without telling anyone. However, now all his earlier conflicts and his vivid phantasies have almost disappeared. He had sexual intercourse once since he has been away, but he has no great urge. Altogether, he is very much satisfied. He never kept a job as long as this and he never felt so settled.

Fate, however, was not kind for very long to David. The company which employed him went into bankruptcy during the depression. David came home and again for a time was jobless, but withstood the situation better than earlier. Then he found a job, is working steadily, and turns in his wages to the family. Again he feels settled and satisfied. He plans to go to night law-school next year and become a lawyer. But this time he is sure that it is a real rather than a phantastic plan. His mother always wanted him to become a lawyer and he hopes that he may realize her ambitions.

The reconstruction of David's personality problems is not difficult on the basis of this material. It is evident that he was very strongly fixated in the pregenital emotional pattern belonging to the oral-sadistic (cannibalistic) phase. In phantasy he wants to possess the mother alone, to get rid of all the three male members of the family, but this possessive attitude toward the mother is entirely on the cannibalistic level. He wants to devour her, as is most clearly expressed in the rat dream, in the second part of which he cuts out the heart of the prostitute. Association between prostitute and mother was well established during the analysis. This strong oral receptive attitude is at the bottom of his inferiority feelings. His strong envy is the natural consequence of the sense of inferiority. Another reaction to the sense of inferiority is his phantastic lies in which he develops in phantasy what he does not achieve in reality—

namely, the gratification of his masculine ambitions.

Another consequence of his cannibalistic oral aggression is his violent sense of guilt, together with his tendency to project his hostile attitudes onto others. His running away was a reaction to this intense feeling of guilt, which became strongest when he gratified his grabbing tendencies by stealing or receiving something. Before his analysis, he belonged to the type who cannot stand success on account of the guilt feelings originating from the grabbing, sadistic impulses.

Confronting the psychoanalytic material with the case study of the Judge Baker Guidance Center we find the above analytic construction complemented by the interesting fact that David was indeed the favorite of his mother, in spite of his personality difficulties. There is no doubt that his being favored contributed to the intensity of his guilt feelings. It is a theoretically interesting question whether, if the analysis had been continued, David would have ever come to the insight that his mother really loved him the best. It is possible that a longer analysis would have made him not only realize his distorting and projecting tendencies, but also recognize the fact that this distortion went so far as entirely to deny the real situation, to deny that he was the favorite and that he merely phantasied that the mother preferred Harry. In any case, this fact of the mother's predilection for him which the family study established allows us to make the etiological assumption that David's strong oral fixation and his guilt reactions toward it were caused, or at least powerfully supported, by the mother's attitude toward him. The question whether the explanation of this strong oral fixation had a constitutional basis or not cannot be answered in the present status of our knowledge about the development of personality.

It must also be emphasized that the social-environmental

factors had no decisive importance in David's criminality. Both of his brothers under the same circumstances are well-adjusted individuals. The immediate family and also the relatives have shown no criminal tendencies. The economic pressure was never extreme until the last few months. David's antisocial behavior was entirely a manifestation of his emotional and instinctual conflicts.

It is unnecessary to give more data from David's earlier case history because all essentials appear in the analytic material and there are no contradictions or discrepancies. Perhaps scant justice is done to the extent to which his self-aggrandizements, appearing in the form of his fictitious tales of travel, were related to many people, but even these came out in the analysis.

There is no doubt that David has shown a great personality change for the better since his analysis, which ended two years ago. In the face of great difficulties, much economic stress in the family, his own unemployment at periods, his hospitalization several times, and an operation for a chronic joint trouble which has developed, David has shown a stability and a strength of purpose which are truly remarkable. With his discouragements there have been thoughts of self-destruction, but at other periods an optimism amounting almost to a feeling of elation that he has changed so markedly. He has worked very hard even when he suffered great pain and has been admirable in trying to help his family financially. While it must be confessed that he is still somewhat unstable, allowing his impulses rather than rational judgment to guide him at times, it should be taken into account that his life situation has been terrifically complicated by the chronic ailment from which he has suffered. How he is to meet the world, with his ambitions, his conflicting impulses, his illness and financial difficulties, remains for David a complex problem to solve.

# CHAPTER FIVE

## *A Friend of Animals*

ELMER TOME was twenty years old when analysis was begun, and fourteen when he was first studied at the Guidance Center. A summary of the case record, extending to the time of analysis, runs as follows:

*Family Setting:* Elmer is the eldest of five living children, all residing with their parents: Elmer, twenty; Lee, seventeen; Arabella, fourteen; Donald, eleven; Amy, nine. The first child died at two years of age. Father, fifty; mother, fifty-two; both of Scotch-Irish ancestry, born in Maryland.

*Delinquencies:* Since he was six years of age and up to the time he was fourteen, Elmer had left home on the average of two or three times a year. At first he stayed out for one or two nights at a time; then, as he grew older, for a week or two. He had been many times returned by child-welfare agencies, sometimes by the police. He journeyed to near-by towns or out into the country; he walked long distances, even under adverse weather conditions. The only stealing reported was that he once took a bicycle to go away with, and just prior to his first visit to the Guidance Center he had stolen thirty dollars from church subscriptions which his mother had collected.

Since Elmer was fourteen, he has run away at least fifteen times, seven of these flights being from well-selected farm homes where he had been placed by a child-helping agency, for the most part in response to his own solicitations. He has never wandered to other parts of the country; often he came almost directly to Boston, reporting before long to the Guidance Center or to his relatives. He has slept in barns or lived in cheap lodging-houses, usually having no police contacts. At times he has obtained employment in some town and remained away a month or so. When first placed on a farm, he ran away in a few days, taking money, which he did not entirely spend and which his family paid back. Shortly afterwards, when placed again, he drove off with a horse and wagon, which were not found for several days. Later he once ran away leaving a horse in the town to which he had driven from the farm to go to church. On one occasion he took a considerable sum of money from home after a period when he had been working well and turning in his wages. He confessed to having once abstracted from a man's pocket a small sum for food. He stole the contents of the pocketbook of a person in our own office. Elmer acknowledged having practiced cheating with cards, on two occasions having acquired a little money through this.

At twelve years Elmer had been approached by a homosexual man; later when away from home he found it easy to get lodgings and money from such men, with whom he had various experiences, but always, he maintained, with a considerable sense of disgust and a great feeling of guilt. More recently these contacts have been entirely broken.

Elmer continued his runaway expeditions after he had been in a state correctional institution at seventeen. A couple of months after release, when holding a fairly good job, he left home again, and later he ran away three times from a farm home to which he went voluntarily and where he professed to be and, indeed, seemed to be very happy.

*Heredity:* The ancestry is well known. The direct forebears on both sides have been quiet-living working people of good reputation. The family characterize themselves as Maryland

Catholics, ordinary people, without moral blemish in the family. In Scotland there were ancestors of much better social standing; some treasures of one notable ancestor have been preserved. Distant relatives in this country are much better off, but have practically nothing to do with Elmer's family. No hereditary taint is discoverable.

*Home Conditions:* Before Elmer's birth his parents moved to Boston and during his early childhood his father was doing fairly well in business. Since then and earlier he has sometimes worked for ecclesiastical organizations. Until Elmer was seven the family lived in a rather crowded section of the city, but since then they have lived in a small house in a sparsely settled suburb. The home has always been very well kept and the children well cared for, in spite of depleted fortunes. More recently financial help has been received from relatives, themselves not well off. Occasionally Elmer has stayed for short periods with a maternal aunt.

*Family Characteristics and Attitudes:* Mr. Tome is a big man, meagerly educated, a hard worker, home-loving, taciturn, of good habits, much attached to the church. He spends long hours in reading the ordinary run of periodicals. He has been healthy except for an illness about ten years ago which left him nervous and irritable for a long time. Occasionally even before that he became belligerent about annoyances, and in general took a moderately domineering attitude. He has always been fond of the children, and when Elmer was little, provided him with unusually nice toys and pets. For a long period after the death of his first little boy he was emotionally upset about it, blaming the physician.

Mrs. Tome is short, stout, ruddy-complexioned, with light hair, somewhat better educated than her husband, stable emotionally, a good housekeeper, and intensely religious. She also has some superstitious fears concerning non-religious matters.

Besides her six children she had several miscarriages, and on account of suffering greatly during pregnancies and at the birth of her children, relatives helped her much in the early care of them. She has obtained medical treatment frequently for herself and her children, and as the years have gone on she has improved much in health.

In spite of difficulties, there has been a fairly harmonious atmosphere in the home—the father only occasionally showing bad temper. Both parents had to go to work early and were partial supporters of their own families, and it has been their aim to develop responsibility in their children—responsibility to the church as well as to the family. The mother has been very loyal to her husband and has been quietly patient in her dealings with the children. She took great pains to impress at least the older ones with her ideas about sin and the possibility of punishment in the next world. Her husband states that she has had her own way in the management of the children and that she has been very protective of them, particularly of Elmer. He insists that the female members of the family made a great mistake in their concealment of Elmer's delinquencies, even from relatives. This has led, as we know, to numerous evasions on the part of the mother and the maternal aunt, and the withholding of facts even from each other, although both have been deeply desirous of his reformation. While the father feels Elmer was not punished severely enough, these two women have shown abounding sympathy with the boy, maintaining that he was handicapped from birth and that early he suffered somewhat from fear of his father.

Between Elmer and Lee in earlier years there was continuous friction. Lee had several prolonged illnesses requiring much special care and he has been a willful, bad-tempered boy, taking advantage of his illness, though in late years he has helped the family financially and is regarded as the scholar of the family.

Despite his ailments, this boy, like his father, is tall—both of them are considerably taller than Elmer. Lee at times has been very tormenting and domineering toward Elmer, who is said to have become quite forgiving toward his brother.

Arabella is a tall, healthy, quiet, merry girl, doing well in school. The two youngest children, who are healthy and present no problems, have entered very little into Elmer's life. A maternal aunt, a childless married woman, who physically closely resembles Elmer's mother, has displayed an especial interest in Elmer from the time of his birth. She has been willing to have him come to her at any time and under any conditions. She is very closely attached to Elmer's mother.

The whole family have been naturally much concerned about Elmer's disappearances; his mother and aunt particularly have worried about him and often have made efforts to find him or hear from him. He has always been welcomed back.

*Physical Findings:* At fourteen years Elmer presented a fairly normal physical picture, with rather good development and strength, though a little underweight. Careful medical examination gave negative results. (Three years previously at a psychopathic hospital where he had been taken for an examination by the Travelers' Aid, the physical findings were also noted as normal). Elmer's features were regular and fairly well shaped, but his expression was noted as being far-away, repressed, unhappy. During the ensuing years Elmer has been in good health, but sometimes has appeared very thin and worn as a result of deprivations. His teeth have decayed badly and he began dental treatment several times, never returning, however, for completion of the work.

*Developmental History:* Elmer's mother was ill for months with some abdominal trouble before his birth, and a miscarriage was feared. (Wassermann tests on mother and children were negative.) The birth was instrumental and difficult, with doubts of the survival of the full-term, large baby. Elmer was bottle-fed from the first. (None of the children were breast-fed.) At the end of the first month Elmer was in such poor condition that he was taken to an infants' hospital, where he remained up to his sixth month and afterwards had medical supervision. He walked and talked at the usual age. During childhood he had various diseases, but always in light form; his tonsils were removed early. At nine years he had severe rheumatic arthritis from exposure during a runaway in the winter. At twenty he is of average size and weight, with good muscular strength.

*Habits:* Good toilet habits were established neither very early nor very late. From his early years Elmer has been a fussy eater at home, going without food rather than eating what he dislikes. He exhibited no special cravings, but showed a great distaste for milk and most vegetables. However, in his foster-homes he is said to have shown no dietary peculiarities. He dislikes tea and coffee, but in the last few years has been a heavy smoker of cigarettes. To the age of fourteen he was occasionally a sleep-walker, even dressing himself while asleep. (The next two children are also somnambulists.) As a little boy, his mother discovered him in masturbation; he was threatened with its sinfulness, and his mother believes that this checked the habit.

*Psychological Findings:* Tests given at fourteen years showed I.Q. 98, corresponding almost exactly to the hospital findings of three years earlier. Reaction time on association tests was delayed, with considerable repetition of replies. Memory and learning ability seemed normal and the boy demonstrated a good range of information. Certain tests for apperceptive ability and mental control were poorly done. Scholastic achievement tests showed irregular results. The psychologist found him detached, sad, difficult to contact, but responding well to encouragement.

*School Record:* Elmer started school at the usual age. He had a good record for conduct and was promoted regularly with the exception of one of the times when he was transferred to a church institution. He finally finished the ninth grade.

*Personality Characteristics:* No change of personality was reported as appearing at any age. By everybody, Elmer is said to have been normally active and often very industrious, though slow and deliberate in his movements. When he was about six or seven he had some nice boy friends to whom he was attached, but since then he has had few, if any, intimates and has never belonged to any boys' gangs or clubs. Except for occasional evidences of unhappiness and his obvious sensitiveness, he has appeared emotionally stable, practically never showing bad temper. As a young boy he was much interested in stories of the West and at times has been a great reader. Early he drew many pictures of cowboys, and then, during early adolescence, made many elaborate drawings of religious subjects, particularly of the Holy Cross and the Sacred Heart. From his early years he has shown an especial interest in horses and other animals and has always been a great lover of outdoor life. By the time he was fourteen he occasionally worked on farms and earned fairly well, or picked and sold berries on his own account. His family insist that everyone has liked him because he is so quiet and considerate.

At the clinic Elmer usually appeared frank, clear in ideas, and always willing to talk about himself. After his runaway episodes, when he sometimes reported to the psychiatrist before he went home, he would appear depressed, with tears in his eyes, but at other times, when things were going better, he presented healthy normal attitudes, showing considerable sense of humor.

Concerning his own reactions to his delinquencies, it is to be noted that he generally was penitent and paid back from his earnings a good deal of what he stole. His professed ethical standards were high and for the most part his behavior was exemplary. At home he was quiet and reticent and practically never retorted to admonitions and scoldings.

*Psychiatric Considerations:* Notes of a score of psychiatric interviews during five years show Elmer to be a marked introvert with varying mental attitudes. One psychiatrist carefully considered the question of a beginning psychosis when Elmer was fourteen, but decided against this diagnosis, although there were evidences of a tendency toward being a schizoid personality. In the ensuing years, however, there has been no further development of these tendencies and, indeed, Elmer has withstood very well the vicissitudes of fortune.

As expressed by himself, Elmer's ideas and conflicts centered on the following: thoughts of sin and of punishment after death; what parts of his early teaching he could or should reject. Insisting that he was not making true confessions to his priest, he was urged to do this and then said he felt the better for it. At other times close religious observance made no difference. At fifteen he told the judge that sometimes he had thoughts of selling himself to the devil. When younger, he spoke at length of hearing voices which plainly told him to do or not to do this or that, crowding everything else out of his mind. He heard these voices before he was eight or nine, after he had been much impressed by the alleged therapeutic results of a visit to a shrine by one of his relatives.

Elmer told of his interests in country life, in riding or driving horses. When he had no opportunities for outlets in this direction, he liked to take long walks and phantasy these pleasures. His ambition was to have a farm home and be married.

Elmer had much to say about his family and often seemed contradictory in his statements about them. His father was a very good man who used to beat him when he was young. His brother was a good boy, but Elmer had hated him from the time he was born. His mother was not always truthful, but that made little difference; she would do anything for him, whereas his father would not. Elmer felt he had been punished for things he had not done, and then again he had not been punished for transgressions. He had never been understood by either parent and could not talk to them, particularly his father. Once he casually mentioned a girl relative, Viola, who had been brought up in his family. It was known to the children's agency visitor that her last illness was a great shock to Elmer and that he ran away just before she died, but Elmer denied that this had any influence upon his running away then.

Elmer's earlier expressed attitude toward sex affairs was abhorrence of the ordinary sex talk of boys—it was sinful. At fourteen he denied the homosexual experiences which he had really had, but a couple of years later he gave an account of these and more recent affairs, always insisting that they disgusted him and that he merely played a passive part in a mild way. He told of the care that his mother took to keep him away from bad boys when he was little to prevent him from getting into sinful ways. He expatiated on the contrast between mortal and venial sins. He spoke of swimming naked with a little group of boys and girls when he was seven or eight. His sex ruminations were evidently mostly heterosexual and not excessive. He confessed to almost complete avoidance of girls and great bashfulness toward them. He preferred thin girls and with some scorn once showed to the agency visitor the picture of a stout girl whom the family, feeling that he ought to have more normal companionship, were urging upon him as a suitable girl friend.

Elmer's only acknowledgment of dream life was concerned with dreams of animals, of tigers and snakes, which in some curious way would be "standing up and swaying back and forth," trying to speak to him. At sixteen he gave a vivid account of this.

It proved very difficult for Elmer to give any expression to the causes of his running away. He often repeated that he had a great feeling of wanting to get away somewhere, just anywhere. The impulse might come suddenly or after a period of uneasiness, but sometimes the runaway was planned days ahead. Nearly always he had gone alone. When he was much younger, two or three times he went away with other boys who desired to get into the country. Sometimes his flights had been preceded by some unpleasantness, but then again he had gone away when he had apparently been happy and doing well. Two or three times, when in foster-homes, he ran away immediately after attending church; once he stated that it was because he had borrowed an umbrella, forgotten it, and was ashamed to return without it. In short, Elmer was utterly contradictory about the reasons for his flights, or else he spoke of an utter lack of knowledge concerning why he went, saying once that his mind was a complete blank. Frequently he stated that above all things he would like to know why he so misbehaved and gave others so much trouble. He always readily acknowledged his own weak attitudes and inability to face difficulties. He confessed to a delinquency previously unknown to us—petty stealing from the poor-box of the church with which his father was connected. He could not explain why he was so cowardly about dental treatment. On the other hand, Elmer made very little of his good qualities. For example, he never told us what was well known to the agency visitor—namely, that at two periods, when he was doing well at work, he was almost the sole support of the family.

*Forms of Treatment Undertaken:* Elmer's earliest misbehavior was met by threats and whippings administered by his father. When these proved unavailing, the boy, at seven years,

was placed in a church institutional school, where he stayed
several months and was reported satisfactory in conduct and
scholarship, but peculiar inasmuch as he did not mix with the
other boys. Then after other runaway episodes he was placed
in another church institution at nine years and at eleven years,
the last time remaining a full year, again with satisfactory
reports being given. Between times, the treatment at home had
been relegated to his mother, who on very many occasions indulged in admonitions and warnings about sin and punishment after death. Elmer was always received after his runaway
episodes by his mother, or by his aunt at her home, in the most
kindly spirit.

After his first appearance in the juvenile court at fourteen
years, Elmer was placed on probation and the children's agency
was asked to find him a home in the country, to which he said
he wanted to go. After being placed in two homes, from each
of which he shortly ran away, stealing from one and taking a
horse and wagon from the next, his parents again placed him
in the church institution where he had been twice before. This
time he remained there eight months. The case was filed in
court the next year, when he had been doing well. A few months
later he again reappeared in court, now much ashamed because
he had stolen from his family. To the judge, who endeavored
to take a psychiatric attitude, he told of his prevailing impulses
and his homosexual experiences. Another agency now took him
for placing, putting him under the charge of an energetic and
understanding man visitor. He was given five opportunities
in two country homes, both of which he said he liked very well,
remaining at the longest a few months. The foster-parents were
always willing to take him back because he was industrious
and unobtrusive. It was not held against him in one home that
he had ransacked a box in the endeavor to find some money
with which to run away.

When he was almost seventeen, Elmer was sent to a state correctional school, where he made a good record. After this the agency visitor again found him a place in the country, from which he ran away a couple of times. Other people besides the family were sympathetic with him, and in the earlier days of the general economic depression he was given various forms of employment out of doors, at which he always did well for a time. It was soon after his last runaway from the farm, where he had been once more most kindly received, that the psychoanalysis began. In the meantime Elmer remained on parole from the correctional institution.

In addition to the above forms of treatment, it should be noted that when Elmer was thirteen or fourteen, a young priest worked for a time with the boy in an endeavor to influence him, and that at the Guidance Center he was interviewed more than twenty times in an attempt to understand and guide him. Also the agency visitor gave him a great deal of personal attention, having many confidential talks with him, and one farmer, of the "barnyard philosopher" type, tried in many hours of conversation to instill common-sense ideas into Elmer's head. Nor should there be omitted the efforts of Elmer's uncle, a most kindly man, who has tried to do everything he could for the boy, feeling, as he said at the clinic, that there was too much talk among the womenfolk about sin and hell.

### PSYCHOANALYTIC MATERIAL

Only the main facts of the family history, the delinquencies, and the treatment were known by the analyst. Hence a good opportunity is offered for comparing what was obtained by analysis with data derived by an ordinarily good case study. For elucidation of the dynamic issues, it seems best to deal with the analytic material more or less under the head of topics.

After the first four interviews Elmer made off to New York

with a little money received as overdue wages. He returned a week later, saying that he had gone to look for work, and, not finding it, he wished to continue the analysis.

The fifty-five interviews, continued until the summer vacation, show much repetition of themes. Sometimes associations are free, but often Elmer feels there is nothing to say or that he has told everything. In many of the later sessions, the unemployment situation is so much on Elmer's mind and he feels so hopeless about it that nothing else seems to matter; he feels caged in, with no escape. He frequently comes to the sessions long ahead of time because he has nothing else to do; sometimes he comes directly from employment agencies. Except for this discouragement, he evinces no strong emotional attitudes other than those expressed in his comparatively mild verbalizations. He lies quietly on the couch and speaks in a low, rather monotonous voice. He is always amenable.

In the first four interviews he deals with various features of the family life, the excessive religious teaching, his feeling of being over-directed by his mother and aunt, the reproaches of his people and their suspicions of him, his reluctance to go home. He tells of his own shyness and shame, the many causes for this, the fact that other people know too much about him, his inability to meet people well, the pleasantness and freedom of life in the country, his rather vague memories of early running away. He speaks of the childishness of his phantasies about horses and cowboy life, but he still retains such foolish notions.

It was made clear to Elmer that he indulges in much self-accusation, that his guilt feelings are frequently reactions to feelings within him rather than to external facts, that perhaps this came through his early vast experience with religious prohibitions. His intimidations arise from his own conscience. Elmer gives the details of an argument that preceded his last leaving a farm home and agrees with the analyst that the flight was due to over-sensitiveness. Then he tells about his sympathy with a mentally handicapped boy and particularly with animals who have suffered. It was interpreted that he carries over his self-pity into other fields. Elmer readily sees that he acts out some elements of his phantasy life and that he does this without maturely considering the consequences. In all this he shows almost too great a readiness to accept the views or explanations of the analyst.

When he again begins analysis, he dwells much on the nature of his unhappiness, his loneliness, his feelings of homesickness even when he is at home. Many things bring this on, particularly hearing sentimental songs. He speaks of how his feelings were often hurt during childhood and states that he is sentimental and romantic. He readily tells much about his affectional life in the family circle. His mother and aunt are always doing much for him, but he early centered his love upon Viola, the orphan relative who was brought up in his family. She was fourteen when he was born; she "took all the care of me. . . . I thought more of her than I did of my mother; I said I wanted to marry her; I never played with any other girl; I was her favorite; I think I used to sleep with her." Elmer tells about crying bitterly for days when she was married when he was six years old; he hated her lover. She was the only one who understood him; she was more liberal about religion; she did not say that he would go to hell; he could tell her everything and did tell her about swimming naked with children.

Later, speaking often of his difficulty in getting on with girls, Elmer makes it plain that one reason for this is that he has never found a girl or woman that he could talk to except Viola, and she died two years ago. On account of her own family life with her children, he had seen little of her recently.

"But the only home I really liked was Viola's. Sometimes after I ran away I would go to her house." He is able to give a detailed description of her and shows a photograph of her as a girl of fifteen; he always carries it in his pocket. She was tall, slim, with dark hair; she was jolly and fun-loving. "Somehow, I had a funny feeling for her." In discussing his phantasy life about girls, it appears that from the time he was small his love or sex phantasies have had to do with girls or women some years older than himself, and always they were dark and slim. Viola was a great contrast to his other older female relatives, who are short, light-complexioned, and stout. He tells about the girl whom his family, thinking he needed a girl friend, would like him to make up to. He has never had any success in developing good rapport with her or any strong feelings for her. It appears that she is stout. Indeed, he has never found a girl who was like either Viola or his own phantasies. Elmer once blurted out that he never ran away until Viola was married. Then, with regard to his having been sent to institutions: Viola had been in an orphanage; she knew how it felt to be in such places; he contrasts her with the priest who, with such a hard attitude, advised his being sent away. When he was a child, she sang sentimental songs, such songs as stir in him even nowadays the desire to make off somewhere. After all, Elmer says, Viola married better than his mother did, for her children have the sort of father that he would like to have had. But he has some longing for his mother and pity for her on account of what she has had to endure, and he has a feeling of guilt about not loving her more. He will do something for her on Mother's Day.

By the thirtieth interview Elmer had given many details about Viola and his mother. He readily accepts or directly evolves for himself the interpretation that Viola, from the time that he was six months until he was six years old, was almost a complete mother-substitute for him, that toward her he had a typical Œdipus love, and that she formed the basis of his object-choice. With the loss of her, he had a feeling of frustration that has repeated itself in many situations and has had many dynamic issues for him because of his fixation upon her. His ambivalent attitude toward his mother is equally explainable: On the positive side, it had its root in the fact that his mother loves him greatly and has done so much for him that he has a religious sense of duty toward her and sympathy for her because he identifies himself to a certain extent with her in her having to stand her husband's coldness, taciturnity, and bad temper as he himself had to endure them. On the negative side, she was forever warning him of sins and especially of sexual sins; she never understood him any more than his father did; he did not feel toward her as a mother because Viola was her surrogate. She was affronted by Viola's allowing him to have his own way. Very early she agreed to his being sent away from home. She frustrated his desire to be a real boy among boys. She is the opposite in build to the girl he phantasies for himself.

Beginning with early interviews, Elmer frequently has in mind the fact that it seems strange that he cannot get along with girls. He is bashful with them, afraid of them, although he would like to be with them. And this is entirely different from what it used to be when he was little; then he thinks he was quite forward. He has had chances to kiss a girl, but has never even dared to do this, and though in his phantasy life he has sex feelings when he thinks of girls and he has had dreams of intercourse, yet when with them, he has no sexual response. Even when he was little his parents were always warning him of the sin of sex; it gave him a terrible sense of guilt. He cannot get sin out of his mind. Masturbation was a sin and he was told he would go crazy if he practiced it, but when doing so, he has thought of sex relations with girls. Then sometimes he felt as if he were not good enough to speak to them, though sometimes he has had the temptation to ask them to have sex relations with him. At times he has thought he would like to love an older woman, and then that this was foolishness. He has had a little feeling toward the wives of the farmers with whom he lived, and has felt guilty about this. He is deeply impressed by the fact that girls have the hardest time of it, especially if a boy gets them into trouble. His mother often told him about it. He has never found any girl who confided in him or to whom he could talk freely.

At the ninth interview he brings a dream, the first that he remembers for a long time. *Dream:* There was a bowl full of cuff-buttons. He was looking through them for the right pair. He picked them over and over and rejected many. Most of them seemed to be alike, to have a pearl on top, white, and not what he wanted. None of them were together in pairs and he could not match any of them. He did not know what he was looking for. *Associations:* Superficially these are about a cuff-button that he had in his pocket the day before, about a bowl on a bureau, about a girl who wanted him to take her to places of amusement and he was not inclined toward her. She went to the bad. Elmer readily accepts the obvious interpretation of what looking for the right pair means: "I think that's at the bottom of a lot of it," and immediately speaks of his mind being in a daze, of his not knowing what he wants to do, of having a homesick feeling for some person whom he does not know, of the effect of old songs upon him, of the fact that he used to sing a little with Viola.

When freely associating, Elmer reverts time and again to his remarkable attitude toward girls, usually based on the fact that in some ordinary situation with girls or women he has found difficulty in talking to them. He cannot look them in the eye.

Perhaps he may think about their bodies, but not about any special parts. He thinks of them as being maturely developed in general. He never has specific ideas of breasts or of hair upon the body or of the sex organs. He has never been a *voyeur* and cannot remember ever having exhibited himself. It seemed to him quite natural and all right when he was swimming naked with children and tried some sex experiments with them. Viola knew about it, but made very little of it, merely telling him that he should not do it. He vaguely remembers, however, a great feeling of guilt in wondering if his mother knew. She had already taught him the sinfulness of sexual affairs. Then after he went to a certain church school for the second time, he felt differently about girls and has ever since. There he heard the obscenities of boys and saw older ones hugging little ones. This was reinforced in his next stay at that school, where he saw homosexual advances being made. Viola noted his change and joked him about his bashfulness and about why he no longer wanted to kiss her. His attitudes altered toward girls before he ever had any homosexual experiences himself. Everything connected with sex seemed sinful to him. He never could bring himself to touch a girl, but would like to. Even when he was little, the girls he pictured had well-developed bodies. They were grown up. He thinks if he were married he would be afraid.

Viola used to come to see him in the institution where the change took place in him and he began to feel bitter. That was when he first began to have actual sexual sensations when thinking of older girls and women. He is never interested in phantasying any but tall women, grown up. At the twenty-fourth session Elmer seems quite ready for and accepts an interpretation of the origin of his guilt feelings in incest tabu with Viola as a mother imago. Shortly afterwards he has the following *dream:* He dreamed about two women. He was in a room with a woman who was lying down. He does not know whether she was dressed or not. She was long and thin and had reddish hair that "sort of shone golden." She pleased him. He was not afraid of her. Another woman came in; "she had light hair or was light-looking." He did not like the idea of her coming in. He hit her with a rock or something. He thought he had killed her and was afraid. *Associations:* Once when he was about nine, he threw a stone at a grown-up girl and hit her over the eye and injured her. She fell down and had to be carried in and he was much afraid for fear he had killed her. She had been teasing him, holding him and twisting his arm. "My mother is kind of light in complexion. My mother and my aunt were always warning me about girls. I argued with them about it. Why are they so afraid of sex affairs? Why should they think about it so much?" All his father talked about was religion and the church, but they continually brought forward the idea that if he went out with a girl there might be trouble. They were always lecturing him not to touch girls. "They usually put ideas into my head, and when I was little I always used to believe anything I was told." He has never seen a girl lying down since he was small.

Interpretations that the injured woman in the dream represented not only his mother, who frustrated him by always trying to hold him back with her warnings, but also his own inhibiting ideas that continually interfered in his contact with the female sex, and that he would really like to be rid of these ideas, but would be afraid if he did, seemed thoroughly justified. Indeed Elmer said: "It seems to me that it was probably ideas that I was hitting rather than a person. I would be afraid if I did something that I had been told was wrong—that was like the dream. And objections to my doing things have a lot to do with my actions." Here also is revealed Elmer's underlying conceptions of the masculine rôle as being that of aggression toward women, a conception which is partly the result of his own frustrating inhibitions; then follows a sense of guilt when aggression is shown. (Another point that was not made with him is that the pleasing figure in the dream was not too much like Viola; he thus was prevented from dreaming of her as a sexual object.)

It seems very notable that from about this time in the analysis Elmer steadily reported his growing ability to meet girls in a more normal way, and it so happens that there was ample corroboration for his statements.

From the first until about the fortieth session Elmer's father comes much in his mind. He is a good man. He never even swears. He says very little and then it is generally about the church. When Elmer was a young child, his father appeared huge, towering, and even now he is very much taller and heavier than Elmer. He never seemed like a father to Elmer; he thought that if he kept a roof over their heads, that was all he should do as a father. Elmer can't understand why his mother ever married him. They are mismated, cold toward each other. He crushes his wife's love of jollity. On their honeymoon, when they were under a tree, he went round on the other side and read to himself. He flares up in a temper and orders his wife around and tells the children to be quiet. Elmer never could talk to his father. "He never understood me." When Elmer was little, his father whipped him sometimes. But yet, as he thinks back, Elmer tells of many nice things that his father did for him. The one thing in common they had was the love of animals. His father got a goat and a dog and a pony for Elmer at different times. One of his earliest memories is of sitting beside his father on a wagon or in a buggy and being allowed to hold the reins. His father bought nice toys for him—in particular, a mechanical horse. In recent years his father has been much depressed because of lack of employment and the fact that their favorite priest died. His father always wanted to do what was right, but did not know how. "He was never my ideal of a father, I was always afraid of him. I used to wish he were dead; lots of times I felt bitter toward him. I was always afraid of him. I hate to see a man ordering his wife about. I never saw my father kiss my mother. He was not a real father to me."

In the seventh session Elmer produces a dream of death, all very vague and unpleasant—he is not sure whether it was or was not he who was dying or dead. His associations lead him to tell of a pain that he has had since he was injured a little by a bull. This makes him think that it must have been he himself who was dead. He has wished many times, especially when he was little, that he were dead and has thought of methods of suicide. Then he has wished many times that his brother were dead. When asked if his father and brother were dead he would have had his mother to himself, he quickly begins to talk about Viola. She was the one he wanted for himself, but still he sympathized a good deal with his mother. The next day he reports a long and involved *dream:* He dreamed of killing someone and enjoying it. It was vague except that he twisted off the head of a fellow as chickens' heads are twisted off. The face of that fellow was very clear. It was of an older boy who had authority over him at the correctional school and hit him across the face, and Elmer hated him. In the dream Elmer pulled another boy who was with this fellow from under a building where he had crawled and stepped on him over and over again in a place where there was mud, and the boy went down in it. He was dressed in dark clothes. Since Elmer himself dresses in dark clothes, he is asked if he thinks this boy in the dream represented himself. He accepts the idea and directly begins to discuss homosexual affairs and his shame about them.

Three days later, he dreams of houses tipping over, crashing, and breaking. They were wooden houses in an out-of-the-way place, two of them side by side, one much bigger than the other. One moved ahead and then suddenly tipped over, and the other a little while afterwards. Both were dark and dreary. There was a horse hitched to something that was also turned over. *Associations:* A tornado many years ago in the country town where he lived. A house that was torn down, etc. A horse that he possibly could ride if he goes home in a couple of days. There is some question about his getting this horse. (In a later interview it came out that his family has the feeling that he ought not to spend money for riding-horses.) There is not much pleasure in going home. It all seems so gloomy. They are always downhearted. He feels the dream means something about his home life. The houses and their situation in the dream somewhat resemble the family house. He has had wishes that people were out of the way—his aunt because she warns and accuses him, and his father, toward whom he feels bitter. Elmer has a sort of feeling of duty toward his father and mother and yet he does not see how his staying at home would help them.

While Elmer acknowledges long-standing feelings of hostility toward his father, he several times emphasizes that really his father was very good to him when he was little; he bought him many toys. The trouble was that he was always too distant. But, after all, they always did have in common their love of animals. In these ways Elmer reveals ambivalence and the basis for a considerable sense of guilt because he has such feelings of hostility. His father always meant to do what was right, he assures us, and as far as his own misconduct is concerned, perhaps he sometimes "got away" with more than ever his brother or sister did.

We see plainly that there never was much normal father-identification. It is only because they are both fond of animals that Elmer has ever felt himself like his father or wanting to be like him. On the other hand, Elmer senses that he is considerably like his mother. He gives in easily to authority in order to avoid a fuss, as she does; he has a few of her many superstitious notions. "I am the only one except my mother who has been intimidated." Many times he is sorry for his mother as he is sorry for himself. He has sympathy for girls and young women who are going to have babies; his mother always had a hard time with them and he knows of her suffering. In general he feels badly for what girls and women have to go through because of the behavior of men. He asks why he allowed himself to be dressed up nicely, like a girl; his brother angrily tore off nice clothes when they were put on him. Why, he asks, did he allow these homosexual advances when they were so disgusting to him?—he always took the passive part. It is the pleasant, kindly feminine characteristics of homosexuals that lately have rather attracted him to them. He really only desires to return home when he is away because of his feeling that his mother is there suffering as he did.

From all this we discern that there is a much more mother- than father-identification—greatly complicated by the fact that, through having almost entire care of him from early infancy until about five years of age, Viola, instead of his actual mother, was in any emotional sense his mother—and that there has steadily been going on a conflict between the feminine and the masculine, the passive and the aggressive parts of his nature. Perhaps nothing illustrates this so well as Elmer's repeatedly confessed superstition that he will not live to be twenty-one years of age, an idea that he has frequently expressed to his family. This idea seems to have arisen from a double fact: first, that he was often disgusted with life and wished that he might die; and then that when he was little, there was some talk about whether Viola ought to be married early because she might die of heart disease before the time she was twenty-one. Also it was always pointed out to him that until he was twenty-one he must be obedient to his parents; until that time they had charge of his religious life and had full control over him. There has always been a great ambivalence between his desire for independence, freeing himself from the family yoke, and his feeling of inadequacy for becoming independent. His phantasies and actions, he says, run counter to each other and we know that his gestures toward independence were shortlived, for he always very quickly put himself into a position where he was again under authority and restraint, under such conditions always making a good record, as in the church schools and the correctional institution. He wants to be a man and at the same time he wants to be a child. He wants to evade the age of full responsibility. He wants to be aggressive, but at the same time remains largely passive and feminine in his attitudes and sympathies. Elmer works this out for himself clearly during the analysis.

Elmer's feelings of inferiority date far back. "My father always seemed so big; I always seemed as if I was under someone. I seem to have been in fear of someone ever since I can remember; I have been ruled by fear. For many years I believed anything that was told me; anybody could do anything with me. I was always being sent away; the boys called me the crazy wanderer." Elmer's female relatives felt that fighting was sinful, so when he was little, if he got into a fight, he was dragged into the house and spanked, he tells us, and he was not allowed to get dirty. He was teased by the other boys because he was too dressed up. He envied boys who were allowed to go out and get dirty and fight with each other. He feels sure that a certain cowardliness came over him after he was five or six because of this. After a sex-curiosity affair before he was six, he was told that touching his genitals was a terrible sin; it would make him crazy. He feels particularly inferior nowadays because he is so bashful; he easily loses his nerve with girls, is readily embarrassed. Besides, he does not face things. He lacks will-power to carry things through; he does not act out the wishes which develop in his day-dreams. He is self-conscious; his feelings are hurt easily; at times he has thought he really must be crazy because he thinks so much about himself. He feels sure that he was modified for the worse by the family restrictions when he wanted to play roughly with other boys and again at the church school when he felt nobody cared for him and began masturbation, with phantasies of older girls. This led to his embarrassment. Inferiority feelings came greatly to the fore at those periods. His homosexual experiences and even his curiosity about them make him feel inferior, and, more recently, his utter discouragement about his lack of employment and having no money. He dates back his sensitiveness about not having good clothes to his being early overdressed by the family. In all this it appears how effectively Elmer's relatives emasculated him.

Elmer's early phantasies about life in the West, which he has continued to the present time, and his practice with the lasso, at which he has become somewhat adept, have tended to make him a runaway, but he never got anywhere near the West. He was no sooner away than he felt himself ineffective, taking pleasure, to be sure, in love of the woods and of animals, but soon developing homesickness for the protecting roofs of his relatives. He never had the pluck of the adventurer; his flight episodes were merely gestures of a masculine protest, weak expressions of the desire to be a man. He tells of building a fire in the woods at night with one comrade and talking of the West and singing songs, but he was unwilling to face the difficulties of going very far. He thinks that sometimes his running from farm homes where he had been happy has represented lack of courage in facing some difficult situation. On three occasions he left directly after Sunday church services without going back to the farm. It might have been thought that out of a church service or sermon the boy would have gained strength and courage, but evidently it unconsciously unsettled him—perhaps because of his frequently expressed hatred for the priest who advised that he be punished by being sent away for the second and third time to the church school, when he himself felt that above everything he wanted the affection and understanding that he had lost when Viola had betrayed him by getting married.

Elmer's extremely self-regarding, narcissistic mental attitudes are always shown. Objective reality has the lesser value for him; it is his own thoughts and feelings about himself that mainly concern him. He wonders at times if this is not a mark of inferiority or even of abnormality, saying that he takes some sort of strange pleasure in being lonely and miserable. He has a much greater sense of guilt concerning what is going on in his own mind than about anything that he does. In the midst of poverty, he thinks much about whether his coat and trousers match. He projects these feelings in thinking that other people are noticing his clothes or seeing signs of his thoughts. Elmer realizes his own introverted tendencies and says over and over again that he dwells too much upon his own thoughts and feelings. This strong narcissistic sensitiveness is evidently a consequence of the shame felt at his own feminine and dependent qualities.

During the course of the analysis Elmer gradually came to see clearly the causes of his emotional attitudes toward himself, and in spite of his most unfortunate economic situation during the following summer, he came to express himself in more manly ways, even telling his father the undesirability of a religion of fear. He met boys and girls on a more give-and-take level as far as he was able to do so when lacking funds. As he grew better in this respect he several times said that he marvelled at the change that was taking place in him.

The hallucinations of voices of which Elmer gave a vivid account when he was fourteen, and which led the psychiatrist to consider schizophrenia, have been fully explained during the analysis. Elmer, when freely associating about his religious experiences, said: "They told me people have two angels inside of them, one good and one bad, and they whisper ideas in your ear. If I would tell a lie my people would say: 'That's a bad little voice speaking inside you.' When I was little, I hardly knew what it all meant and said that I did really hear voices because they said so. And even now I hardly know if I hear things or imagine them. It always seems so crazy that I don't talk about it. It all has to do with conscience, and the church telling you that there is a voice inside you which tells what is right and wrong. I used to take religion terribly seriously and had a great sense of guilt. Earlier I could have sworn I heard these voices telling me things, but now I know of course that it was all imagination, but it really is sometimes like a voice. It all began when they told me about those angels speaking in your ear. I had a habit for years of pulling bed-clothes over my head from fear of hearing the voices." In the same session Elmer reverts to what he had once mentioned before—namely, that sometimes he has the sense of having known beforehand that certain things were going to happen. It is as if he had heard about them.

Many times Elmer mentions his attitudes toward his brother Lee, emphasizing his own long-standing feelings of unfairness. His brother is just as bad as he if not worse. To be sure, he never ran away, but he is bad-tempered and treats his mother abominably. In that, Lee is like his father. "He was supposed to be sickly," and had a lot of attention; he became the favorite. Elmer has a vague dream about being dead; his associations lead him to speak a little of his thoughts about suicide, but much more about his many early wishes that his brother were dead. It seems very strange to Elmer that Lee has shown no fear of his father—both of them want to be the boss. Elmer's very earliest memory is concerned with going to the hospital when he was three years of age and seeing his new-born brother. "I said then that I hated him, and I have hated him ever since." The two boys did play together somewhat when they were little, but it seemed that Lee was never interested in anything that Elmer cared for; all Lee liked to do was to read, and he was a tattle-tale. Elmer was sent away many times, but nothing was ever done about Lee's faults. If only his father and Lee were in the home, Elmer never would return; Lee has said that it would be better if Elmer stayed away altogether. Elmer's good times at home are with his sister.

Elmer sees clearly that there was a jealousy situation and that his first dislike of his brother was based upon his assumption that his own position as the center of attention was to be usurped. But then he found he was able to have Viola for himself. At the time she left the household his brother was very sickly and demanded a great deal of care. Elmer was now without special attention and unhappy. Then a year or so later he felt himself shoved out of the family circle when he was sent away and his brother remained at home. Thus the hatred and jealousy continued. From recent family reports we have reason to believe that with the progress of the analysis Elmer gained much insight into this matter and came to realize some of the better qualities of his brother. He has become more tolerant of him.

Elmer's love of animals and kindness to them has been commented on by various people. He speaks of it much himself.

He was allowed to have many pets and took good care of them, before long becoming much interested in healing their wounds. Before he was sixteen, he learned how to aid cows in calving and was proud of his success. He feels a great deal of sympathy for animals—"I can feel cruelty to them more than they feel it themselves." When he sees them beaten he remembers his own beatings—people are merely giving vent to their own feelings of anger when they hit animals. It has filled him with delight when animals have shown affection for him. He thinks he can get better work out of animals by being kind to them. He feels a comradeship with animals, perhaps because they do not talk; he hates people who, like his father and brother, are shouting all the time. When he is lonely, he has a great feeling of affection for animals. He frankly tells of seeing some sex perversions with animals on one or two occasions, but it has filled him with disgust. He never felt inclined that way. His interest in them seems to be based on a sort of identification with them as being quiet, passive creatures who are lonely and often suffer and who keep their feelings to themselves. There can be no doubt that all this represents the feminine side of Elmer's attitudes.

But Elmer's masculinity is also much involved in his feelings for animals. He is interested in horses and talks a great deal about them. His free associations lead him to frequent reiterations of his early pleasure in playing about horses, his surprising lack of fear of them, his joy in being placed on a horse's back and of being allowed to play at driving them. Later, when his father had no horses, one of his chief incentives for running away was to find a place where he could be with horses. He can think of no greater pleasure than riding over the fields on the back of a horse; it gives him the greatest thrill. He sings then. Perhaps that is the reason why he has never cared to learn to drive an automobile—one of the earliest ambitions of other boys. In his earlier wanderings he frequently walked many miles to see a certain pony he had much admired in a field. Sometimes he used to ride on a pony when he was a little boy. He thinks he has more affection for horses than he ever had for anybody except Viola and his sister. He forgets everything when he is on a horse. The farmers complain because they say he admires the beauty of horses too much and works too hard at cleaning them, "but I clean them after work just as I like to take a bath after working." He wonders what they are thinking about; he looks into their eyes. He often phantasies having an affectionate beautiful horse, and his dreams often include horses. The companionship that he has always sought he has never found except when with a horse. When he is riding is one of the few times that he is ever happy. Speaking of his singing while riding horseback leads him to remember his very earliest feeling of pleasure and singing when on the back of a mechanical rocking-horse that his father bought him when he was very little. He had a saddle and stirrups, and as it went up and down it gave him a sensation of thrilling motion. It would go up high and then drop down; galloping nowadays gives him the same sort of sensation. In describing the type of horse that he likes best, it turns out that it is of mixed colors, "a calico horse," and is something like the dappled coloring of the mechanical horse.

Once, when speaking of a strange creepy feeling he has when he sees snakes, immediately he says that it is nearly like the sensations he has when he is riding—some strange pleasurable feeling. He remembers that he had that always, from the time he used to be on the rocking-horse. *Dream:* He was sitting on the driving-seat of a yellow wagon, which was moving, but he could not see the horse. *Associations:* When he was little he had a wagon big enough to sit on and his father would pull it around. Elmer held the reins and whip. "I had power over

him then, I was master over him, I hit him with the whip."
Once, on the farm, when he was driving, there was an accident; a horse went out of the shafts and left him up on the
driver's seat.

Elmer often speaks of his desire for and pleasure in "for-
getting everything." He can do this best when having the thrill
of riding. He readily interprets with the analyst that driving
a horse or riding one gives him a sense of masculine power,
and the latter particularly gives him feelings that are closely
analogous to sexual sensations. He thinks that the mechanical
horse gave him childish sexual feelings. Sometimes he has
erections while riding. Through these activities he has a sense
of mastery which he otherwise lacks—he loses then his feeling
of inferiority, he becomes virile. Even when a child, he could
assert himself and forget his fear of his father while the latter
was pretending to be a horse.

For a country boy, Elmer has curious feelings about snakes.
He has repeatedly dreamed about them. During the analysis,
after killing one, he dreamed that a lot of snakes were chasing
him and he climbed up on a ladder to the roof of a cottage.
When he came down, a snake again chased him and he called
for someone to open the door. When he went in, snakes went
in after him. *Associations:* His mother hates snakes and he
does too; although he is not exactly afraid of them, they give
him the creeps; he always wants to kill them. He is fascinated
by snakes. He used to think he could hypnotize them, as he
has seen snakes hypnotize a bird. Other things that have fascinated him and that he has been afraid of are women and
guns. He was not allowed to have a gun, but once secreted a
little rifle. Sexual matters have fascinated him too, and he is
afraid of them. That goes back the farthest. It started, when
he was very young, with a little boy in some curiosity activities.
Homosexual people cannot be so terrible and he likes them

because they are pleasant to meet, but yet he avoids them, and that is one reason he does not like to be in the city. He might meet some of them. He gets a curious pleasure out of hearing them talk. He has avoided girls more than he has these homosexual people. He is curious about the human penis and has a sort of fear of it. It seems dangerous. After all, he is not exactly afraid of a snake, but he seems to have to go ahead and kill it. Putting a forked stick over its head seems to be the best way. After he has killed it, he looks it over and examines it. If he is working in the country and he steps into a little hole, it makes him nervous; he is afraid that a snake may come out.

In the thirtieth analytic session the interpretations of important parts of the following dream were all made by Elmer himself. *Dream:* A long and involved dream begins with his riding through the woods on a big dog, hanging on by a silver chain around its body, and a fierce-looking peculiar little dog with human skin going along close by him. He had some fear of the big dog and got off and walked, holding on to the chain. He looked around and saw that instead of a dog it really was a big snake that he was riding on—about one hundred feet long. He thought that he would fool it and elude it, so he suddenly turned the other way and let go of the chain and ran. Then, as he ran, the smaller dog followed him and he was much more afraid of it. He tried to get rid of it. He stopped once and held out a stick, hoping to coax it near him so that he could hit it, but it ran back into the woods. Then Elmer ran on until he saw lights and came to a big house. He went up into a room and got into a bed with two or three other fellows. Two women were in another bed. He woke up and found nobody there, etc.

*Associations:* Once after swimming he rode a young bull with a rope around its stomach as they do in a Western rodeo. Seeing a dog with a silver chain around it in a circus. Seeing a man, a parole officer, of whom he was afraid, who has eyes such as he noticed on the big snake. He was thinking of that man yesterday. But the little dog was the most fearful thing in the dream. He wanted desperately to get away from it. He had read of a dog that was a human being, a story of black magic. There are dozens of things in himself that he would like to get away from—his conscience, his self-consciousness, every rotten thing that he has done. He would like to forget his homosexual experiences, the money that he has taken. He cannot seem to get away from the thoughts of them. He has tried the confessional. He is disgusted with himself nearly all the time. The house that he went to in the dream had halls like a hotel lobby. With a homosexual man he once went to a big hotel of poor repute where he saw some fellows and two girls in bed, though he himself did not go into the room. Thus, Elmer makes it plain that his conflicts and his fear of men (a reaction to his aggressions against his father) appear in his dream life, that riding has sexual significance for him as shown by the symbolism, that his conscience accompanies him much, and that he would like to escape from it by running away, but when he tries to do so, he finds himself involved in other bad situations (homosexuality).

At this point we can with much certainty formulate the main factors in Elmer's personality-development.

1. The early beginnings of the normal masculine drive were largely frustrated through intimidating experiences, centering in the Œdipus complex, which have been brought out so clearly in the analysis.

2. These intimidations and his negative critical attitude toward his father favor a female identification.

3. This feminine identification creates, as we see, a deep sense of inferiority.

4. As a result of the last there is an over-strong masculine

protest, with the reactive, aggressive, and somewhat sadistic masculinity shown chiefly in phantasy. As mitigated in actual life this appears only as Elmer's pleasure in horseback riding.

5. These strong masculine aggressions, particularly in the form of the wish to overcome or emasculate the father, lead to a secondary enforcement of all the early religious and moral restrictions, with a strong castration fear in connection with sexuality. Herein we have a reinforcement of Elmer's female tendencies and establishment of the typical neurotic vicious circle—the feminine identification once more hurts his masculine pride and drives him again and again to protest reactions. The running away and the stealing are obvious manifestations of this reactivated aggressive masculinity. To ride is the non-criminal manifestation, to steal and run away are the asocial manifestations of the masculine protest reactions.

Elmer's conflicts about sexual matters and religion are closely intertwined. These appear frequently, but were especially focused in his associations to a certain dream. *Dream:* he was at a table talking to some woman about whom there was something he liked. She was not old or stout and he enjoyed her company. Other people were there. He found himself going up in the air and rather pleasantly swimming as if in water on the side of the long table. *Associations:* Yesterday he was alone with a man's wife and was rather afraid to talk to her when her husband was out of the room. He is always afraid of thinking things that he should not think. He is afraid that under such circumstances he will have sexual thoughts about a woman. He is afraid that he will have an erection or that she will know what he might be thinking of. On a couple of farms the husbands talked of sexual matters and then he had some thoughts about their wives. That is wrong. He was reading yesterday a philosophical treatise on ethics, and if he could have had such books to read earlier, he would have been able to do better with his life. He has too much sense of guilt. When Viola was married, he cried so much that he was teased about it, and later about not talking to girls. He used to say that he was never going to be married. He had feelings of love for Viola. His father and mother are cold-blooded. They were not in love with each other. He has had other dreams of going up in the air and they are something like his feeling when he rides on a horse. He never had any sexual feelings toward a girl except in a dream, toward the one that his people picked out for him (a stout girl), and somehow he can't get along with her. His family all feel that he has to have somebody over him, to give him advice. He has fear of something when he thinks of sexual intercourse. It was always supposed to be a terrible sin. In recent years he has tried to lose that sense of guilt because he knows that God put sexual feelings into mankind. His brother was once fooling in some partially sexual way with his sister. His mother told his brother that his father would burn his hand for it and that he would go to hell and burn there for it. After Elmer as a very young boy was playing with the other children at the swimming-hole, he went to Sunday school and there they talked about the sin of sexual things as his family did. It was supposed to be a sin to have any sexual practices or thoughts. He had fear of his father's punishments.

At many other times Elmer deals with the same topics. In one interview he says his parents were always warning him about bad men and bad women. "There are a lot of things that a fellow thinks which he gets to feeling guilty about if he is talked to like that." He was threatened with whippings if he did not learn his catechism. Once, in the city, a man made some sexual approaches to him, he does not remember what, but the man gave him money or candy and he felt ashamed. He did not tell his parents about this. It was a priest who advised his being sent away to the correctional school. The church seems ruled by fear, but he does not believe that God rules by fear. When, in more recent years, he has spoken of that at home, the family have accused him of turning Protestant. For a little while he once knew one young priest who told him there was no sense in talking so much about hell. Now he does not know what to believe. The prayers that he learned by heart he does not think are as good as prayers in his own words. He feels that people who read prayers and say beads are often hypocrites. Viola was more broad-minded. She knew about his bathing naked, but did not think it was any great sin. When he first went to school, he was one of the most forward of the boys, and ever since that period he has had no confidence in himself. In a childish way he tried to have intercourse with a girl at the swimming-hole and even before that. He remembers that he and another boy tried some sexual play together and he got a whipping for it. It was impressed on him that it was all terribly sinful. They had prayers morning and night. So whenever Elmer's thoughts have turned on sexual matters, at the same moment he has had feelings of guilt derived from his early religious training. His mental and emotional life has been colored by this to the extent that his normal instinctual cravings have been met by inner frustrating ideas, leading even to constraining interference in Elmer's ordinary social contacts with girls.

Elmer's stealing seems to have represented nothing more than taking money for the journeyings which were partly determined by the desire to assert his masculinity. When he stole at home, it seems that he merely seized some cash without even knowing how much he took. We have wondered whether the stealing from the church poor-box and the taking of the money that his mother had collected for church subscriptions was unconsciously an act of revenge against the church. This may be possible, but we have no proof of it.

During the analysis we learned of one theft which seems remarkable. When Elmer was eighteen and away from home, he met an unfortunate young fellow, not a delinquent, who had lost his position and had no money to pay for his lodgings. Elmer spent the night with him. There had been a little talk between them about homosexual affairs, but Elmer assures us that nothing happened. In the morning, without breakfast, both of them went down-town feeling very discouraged and impotent. They half-heartedly discussed the possibility of breaking in some place to get either food or money for food, but neither was willing to try this. A department store was open and they walked in a little way. Suddenly Elmer seized an umbrella and walked out with it. He was arrested at the door. Several times Elmer has said that this was one of the most inexplicable things he ever did. To be sure, it was raining, but he never used umbrellas, he always scorned them at home, he never minded being rained on. While he has always despised umbrellas, however, he has always wanted canes and walking-sticks. Knowing Elmer's castrative tendencies from his dream life, it is obvious that this umbrella as well as canes unconsciously represented for Elmer a phallic symbol of potency. Elmer several times has brought up the problem of this theft and said that his taking of this umbrella must have had a meaning, but he cannot imagine what—there was no conscious reason for his taking it and especially there was every reason against his doing so, because he was already on parole from the correctional institution and if this theft had been known to the parole officer, he would have been returned to the institution, which above all things he consciously wanted to avoid. (However, it is to be remembered that Elmer was fairly happy in that institution and in some ways being back there was better than being unemployed and without funds.) As against this conception of an unconscious desire to return, there is the contradictory fact that Elmer successfully avoided letting the parole officer become aware of this petty delinquency, and was merely placed on probation when he had his hearing in court.

The last of the analytic interviews were almost unproductive because Elmer felt so keenly his reality situation. After visiting employment offices he would sit for long hours on a park bench without eating; he slept very poorly, smoked excessively, and was, very naturally, utterly dejected. Then during the summer he tried various devices for earning money, but with little success. A couple of months later he reported to the analyst, looking better and seeming much less discouraged. He evidently was proud of a new attitude of manliness that he had assumed; he had been standing up for himself in arguments at home, not merely keeping quiet and feeling sensitive, as formerly. He was enjoying frequent visits with boy companions to the home of a girl who he said was a tomboy. The family thoroughly disapproved of his visits, and after an argument in which he defended her, he came into town and walked the streets most of the night. (His family reported that Elmer had developed a new manliness and seemed more happy, they joked about his standing up for himself in arguments, but they could not approve of his night hours in the home of this hoydenish girl.)

A few weeks later Elmer was held under arrest for having attempted, while armed, to break into a small shop. Visited in jail by the analyst, Elmer said he had been a fool, but he had been terribly discouraged by the continual talk about possible loss of the family home and he had been unable to earn anything to speak of. With younger companions he had been going to the girl's house, and felt desperate because he had no money to reciprocate by taking her out. As the boys left her house one night, they planned breaking into a store and getting some money. One brought a revolver, which Elmer carried. They were frightened off before they committed the burglary and Elmer ran. However, a young boy was caught and told who the others were. Under arrest, Elmer readily confessed. It also came out that just before Elmer had reported to the analyst, with some of these same boys he had entered another small store and had obtained cigarettes and a little sum of money without detection. He was sentenced to several months in jail.

After release, there followed another winter of unemployment and family hardships, but there was no more running away and no delinquency. Elmer made occasional visits to the analyst, often saying that he wished himself back in jail, where he had been well treated; he was ashamed to be seen on the streets. In the spring he made sincere attempts to get to the Pacific coast, where he had promise of employment. He tells us that with the little money which his family advanced he did reach Indiana, but could get no farther and returned. Then he decided to work on a farm in New England, even if only for his board. There he remained for a few weeks, but became tired of the hard work for no pay and returned home, again seeking employment.

Now, two and a half years after discontinuance of the regular analytic sessions, Elmer presents a much stronger appearance, with a firmer and happier expression. Nearly a year ago he obtained work—an arduous job which he held for four months, until the factory shut down. He earned well and aided his family very materially. Since then he has had only odd jobs. But Elmer makes much more of the improvement of his attitude toward women as bearing upon his personality-development and of the fact that he is now able to "stand his family." He feels much more of a man and attributes it to an affair that he had with a young married woman who had left her husband. He found himself for the first time adequate to meet the advances of a member of the opposite sex. Unquestionably his mental conflicts are largely resolved and his neurotic tendencies greatly bettered. He has neither run away nor been in any delinquency for over two years. We have a strong feeling that if, directly following his analysis, employment could have been obtained for Elmer, he would have done well then and probably not been in his subsequent difficulties. His ego needed to be bolstered up by achievement. His subsequent history seems to indicate that this was a rather necessary first step toward the development of normal heterosexual attitudes.

Comparison of the analytic material with the long case record shows no contradiction but, rather, many additions which for the first time bring to light many sharply defined issues which, put together, form the mosaic, rather unpatterned, which is at the basis of Elmer's personality-development and delinquent trends. It is not a little curious that in the analysis the first is heard of Viola, the mother-surrogate, with all of the immense bearings that she had upon the development of Elmer's emotional life. (Since the analysis Elmer's relatives have been seen and they have corroborated the overt facts, not only in regard to Viola, but also concerning all the other matters of family relationships which Elmer brought out in the analysis. It was interesting that Elmer's aunt brought forward the fact of his mother's extreme antipathy to all that pertained to sexual life. Evidently the family had thought so little of all these things that they had not revealed them, or else with a certain sensitiveness had covered them up, as indeed Elmer himself had very largely done in the earlier psychiatric interviews.)

It seems almost unnecessary to reiterate the crucial subjects of the family romance, the peculiarly mixed-up Œdipus situation, its complication and neurotic solution, with much frustration and repression of Elmer's ardent love of the mother-substitute. Then we come to the matters of Elmer's fixation on his love-object choice, his partial parental identification with the development of passive feminine attitudes, his feelings about having been made impotent, the fears of his father, religious conflicts, inferiority attitudes, ambivalence of emotional reactions, undue repressions of libidinal life, zoophily based on libidinal and identification components—all these stand out plainly enough in the analysis as for the most part entirely new material for understanding the individual career. It is clear that we have before us a young man inclined to introspection, sensitive and sentimental, who for all the above reasons existing in emotional and ideational life, in circumstance and experience, has failed to consolidate his masculinity. A weak ego, unable successfully to meet reality, unable to sublimate adequately, brought to its aid a strong but neurotically isolated Super-ego, resulting in a great sense of guilt and willingness to accept punishment.

# CHAPTER SIX

## *A Favorite of Women*

FERDINAND PEREZ was thirteen years old when first seen at the Guidance Center; twenty-eight years old at the time of the analysis.

Ferdinand had appeared in the juvenile court as an habitual truant. Until he entered the fifth grade at eleven his attendance at school was very satisfactory; indeed, some years it was perfect; but during the last two years his absences had become more and more frequent. The school principal said he was a most difficult boy to understand since no basis for his dislike of school could be found.

At the clinic Ferdinand stated that he hated school because of the restraint; on Fridays he experienced an immense sense of relief because there would be no school until Monday. His family reported that he would say: "Now I can have peace for a couple of days." The boy's story was that he had liked school in the earlier grades, and his family saw every evidence of this. Then when he was eleven another boy inducted him into the delights of truancy, but after a few days of street adventure with this other boy he truanted alone, spending his time on the street, in the movies, or doing odd jobs when he could get them. Ferdinand has always asserted that schoolroom life made him feel dizzy and ill at this period of beginning truancy, but he had to confess that he was not at all uncomfortable at the movies or in a closed room at home.

Ferdinand was the youngest of seven children in an American family of mixed Spanish and Scottish ancestry. His father, a man of good reputation and the disciplinarian in the family, died when Ferdinand was eleven. The mother was a thoroughly good woman who had no trouble in bringing up the older children, but found herself incapable of managing her youngest boy after her husband died. Her death occurred when Ferdinand was fourteen years old. The children of this couple consisted of five girls, two of them married by the time Ferdinand was seen at the clinic, then, in order, a boy who was six years older than Ferdinand and a girl four years older. The entire family was devoted to this youngest child, and though the brother tried to discipline him he had little relationship with the boy as compared with the women in the family. This older brother died when Ferdinand was seventeen years old.

On examination Ferdinand was found to have no evidence of physical disease or defect, but he was an extremely restless boy and his nails were badly bitten. He did well on psychological tests, having an I.Q. 100. (We have the record of later examinations at psychiatric clinics where findings were practically the same.) On account of his disaffection for school, tests for learning ability and memory powers were given, but no evidence was found of any disability that would interfere with school accomplishment. Nor could one ascertain from the developmental history that there was any physical cause for his restlessness and dislike of school. He had been a remarkably healthy child, although at thirteen years he was decidedly short and slight in build.

The home was clean and well kept, but located in a poor neighborhood. The older children worked and contributed regularly so that there were comforts and good summer vacations. The family relationships were those of pleasant harmony.

The sentimental mother and the sisters were deeply concerned about Ferdinand, they were always ready to shed tears about him, and it was the judgment of many that earlier and later they showered attention upon him.

The school people made a couple of changes for the boy, but his behavior remained unaltered. He was then sent to a home in the country, where he remained the better part of a year and attended a country school regularly. His explanation of this was that more outdoor life and a freer school régime made school attendance there more tolerable. When he was less than fifteen Ferdinand obtained employment, and when he was fifteen and a half he managed somehow to join the Navy and was soon sent to China. He came home after almost three years in the service. Since then he has been in various fields of employment, sometimes working as a chauffeur and sometimes as salesman. These two types of work he has evidently enjoyed most.

During the last ten years Ferdinand has been in court at least fifteen times on various charges and has served seven sentences in correctional institutions, some commitments being only for thirty days; the last sentence runs six to eight years. The charges against him have been mainly for such offenses as drunkenness and violating automobile laws, but several times the stated offense was larceny or burglary.

In spite of this record Ferdinand has never given the impression of being the least bit hardened or vicious. His offenses have usually been committed under the influence of alcohol and in company with criminal companions. It is very doubtful whether he was guilty of a burglary, which was the last charge against him. It is true that he was found inside a house, but he was intoxicated. One is inclined to believe his story that he crawled into this place without the slightest intention of stealing.

In prison life Ferdinand remains the same eager contrite individual that he has always been. He is restless, somewhat nervous, and naturally irked by his confinement, but he is amenable, studious in the attempt to make up for his earlier educational deficiencies, and well liked by the officers and his fellow-prisoners.

In prison he was given a Rohrschach test by an expert who states that Ferdinand very largely "lacks extrovert qualities, that he shows comparatively little conscious will for rapport with his environment, that in his affect life he is stable, that there is evidence of inadequacy of the ego." The prediction was made that in his home life he is prone to be tyrannical and nagging, and that he is easily led by companions. (It seems only fair to say that these and other evaluations from this test do not agree entirely with the characteristics observed by those who have known Ferdinand over a long period and which are recorded in the extensive case history.)

Ferdinand married when he was twenty-three years old and his wife and even his father-in-law agree with others who knew him best that he is kind, considerate, affectionate, and that he loves his three children most dearly. He is not lazy and sometimes has been quite successful at employment. A curious fact is that earlier, when after having almost served one of his longest sentences, with only a few days before release, and when he was a "trusty," Ferdinand ran away and was returned to serve a longer sentence on account of it. His explanation is that a fellow-prisoner smuggled in some whisky and after a couple of drinks came the idea of escaping. About this especially—indeed, about his whole career—Ferdinand has long felt himself an enigma and he readily grasped the opportunity for psychoanalysis.

The above is only a summary of a very long case record; as in the other cases, only the bare factual outlines were known to the analyst when he began to work with Ferdinand.

### PSYCHOANALYTIC EXPLORATION

The analysis of Ferdinand Perez which was undertaken for exploratory purposes and extended over one and a half months, revealed much of the unconscious dynamic background of his behavior, although the development of his personality can be reconstructed only in its main features. One of the principal themes of Ferdinand's analysis is the memory of being pampered, as the youngest in the family, by his mother and particularly by his older sisters. He evidently was an attractive little boy who had been given everything he wanted. He often speaks of his sisters as beautiful girls; one of them, a tea-room hostess, was especially beautiful. Ferdinand liked to visit her in the tea-room, where he was given all kinds of little gifts by her and the other girls. He very soon learned how to win people's favor—especially women's—by performing little services for which he received money. He helped in other restaurants and received candy and roast chicken and other delicacies from the waitresses.

Not only in his childhood but also later he always remained the favorite of women. During his last imprisonment various social workers have showed great interest in his case and often visited him in the prison, and his wife and sisters have always been most kindly in the periods of his previous incarcerations. He enjoyed and impatiently looked forward to the visits of these different women.

It is quite natural that the pampered little boy hated school as soon as he felt that it interfered with his sovereignty, since he considered having his own way as a natural right, and reacted with truancy and negativism to discipline. The early school-years are covered by an extensive amnesia, but he remembers that from the fifth grade on he hated school, especially a parochial school where he particularly resented the prayers.

His associations show that his stealing was, partially at least, a reaction to his school life, though he started very early to indulge in petty stealings in spite of the fact that he made himself especially popular and could win affection and bounties. Very early he stole nickels from his mother in order to go to shows or to buy candy. He stole whisky-bottles and sold them. He also liked to cheat people. He remembers cheating a drunken woman out of her change when he sold empty whisky-bottles to her. He would steal cigarettes and peanuts, sneak into movies, and often cheat his comrades. Once he stole five dollars which he had collected, for carfare for an excursion. His very early stealings do not need special explanation. They fit into the attitude of the little pampered boy who thought that the whole world belonged to him. Later his stealing not only continued but evidently became more intense, probably as a reaction to the increasing discipline of the higher grades in the school. It may be that in the first years he had no difficulties in school, probably as long as the teacher continued to show toward the nice little boy affection and consideration such as he was accustomed to at home.

This reaction is typical for children who experience a transition from an extremely pampered situation at home to the discipline of school. They feel that their natural rights have been unjustly taken away from them and they take now by force what they received before as gifts.

Aside from his reactions to school life, his being indulged in the situation of the spoiled baby of the family, who gets everything he wishes, was not without an inner conflict. It is quite impressive to observe that, whenever he begins to bring up associations and memories describing his receptive tendencies and dependent attitude, or stealing, a reaction takes place;

his thoughts carry him in the opposite direction and he begins to speak of his bold deeds, of his fights, of his aggressions against older boys, especially against the suitors of the older sisters.

It is obvious that his babyish attitude toward the sisters and mother hurt his pride and he tried to compensate for it with excessive aggressiveness and a belligerent attitude. This is typical of his actual behavior and of his associations. It is also obvious that the stealing was a compromise between his receptive tendency and aggressiveness. Instead of receiving he takes what he wants by force. All this can be well demonstrated by the following excerpts from our analytical records:

. . . Thinking of New York, going around to cabarets and movies, and drinking. Always well dressed, although he worked hardly at all, but got the money from homosexuals. Thinking of his mother when she died. He sold newspapers as a child. How he liked to give her the money which he got from selling newspapers. She also liked him to give her everything. Still, he often stole from his mother because he did not like to ask for money. Also took pennies from sisters. He once drove a truck for a man. A girl from the neighborhood fooled with him, but when he started intercourse, she ran away. . . .

There was a liquor-store from which he used to steal whisky-bottles and then sell them. This was when he was nine years old. Sometimes he drank a little himself. Sometimes he was kicked out. Stealing little chickens from a store and raising them in the yard. Climbing on roofs and going into houses, stealing dimes and other coins. He never took a large amount of money even if he found it. He never was afraid to climb anywhere. Once he came home and said that the moon was chasing him. He was five or six years old. They teased him for that. A young man who went with his sister gave him a nickel every night. Once he threw it back, but he does not know why he did not want to take it.

The typical sequence of associations about stealing and receiving gifts and bold aggressive acts repeats itself constantly. Here is another example:

. . . He bit his fingernails. His sisters offered him everything not to do it. A red-headed boy played with his penis in a little club. He was given a cent, sometimes nothing. Stealing from a Greek, peanuts and bananas. He also stole pickles and ate them. The American Express had electric trucks. Driving them as a boy. He could drive before other boys could. . . .

He maintains that when he was twelve years old he already had a license for driving an automobile. He drove for a tire company at that time. He lied about his age and said he was sixteen. Once he had an accident and then it came out that he was twelve years old and he lost his job.

Again the characteristic sequence in his associations: memories of stealing and afterwards of driving a car, which the other boys could not do.

Similar dynamic relations can be seen in the following train of thoughts:

From the fifth grade on, he remembers that he did not like school and wanted to leave and go to work. How he got to his sister's home after his mother's death he does not remember. He remembers the funeral. He had to hide behind a carriage to smoke. The beach in Maine where he went on summer vacation with mother and sisters when he was eleven years old. There was a cigarette-stand from which he stole cigarettes. Then he took the train back to the city alone. He ran away. . . .

Again memories of stealing and directly afterwards of a very independent act: riding back alone to the city.

Then he continues: He went back to Boston probably to

play with the kids. He did not like it at the beach because there were no kids. Remembers two new songs which his sister played on the piano. If he hears them even today, he thinks of the beach. Thinking of the lady who visited him today. She gave him a lecture and discussed his case. He has a pain in his stomach. The woman's store where he sold the bottles. How little he can remember of his past history. He should remember more. Whether he acted abnormally as a child. Thinking of his mother, how good she was to him. She never drank and neither did his father. She bought him clothes and everything. When he lived with his sister, he hired a bicycle and did not want to return it. His brother-in-law made him give it back. . . .

Bicycle- and auto-riding served him for increasing masculine pride and we see often that memories of stealing or being pampered or given things are followed by associations about riding. This is also very clearly seen in the following example:

The tea-room was ten minutes from his home. He often went for his sister. All the girls played with him, gave him ice-cream sodas. He liked to go there. One sister was a stenographer in an office and he liked to go there too, because the people there gave him all sorts of things. This sister he did not like as well as the others, but he liked all his sisters. In the neighborhood there was a big hotel on the corner. Automobiles were parked behind it. He took the cars and drove them around and brought them back. . . .

The analysis soon revealed that his belligerent attitude and his extreme predilection for fighting are also reactions to the passive receptive longings in which he indulges profusely, but then he feels the need to compensate for them in order to emphasize the masculine side of his nature. His drinking is closely connected with this; under its influence he overcomes all fear and can become aggressive and pugnacious. Almost all the acts of violence and the offenses for which he came into contact with the police were committed under the influence of alcohol.

When he was fifteen years old, he enlisted in the Navy, chiefly to show the sister with whom he lived that he "was not a baby and was not afraid."

The following incident, which happened when he was a sailor, may illustrate his way of dramatically exhibiting his aggressiveness. On one occasion, in Shanghai, he went ashore to a notorious bar frequented by sailors. In front of the barroom he saw a young American sailor weeping. On learning that this American had been thrown out of the bar by a group of English sailors, he went in and asked for the man who had attacked his comrade. The first one who responded he knocked out, and he then attacked the others. A violent fight ensued. Our sailor's energy was stimulated not only by the presence of an external enemy but also by his need to deny the passive tendencies which he had to overcome. He had to demonstrate to himself that he was not a little baby, the pet of his big sisters, and this inner conflict worked like "dope" in the ear of a racehorse. The fight ended in a complete victory and he was hailed as "the brave American sailor." Now that he had proved what a great fellow he was, he could allow himself to give in to his passive tendencies. In fact, ten minutes later he invited two of the hostile English sailors to have a drink, and the drinking party resulted in a great friendship.

Similarly determined was his relationship to his best friend, with whom he had at least a dozen violent fights, always while drinking. The fights usually ended in an excursion together to a house of prostitution. His fighting spirit had a long history. When he was twelve years old and an usher in a theatre, he attacked a man who had insulted a young lady in the audience. Yet at the same time, in contrast to Vorland, he indulged his dependent tendencies, accepted aid from women, and liked to be cared for in every way.

We see here a most interesting interplay between two sides of his nature and alternating gratification of both. In Vorland the receptive dependent attitude was repressed and entirely eliminated from the ego, which showed only compensating reactions (reaction-formations). In Perez, however, prolonged indulgence in the pleasant rôle of the petted baby of the family did not allow the above solution of the instinctual conflict. He could not renounce the dependent and receptive rôle, but yet could not yield to it entirely because of his masculine ambitions. The result was a kind of alternating gratification of both categories of tendencies. The analyst had the distinct impression that the patient could indulge in his dependent tendencies only if, from time to time, he proved to himself that he still possessed his aggressive masculine potentialities. This pattern of the solution of the instinctual conflict betrayed itself in his sexual life as well. Not only passive dependent tendencies, but passive homosexual strivings also could be tolerated by the ego. He was overtly bisexual and in his sexual relations to men played both the active and the passive rôle. The active rôle, which especially in phantasies took the form of rectal intercourse, was manifestly a reaction to passive gratifications which hurt his masculine pride. He could accept the female rôle only after he had proved that he could be a man also, if he wanted to. In his homosexual phantasies he made a woman of his sexual partner, whereas in reality he often took the passive rôle.

His sensitiveness which arose when he accepted the passive rôle can best be seen in the following episode: While still in young adolescence, he was picked up in New York by an older homosexual. In the park they passed two men who made some remark. Our patient immediately turned around, knocked out one of the two men, and attacked the second. A long and violent fight ended finally in the patient's victory.

When the analyst first had opportunity to call the patient's attention to the conflict between these two sides of his nature, he accepted the interpretation as being evidenced by what he had related and then produced very corroborating material. He confessed how extremely sentimental he is. He wants to be loved by everybody. He loves his wife more than anybody else, but likes other girls too. He always wants to repay a thousand times what others do for him. In phantasy he wanted to give much money to his sister and buy a beautiful house for her. In the Navy he was ashamed of the homosexual approach of the older men. He likes to talk and would like to write, but he does not use English well enough. He always wanted to do something great, but in later years he was so nervous that he could not do anything. When he was a child and did something wrong, if one sister slapped him, another stuck up for him. There was always somebody who defended him. When he first went to prison, he always wanted to talk to the big gangsters. He can remember that he was jealous of his brother and wanted to be able to lick him. His brother kicked him sometimes and never let him go out with him. He wanted to show his brother that he "was also a man and not a kid."

This material leads up to his relation to his older brother. It becomes gradually clear to him that the main reason for his conflict about his babyish attitude was the older brother. He could not enjoy without inner conflict the privileged rôle of the pampered child in the family because of the example of his brother. The relation to his brother stimulated his masculine aspirations, and his chief aggressions centered on his brother.

When he was seventeen years old and in the Navy, he heard of the death of his brother and immediately left the Navy and came home, and soon afterwards there happened what he called his nervous breakdown. The chief symptom was extreme palpitation, which he tried to explain as resulting either from drinking too much alcohol or coffee. Since that time this palpitation has not left him. He is afraid to lie on his left side because then he feels the palpitation more clearly. Another hypochondriacal apprehension took the form of fear of dying from consumption, which was the cause of his brother's death.

The dynamic connections are now clear. The long and extensive indulgence in the passive receptive rôle of the little child created a strong sense of inferiority toward the brother, increased the jealousy and aggression toward the brother, which in turn led to strong guilt feelings and inhibitions and the hypochondriacal fears. A competitive attitude, similar to that felt toward the brother, can also be seen toward his brother-in-law who married the "beautiful sister." He maintains that the chief cause of his sense of inferiority is this brother-in-law, who always teased him. He teased him for biting his fingernails and called him a "little nut." "I wanted to show my brother-in-law and all the boys who went with my sister that I was as good as they were." One fellow who went with his sister gave him a nickel every night, but once he threw it back.

Hostile tendencies toward his brother-in-law and brother appear simultaneously with hostile feelings toward the analyst. He begins one interview by showing a clipping from a newspaper which states that Dr. Gustave Alexander, a nerve specialist, had died. He thought that perhaps this was a relative of the analyst. Then he tells the following dream:

His sister spoke harshly to him. It was on account of eating something or drinking a bottle of milk. At the end of the dream he saw three little bullets which had been fired, but he did not see the gun.

We see that the dream starts with his conflict about his oral receptive tendencies (sucking attitude—drinking a bottle of milk), but then the typical compensatory reaction takes place and at the end there is reference to a very aggressive theme: three bullets had been fired.

In associating to this dream he remembers that a few days before he had said to his sister, who visited him in the jail: "If you had not petted me so much, I would not be here now." The further course of associations led him to his fears of consumption and then to his brother-in-law, who got a job for him in an office. The same day he got influenza and had to go home. After this he found another job—teaching people automobile-driving. He drove before his brother could drive and taught his brother. When he was a little boy, his brother-in-law—the one who gave him the nickels every day—needed a truck for transporting furniture; Ferdinand got a team for him. They put the furniture on, but the back wheel got stuck in the car-tracks, and his brother-in-law fell off and broke his thumb. These associations, like the dream, start from the conflict about his sucking baby attitude (drinking milk), but then lead to the conflict with the brother and the brother-in-law and the hostile tendencies toward them. This hostile attitude caused fear of retaliation, as is clearly seen in the following dream:

He dreamed he was at a party. Everybody left. Suddenly two men grabbed him, one at the back of his neck and the other at his testicles, and pulled him down. They wanted to rob him. The men came from behind. He awoke in fear.

The basis of his aggression was the envy of the older brother and the brother-in-law's greater strength and potency, and in this dream he is beset by two men who attack his genitals.

His receptive and dependent tendencies (oral receptive attitude) he identifies with femininity, as is clearly revealed in the following dream:

He was in a house or in a home. His sisters were there and

a little girl, who was singing. There was an open door and no fence. It was high in the air and he was afraid that the little girl would fall down because she was standing near the door. He went to pull her back, but his sister resented that and did not like his pulling the girl away. He was very angry and said she ought to mind her own business; he was so provoked that he did not want to speak to her at all any more.

Asked for associations to the little girl, he begins instead to associate to his sister. His beautiful sister always criticized him, criticized the jobs he got, the way he dressed, said that he was too conspicuous. She was angry with him when he got into trouble. If he said something she always resented it.

Associations to the little girl: she was like his oldest sister's little girl.

Associations to the singing: earlier his eldest sister sang much.

Analyst: "And who else?"

Patient (looking around, manifestly embarrassed): "I sang."

Analyst: "And you are the little girl in the dream. You told me yesterday that you are afraid of being on high places. You said that you sang well as a child and yesterday we started to recognize your female tendencies, which you want to get rid of by drinking. In the dream you resented the fact that your sister did not allow you to take care of this little girl, but I think what you really meant was that you resent that your sister does not take care of the little girl, alias you. This friction between you and your sister is probably based on the fact that you wanted to remain the little boy of the big sister and she wanted you to become more masculine, more adult."

He admits his femininity and sensitiveness and his tendency to make believe he is a man; that he is afraid of not living up to what he would like to be. Yesterday he said that he never would touch anything which does not belong to him. This resolution gives him satisfaction in the feeling that he can resist.

Analyst: "Probably in your stealing there is also a factor which comes from this same side of you—taking away from others because you have no confidence in yourself and a feeling that you have not what others have. But it is rather easy to understand how these female tendencies become so strong in you. You were the youngest in the family, and to be the little baby was connected with the greatest advantages. You became accustomed to these gratifications of the little boy, and your environment fostered this attitude of yours, but when you became older, when you compared yourself with other boys, naturally you began to be ashamed of these sissy tendencies and so the conflict was created."

It seems contradictory to this picture of Perez's personality that he, who married when he was twenty-three years old and became the father of three children in the first four years of his marriage, was a good and considerate father, who assumed much responsibility toward his family. The analytic material, however, shows that this marriage and fatherhood played the same balancing rôle in his emotional conflict as did his criminality. It was a constructive solution of the same conflict that also determined his aggressiveness and pugnacity. He compensated for his strong dependent and receptive tendencies by his great generosity and the responsibility assumed toward his family. In his associations he expressed repeatedly the wish to repay a thousand times everything which he received from his mother and sisters. Being a responsible husband and father who supports his family was a good compensation for the strong and even conscious desires for help and dependence.

In the emotional relationship to the analyst the same conflict between his passive receptive attitude and his hurt masculine pride repeats itself. This is clearly manifested in the following dream pair:

*Dream 1:* He went to the analyst's home and waited to have an interview. It was in the evening. The analyst came, but was going away again. The wind was blowing and it blew the analyst's hat off in his direction. He caught it and gave it back.

*Dream 2:* He was with his wife and oldest son on the beach. The water was rolling up. There was a hole there and his son stuck a stick into it and found a hundred and fifty dollars. His son wanted to give the money to him. He said: "You can buy some ice cream for yourself." He thinks the boy was crying.

Associations to being in the analyst's home: "Nothing except that I don't remember where it was, but it was during the night time."

Associations to the fact that analyst was just going away: "The way you hurry away from here after you have finished with me."

Associations to the wind blowing off the analyst's hat: "I can't think of anything. I think the wind blew off another man's hat and I caught that one too. I can't think of anything. I can't associate anything else."

Analyst: "Is it not evident that in the dream you create a situation in which you help me? At first you come to my home at an unusual time—you cannot even wait for your regular hour—but then you help me to get back my hat. In that way you can balance getting and giving and you relieve your sense of inferiority for being helped."

Patient: "I see that perfectly clearly. Do you think that if I would pay you for my cure, I would not have had this dream?"

Analyst: "I think you would."

Patient: "It means that I always want to give more than I get in order not to feel inferior."

Analyst: "Exactly."

Associations to his son's finding the money in the hole: "Finding this money here the other day." [1] Sometimes his little boy gives him a cent and says: "Have a cent and go and buy something for yourself."

Analyst: "Your son behaves as you do in the first dream; as if you would say in the second dream: 'It is not I who am playing big and want to help the doctor, but my son is the silly little boy who wants to give me money and help me, his father.' You project your own childish gesture of superiority onto your little boy."

During the process of analysis Ferdinand involves himself more and more in this very conflictive situation. His analysis was discontinued mainly because of external circumstances, but in the last days he developed an extreme resistance and at least partially was glad to stop the analysis. His last dream reveals quite directly his emotional difficulty in regard to the analysis. At this session he starts by confessing that he hates to lose the analyst but he feels he would not be able anyhow to get much farther in the three weeks in which he could still work with him. He knows that he would not be finished in this time and later, after he is out of prison, he would have to continue anyway. Now he feels well and very contented with what he has got out of the analysis and thinks it is the best moment to stop. He admits that he must have some emotional resistance against the continuation of the analysis and that somehow he welcomes the possibility of stopping, even if at the same time he hates to do so.

Then he tells this dream: His son was lying on a bed. He kissed him, but the boy was very disobedient and unpleasant He went into another room and cried because his son was not

[1] The patient found seventy dollars hidden in his cell under the mattress and returned it to the guard. This honesty made a great impression in the jail and the deprecatory attitude of the guards and officers toward psychoanalysis as the result of this episode was considerably changed.

properly trained.

He states immediately after telling the dream that he sees it contains his own problem.

The analyst explains to him that obviously the son represents a part of his personality. He represents the patient's reluctance to continue the analysis because the analysis now hurts his pride. To be analyzed means to give in, to accept the passive attitude for which he always has to compensate with display of masculinity and independence. He has developed the same dependent attitude toward the analyst, and also the reaction against these feelings; therefore he has to fly now from the analysis, which makes him feel too passive and receptive, but at the same time he would like to give in to the receptive tendencies: in the dream he (his son) cries because one portion of his self does not allow him to continue the analysis.

Ferdinand accepts this explanation entirely and says that the analyst has really verbalized something which is almost conscious in him. He feels that with one part of his person he would like to continue the analysis and he has decided to continue after his release from prison. As he was only transferred for a limited time to the jail in which the analysis has taken place, he had to go back to the prison to which he was sentenced.

The dynamic picture of Ferdinand's personality-development in its main features can be fairly well reconstructed from this material. As the youngest in the family he was spoiled by his mother and five older sisters and enjoyed this baby rôle until the comparison with his older brother and the contact with other children began more and more to disturb his inner peace. It is the unavoidable defect of such relatively short analytic explorations that many important but deeply repressed emotional events cannot be evaluated sufficiently. Thus, for example, we know little about Ferdinand's relation toward his father, and not even his reactions to his father's death, which occurred when he was eleven years old, have been revealed. Probably the very similar and parallel emotional attitude to the older brother overshadows the father-son relation. The ambivalent feelings toward the older brother necessarily become conscious much more easily and earlier than the deeper repressed hostile emotion toward the father. But be that as it may, having accepted so extensively the dependent rôle, his feeling of inferiority and his aggressive jealousy toward the older brother became very accentuated. As a reaction to his extensive hostility, guilt feelings and, in consequence, self-destructive tendencies have developed. Both the continual nail-biting (self-mutilation) and the hypochondriacal fears of consumption and his palpitations are related to this guilt reaction toward his brother. Later he transferred the same attitude to his brother-in-law, the husband of the most beloved sister. These guilt reactions, self-destructive tendencies, fears, inhibitions, drove him back again to the dependent passive-receptive attitude, and in a vicious circle this infantile regression again hurt his masculine pride and drove him to an over-emphasized display of aggressiveness and bravado.

The following diagram may give a schematic view of this dynamic relation (vicious circle):

Fixation in the receptive dependent attitude (oral receptive phase), due to spoiling by mother and sisters. } Oral fixation

↓

First interference with the uninhibited gratification of these dependent tendencies through school contacts and competition with older brother leads to sense of inferiority. } Sense of inferiority

↓

Sense of inferiority intensifies jealousy of brother and leads to hostile attitude toward brother and brother-in-law. } Reactive jealousy and hostility

↓

Aggressions toward brother leads to sense of guilt and in consequence to self-punishing tendencies (hypochondriacal symptoms). } Guilt, self-punishment, neurotic fear

↓

These self-destructive tendencies and fear reinforce the sense of inferiority, which intensifies jealousy and hate, which in turn again reinforce fear. } Neurotic fear, aggression, neurotic fear

↓

Fear drives him back to the infantile fixation—dependence and receptiveness. } Regressive reinforcement of dependent receptive attitude

↓

Criminal behavior as an over-emphasized display of aggressiveness and bravado, which is a compensatory reaction to his infantile regressions.

His criminal behavior is thus largely a direct expression of the over-emphasized masculine behavior. A number of the offenses for which he came into conflict with the police have been on account of violence, usually fighting, under the influence of alcohol.

There is very striking similarity between the dynamic background of Ferdinand Perez's and Richard Vorland's criminal behavior. In both cases the reaction to intensive or oral receptive and female passive tendencies is of decisive importance. The instinctual conflict between passive receptiveness and masculine aggressiveness in both cases is the same. In Vorland's case, however, the conflicting tendencies are strongly repressed, and the conscious ego rejects the passive female trends and shows only defense mechanisms against them, whereas in Perez's case the conflict is fought out in the conscious ego, which is dominated by both passive and aggressive tendencies. The explanation of this difference may be found in the historical fact that in Vorland's case the rejection of the infantile dependent attitude was a reaction to deprivations, whereas in Perez's case the passive dependence was the result of spoiling and the direct continuation of the patient's early infantile situation, which in reality was never changed. Perez has good reason to accept and indulge in his passive dependent attitude, an attitude which has yielded him so many pleasures and advantages in his earlier and more recent life.

COMPARISON OF EARLY CASE RECORD WITH THE PSYCHOANALYTIC
MATERIAL

Comparison of the psychoanalytic material with the case record shows strong agreement concerning the part that women have played in Ferdinand's life, his dependence upon them, the response which he has always obtained from them, and his failure to grow up and fully play a man's part. These early studies, however, did not reveal anything about the dynamic causal relation between his dependent receptive trends and his criminality, which in the analysis was shown to be a compensatory attempt to restore the inner prestige which was so badly damaged through the indulgence in his infantile and female gratifications.

No deep psychiatric study was undertaken in early adolescence, because it was felt that an environmental change was absolutely necessary. The boy wanted the freedom of country life and a different school régime; however, while his truancy ceased when he was placed in a farm home, his fundamental characteristics were unaltered—the bettered environment was not sufficient. Later casual contacts with the boy were for the most part when he was in trouble and after he left the Navy. There has been much attempt to help him, but entirely from a case-work standpoint.

It is only to be expected, then, that much revealed by the psychoanalysis has not been known to the many social workers, male as well as female, who have tried to aid him because he has always seemed to present so many assets for reform. Neither the family nor the court knew anything about Ferdinand's pilfering tendencies at the period when he was complained of for being a chronic truant. At the clinic he was then found to be a furtive, evasive little boy who hated school because of the confinement and because he had discovered that the movies and street pleasures gave him more enjoyment. The early sex experiences that he revealed then were regarded as nothing peculiar, and in his later contacts he gave no indication of the many heterosexual and homosexual affairs that he had been in, the latter being so illuminating concerning some of his hidden tendencies.

The case record contains a number of allusions to Ferdinand's generosities; he liked to give to others. One foolhardy affair that he was in trouble about was caused by his generously aiding a "buddy" who proposed some criminal act. In the analysis Ferdinand made a clear revelation of all the criminality that appears on the record and beyond this tells of the early pilfering that was not known at all, as well of as much other delinquent behavior. It is astonishing with what regularity he has been apprehended for his delinquencies and how often he has suffered incarceration for them; he is anything but a shrewd, calculating criminal. And it is probably true that, as he has often said in his letters and as his sister maintains, he has never really meant to do wrong.

Another point is that none of those who knew Ferdinand early characterized him as being a fighter; he was then quite small for his age and in general was regarded as likable and fairly mild in behavior. His fighting qualities were evidently brought on by alcohol, as he states in analysis. His early memories concerning this are probably distorted, as they certainly are in regard to the early age at which he states he obtained an automobile license—this last would be impossible for a boy of twelve, less than four feet nine inches in height. His story of being a theater usher at twelve years and attacking a man is unquestionably likewise antedated. But all these distortions go to prove the great need that this spoiled, receptive fellow has for picturing himself to himself as an unusually and even prematurely masculine and aggressive personality. It is in line with his actual enlistment in the Navy at less than sixteen years of age, which must have been through falsification of his birth date. However, by then he had grown considerably in size.

Many of Ferdinand's letters contain statements that he is a puzzle to himself. He said the same thing just after he returned from the Navy, when he was eighteen. He had obtained release from service because he had heard of his brother's death, but instead of returning straightway home, he stopped in many cities on his way across the continent, spending his accumulated pay in whatever pleasures the places afforded. When interviewed at that time, Ferdinand seemed to have a much broken morale and to be rather confused about his past and his future. It was noted that he found it difficult to reconstruct the details of his school-history, or even to remember just how old he was when his father died. Perhaps these partial amnesias have always offered a possible chance for some little glorification of the part that he has played.

While Ferdinand as a younger boy seemed furtive and evasive and was generally regarded as quite untruthful, he now remains the engaging personality he has always been since later adolescence. He is not dramatic or self-seeking, nor does he ever appear to be purposefully deceitful. He is fairly good-looking, with well-marked features and a pleasant boyish smile, having a direct and simple approach that is rather winning. It is no wonder that he has retained the affection of his relatives, or that his wife has always stood by him. Indeed, she states that in some ways he deserves her help because he has been wonderfully kind in his family attitudes. Neither is it surprising that prison social workers have always felt that he was such good human material. The many letters that have come from him during his prison life express much appreciation of love and friendship and of what has been attempted for him, as well as contrition and optimism about his conduct in the future. A prison magazine published a rather beautiful little poem by him on friendship. With more than ordinary persistence he has attempted to educate himself in several directions, that he may be able to get better types of employment when he is released.

Applications for pardon or commutation of sentence have been made on the basis that Ferdinand is no ordinary criminally-inclined offender, but his long record as it shows on paper has steadily been deemed sufficient reason for denying the applications.

Now, a year later, we find that Ferdinand has been on parole for about two months. He appears attractively well and very energetic. He has been found temporary employment and is taking great delight in supporting his family. As always he is immensely interested in his children. With contagious optimism and forcefulness he seeks a better and more permanent job. He feels that he profited much by his short analytic treatment, but circumstances make it quite impossible for him to continue the analysis.

# CHAPTER SEVEN

## *The Solitary Offender*

HENRY ELTON was thirteen years old when his case was first studied at the Guidance Center. Both parents were seen as well as the boy. The mother was forty and the father forty-eight. They came to Boston from Jamaica when Henry was three years old; both parents were of English ancestry. This couple had lost two children in infancy before Henry was born; now they had another boy, almost exactly seven years younger than Henry.

The father was a hard-working artisan who supported his family comfortably. He was a man of thoroughly good character and reputation. The mother was an energetic, intelligent woman who complained somewhat of nervousness, but had never been very ill. At the Center both were found thoroughly co-operative and able to give an evidently reliable account of themselves and of the problem with Henry.

The pregnancy with Henry was quite normal; he was large at birth and was nursed five months. There was no feeding problem with him and his diet was carefully scheduled. Indeed, he seemed a very normal, happy baby and showed no peculiar habits all through his younger childhood. When he was about five, Henry began to have asthma; at first this was very severe and it continued in minor degree until he was thirteen. Aside from this he never had any serious illness or injuries. He responded to sphincter training very normally.

Examination at this time showed a well-developed boy of normal strength and apparently healthy, but in features and expression he appeared quite soft and sensuous. He was already much of a smoker, having begun smoking at nine years, and was reported to be very fond of eating, particularly of sweets.

In general intelligence he rated as highly superior; I.Q. 133. He evidenced remarkably good memory powers and worked well with tests involving language. He was then completing the last grade of grammar school, but not getting good marks; the teacher said, for lack of attention.

On account of his asthma the family doctor had proscribed many activities for Henry; between the ages of five and ten he had not been allowed to play rougher games with boys. He had mechanical toys and read a great deal, besides making normal boyish collections. He was able to attend school regularly and made normal progress, and he attended Sunday school for five years or so until he began to lose interest. It was stated that Henry seemed particularly fond of children younger than himself and was always kind to them.

Apparently Henry was a very good young child, who never had to be punished until he began to steal. He was quite affectionate, but his parents were not especially demonstrative. His mother characterized him as an adorable child until about his ninth year—she evidently rather easily forgave his earlier stealing because of his good qualities. Henry's personality and behavior characteristics as observed at the clinic and as reported by his relatives appeared to be the following: Fretful, peevish, pouting, cries easily, selfish, tricky, sensuous, always demanding, scheming for his own benefit, soft, cowardly, avoids fights, obstinately argumentative and protesting, energetic and a good worker for very short periods, shows initiative, occasionally becomes very angry at home, lies readily.

The family attitudes seem to have been very reasonable; there was no friction about discipline and the parents were fond of both children. In his occasional spare time the father was quite companionable with Henry; for example, he took him on fishing excursions. It was only after he had been stealing a good deal that the father resorted to severe whippings, and this was when he had failed to respond to other forms of punishment, such as ordinary scoldings and deprivations which his mother used in an attempt to curb his delinquency. The parents did not feel that they had ever shown any partiality; indeed, the mother was very fond of Henry; nor did they know that Henry showed any signs of jealousy toward his brother, a very well-behaved boy.

The pastor of their church advised the parents to bring Henry to the Center because of his excessive stealing from home, neighbors, and relatives, as well as from shops and at the church. Evidently the stealing had begun some time before the mother knew about it, but it certainly increased greatly in extent and seriousness during Henry's eighth year.

The father made a special complaint about the boy; he said that it made his blood boil when he saw how Henry would not stand up to other boys in a fight, although he appeared so large and strong. He stated that he had used his best ingenuity to make the boy more manly and to reason with him about the wrongfulness of stealing.

In interviews with Henry the psychiatrist found him a little deceitful, quite glib and plausible, but almost boastful about his delinquencies. He told definitely of having begun his stealing at five years with another boy and how this pilfering of small sums had gone undetected for some time. He spent the money for candies and eatables, at first enjoying these with others, but soon turning to stealing entirely for his own benefit. It was not until he was about eight that he began purloining things so extensively from shops, and money from other places than home. More recently he had developed a shrewd scheme for returning stolen articles to stores as if they had been purchased and receiving a refund for them.

Henry was full of promises of reformation about everything except his smoking—that, he said, he must continue to enjoy. He frankly told of ordinary boyish interest in sexual matters; he made much of his physical disability induced by asthma; he said that he had to steal in order to get the enjoyments that he wanted and to treat other boys so that he could keep in their favor and not be "licked" by them. He said he hated his father for nagging about the stealing and that he liked his mother a thousand times better.

An improved régime for the boy was planned by the parents; he was allowed more freedom and more spending-money and for a short time Henry's behavior was bettered. Then Henry thought if he got away from home entirely all would be quite well with him. He was placed in a foster-home where other boys had done well, but there after a short time again much stealing developed. His pilfering was regarded as peculiar because he stole not only things to eat but made whole collections of articles that he took. He remained away for about a year and then his parents thought that they would like to try again with him. At infrequent intervals during the latter part of the time he was in the foster-home and after he had returned, an analysis of the Adlerian type was undertaken, but the boy reacted to this with a tremendous show of peevishness, discontent, and protests against his parents, accompanied by many demands for things that he wanted.

At one time earlier Henry stated: "I have been a common thief since I was five years old. They whipped me; all right, I said to myself, I will do it again." Even when his parents were generous, he always wanted more than he could get—"I just wanted things, I wanted a good time." In later interviews Henry acknowledged his jealousy of his brother, though before the latter was born he thought he would like to have a brother. Henry gave the impression of enjoying being the center of attention and of playing with his own problem. He seemed insincere as he moralized about his own behavior; on the other hand he rather boasted about how he was "raising the devil" by stealing so much.

When Henry returned home he engaged in a new orgy of stealing and was taken to the juvenile court; his parents made arrangements for him to go to a private institution for delinquent boys in another state. During four months there he rifled the lockers of other boys, ran away three times, and committed serious burglaries in neighboring towns. He was apprehended and sent to a state correctional school, where after three weeks he ran away. He made his way to a Western state, where he was arrested for carrying a gun and sent to a local correctional school. After eight months he was allowed to return home.

Henry was now sixteen and his father was dead. The family had fallen on hard times, and his mother had taken a friend of the father's to board, together with his lame child. A year or so later she married this man, who was of thoroughly good reputation and who tried to be a father to Henry.

After he was sixteen, on account of his good appearance and address, Henry rather readily obtained employment, but he stole from his employers in several places and after committing a burglary he was sentenced to the reformatory, from which he was paroled after twenty months. He then worked irregularly and for a time travelled with a circus, being dishonest in various places. He once returned to his former foster-home and was welcomed there, but stole a considerable amount from a man in the town who employed him. New warrants were now out for him in two states. It was at this time that he heard through his family that inquiries had been made to see if he were interested in being psychoanalyzed. He appeared at the Guidance Center and agreed to give himself up and serve his extended term as a failure on parole in order that he might have the opportunity to be analyzed. He said he was willing even to be regarded as insane if he could be studied and it could be found out why he so foolishly kept on with his career of stealing.

## PSYCHOANALYTIC MATERIAL

When the analysis of Henry Elton was begun in the jail he was twenty years old. He came there under very unusual circumstances. When he was on parole for the unexpired portion of an earlier sentence he heard of the possibility of being analyzed and gave himself up in order to undergo this. There were warrants out for him on account of offenses committed since his release. He knew that his added term would be about two years, but hoped that he might earlier than that obtain another parole.

The analysis was undertaken with the distinct understanding that on account of this boy's weak attitudes it might not be possible to get his co-operation for a complete analysis. It was felt, however, that enough material could be elicited for a more or less satisfactory research into the etiology of criminality.

Henry appeared neat and cleanly, a soft-looking boy, alert and quick in expression and movements, with pleasing manners, and rather glib of speech. He quickly stated that he had been an incorrigible thief since childhood. According to his memories, he began stealing at six or seven years and started by taking small sums of money from his mother, then toys and books from shops. At thirteen years, on account of his stealing, he was placed in a foster-home, but there his thieving continued. When, after a year, he returned to his own home, he engaged in an orgy of stealing from stores. He mentions that since then he has broken into houses, rifled lockers, stolen repeatedly from employers, and swindled much through collecting subscriptions and retaining the money. He has changed many positions which he has held, often without any objective reason.

The impression gained from him is that he comes from a family of very decent standards; his father, who died about three years ago, was able to support his family in moderate circumstances. The personality of the mother, as it is reflected in the analysis, seems to be that of a somewhat strict and moralizing woman with an over-protective attitude toward both her children, Henry and his brother, seven years younger. It would seem as if she had too little understanding and intuition concerning the emotional needs of her children. Doing everything with the best intention, her tendency was to deprive the boy too much of infantile pleasures. As Henry looks back on it, he thinks that he had less than his companions— less sweets and pocket-money and fewer toys—and when he grew older his ambitions for independent play and adventure were even more thwarted by his mother's control.

The mother's marriage soon after the father's death did not essentially change the family situation, nor did it have much effect on Henry, because at that time and later he was very little at home.

Henry starts the analysis by freely confessing his stealing and emphasizing the fact that, especially as a child, he never felt any regret about it, never felt that he had done anything wrong. He acted with a feeling of full justification. He talks about being very frequently caught in his thieving, but later in the analysis he confesses to quite a series of greater thefts which were never known, either to the police or anyone else. His cynical attitude toward stealing has never changed, though recently he has begun to feel that he should cease his delinquencies, more, however, from rational reasons than from self-condemnation.

His reaction toward punishments by his mother is not entirely clear. They were mostly in the form of deprivations—for example, taking away his bicycle—rather than spankings. There is an element of spite and some feeling of wanting to offer provocation for being punished. But the basic attitude toward his mother is that of demanding. The punishments help him to get even with his mother and stick to his claims. This attitude has never been fundamentally changed and has been transferred from his mother to other persons or, in general, to society in some degree. His most conspicuous character trend is centered on these claims and demands which he feels toward his mother and which have never been overcome. The meaning of much of his general behavior and of his attitude toward stealing is quite obvious: it is as if he said: "I must get something from my mother. She owes me something, and because she does not give it to me, I can take whatever I want."

The sense of justification which he had in stealing is very characteristic, the fact is that he not only has no guilt feelings toward persons who have treated him well and whom he has robbed, but sometimes he shows just the opposite, anger and accusation. Recently he robbed one of his employers who in spite of this still had some affection for him and wrote him a very kind letter to the prison in which he offered to consider the whole thing settled without prosecution if he would pay him back in installments. In showing this letter, he was full of criticism and aggressiveness against the employer, accused him of mentioning a bigger sum than he really stole, and showed very little appreciation of the friendly tone of the letter. It sounded as though his employer had committed something against him, not the opposite. He repeated again and again: "I am not angry with him," but a moment later he was full of emotion and accusation against the employer. It is, however, not the usual projection of guilt that is behind this, but the simple, almost naïve conviction that he had the right to take money, that in general he has the right to take, and everybody who interferes with this wish is his enemy.

Although this egocentricity and reckless receptive demands are predominant features, they alone do not give a complete picture of his character. As the analysis in many details has shown, he needs certain justifications for his demanding attitude, which became most evident in his reactions to the approaching Christmas. For seven years he had been in prison at Christmas except once. He emphasizes this fact in connection with phantasies in which he wallows in all the good things which he is going to receive for Christmas. It looks almost as if he would need to be in prison to have the justification to indulge in these orgies of receptive and demanding tendencies for Christmas day, which is the day of presents. This attitude of accepting, or perhaps even seeking, suffering as a justification for demanding shows that there is a conflict in his personality and that it is not a case of a simple conflictless oral fixation. His demanding tendencies, although they exhibit in many respects the unsublimated oral characteristics (wish for good food, cigarettes, sweets), are not simply accepted by the ego. He needs to create an external or internal situation in which these demanding wishes are justified.

Another reaction-formation to this oral fixation is a peculiar protective interest in small children. He plans to become somehow a worker for children; he is extremely upset if he hears of little children who are maltreated; he enjoys taking care of little children, giving them pleasures. He seems to understand how to deal with small children. He wants to write his life-history so that other children shall learn and profit from it. This interest has many sources. One of them is the tendency to over-compensate his childish receptive and dependent attitude by having authority over children. Another is that in caring for little children he identifies himself with the little child, and at the same time also takes the place of the kindly mother who grants to little children all the pleasures they want. He plays the rôle of the mother whom he wanted to have; in identifying himself with children he gratifies his receptive wishes in this indirect way. Thus, taking care of children has three advantages for him: first, it relieves him of his sense of inferiority deriving from his receptive infantile attitude; second, it enables him to enjoy these receptive pleasures in an indirect way through identification with the children. The third factor is a guilt reaction derived from his attitude toward his brother, eight years younger, and consequently can only be understood if his relation to his brother is known.

He reacted to the birth of his brother with strong jealousy and the feeling that he had lost his position in the family. This feeling became conscious only in later years. At the beginning he repressed it, but there is at least one rather reliable piece of evidence for its presence from the beginning in spite of the fact that there were also ample manifestations of love, curiosity, and tenderness toward the newcomer. He has one vivid memory of a seemingly quite unimportant episode which happened when his brother was born. He remembers that he spent the night his brother was born at a neighbor's house and he remembers all the details of the breakfast. He could take all the marmalade he wanted. The fact that this isolated memory was preserved so vividly can be interpreted in different ways. One could say that he remembers this fact on account of his strong oral tendencies, which were always checked at home.

This day, he took breakfast in another home and here he was treated differently, without the restrictive attitude of the mother—this might be the cause of this unimportant little scene sticking in his memory. On the other hand, the vivid memory of this breakfast, undoubtedly a screen memory, seems to be the most significant proof of his envious attitude toward the little brother. The vividness of this memory, which surpasses the clarity of all memories of this time, can be explained by the fact that that was the last breakfast which he ate before his brother was born. In remembering this, it is as if he said to himself: "Before my brother was born, I could eat as much as I wanted. I could get everything myself; there was no limitation." The vividness of this memory might come from the forgotten—that is, repressed—memory of seeing his little brother being nursed by his mother. He recalls some details of the infancy of his brother—his mother changing his diapers, his brother lying in the crib—but he does not remember anything about the nursing. The scene of his mother's nursing the baby, as it occurs so often, probably aroused the strongest envy in him. Therefore he repressed this scene of feeding and vicariously remembered another more pleasant scene connected with eating—namely, the last of his own meals which he took before his brother was born.

It seems also of significance that he spontaneously emphasized that he did not notice at all his mother's pregnancy, although consciously he wanted to have a brother. He remembers only that he knew of his brother's coming on the night before his birth, when he was sent to stay with the neighbor. A pronouncedly neurotic fear which has had a fatal significance in his career seems to contradict this statement. He has the irrational fear of losing his position on a certain date, which he usually cannot even rationalize very convincingly to himself, and actually several times he gave up his job without real reason only because he anticipated that he would lose it on a certain day. Once he gave up his job in a bakery because, without any tangible reason, he expected that he would be fired in September. Once he robbed his employer because he was afraid of the future, when he would lose his job. The same senseless changing, giving up his job for fear of the future, has happened again and again. There was an emotional pattern imprinted in him, some old fear of a certain date when he would lose his position. It seems that the event which he feared in the past was the birth of his brother, whom partially he wanted to come, but at the same time, he was afraid of his coming, which would mean losing his privileged position in the family. In a boy with his strong receptive oral attitude, such anticipation is very understandable.

Once, in connection with a story about giving up a job when he was sixteen years old, we discussed his irrational fear of losing jobs. The analyst asked him what was the basis of his fear at that time. He gave the quite disconnected answer: "A sixteen-year-old boy cannot do a man's work," as if he would say that his fear was connected with his feeling of being too young. If we accept the apprehension of the birth of his little brother as the basis of this fear, we understand the unconscious meaning of this answer: "I still felt too young to become independent when my brother was born. I still felt the need of being the center of my mother's interest." The irrational feature of this quite neurotic fear of losing his job, and then the memory of the "last breakfast," can both be explained by the assumption that Henry knew about the newcomer, expected but dreaded the day of his birth, and remembered the breakfast in the neighbor's family as the last one in which he had not yet had to share the oral receptive gratifications coming from the parents. His peculiar stubborn insistence on being transferred from jail to another prison on a certain date may have had emotional connections with the infantile apprehensive expectations which have been of such fatal significance for his life. He once made the remark that his life would certainly have taken another course if he could have stuck to one job, stayed in one place. This restlessness and irrational wish for change, connected with certain unmotivated apprehensions, was perhaps the only abnormality which he recognized in himself and which he wanted to get rid of.

To return now to his wish to be a social worker for children, the third gratification which he receives from this kind of profession is the relief of the sense of guilt which he has felt toward his little brother on account of the jealousy and death wishes against him, which later he remembers to have had quite consciously. Of course, these aggressive hostile feelings could only become conscious when he could connect them with certain rational motivations, as when his mother allowed the little boy to take away and break his toys. As a child, he used to have electric trains, and liked very much to play with them, but his little brother sometimes took them and broke them. His mother always allowed the little one to play with his toys. His brother used to let the air out of the tires of his bicycle only to hear the escaping air hiss. He was furious. In telling of this memory, he becomes very emotional and bitter. Naturally, then, as a reaction to such things, he used to tease his brother a lot. He says that it is not a nice thing to do, but he did it.

The relation to his brother seems to be closely connected with his stealing. It could not be established with certainty how much he stole before his seventh year, the year in which his mother was pregnant. Stealing, however, in this very early period, in the fifth or sixth year, is not at all extraordinary and needs no special explanation. It corresponds to the infantile tendency to have everything which is wanted, at a time in which this wish does not have to cope with strong inner moral restrictions. In the case of a little boy with an over-protective and at the same time somewhat restrictive mother, a stronger manifestation of this infantile stealing is nothing unusual, but what needs explanation is the continued stealing up to the adult age.

The analytic material, which is based greatly on direct memories or self-evident reconstructions, leaves no doubt that he felt his brother's birth and presence as an interference with his infantile rights and an addition to the restrictions which his mother's attitude had already brought to bear upon him. With his demanding traits this contributed to his tendency to take everything which his mother did not grant him. Apart from this, it explains also his peculiar feeling of justification, the lack of guilty conscience and remorse for his stealing. The appearance of the brother was considered an unjustified injury and he felt it absolutely right to make up for it by taking the things which he liked and which were denied him. This tendency to make up for deprivations manifest itself very clearly in the way he uses the stolen money. He goes to good hotels and enjoys the luxurious atmosphere. He describes in great detail how he enjoys comfortable, pleasurable living. He arises late and eats a good breakfast in his room. He buys nice clothes, makes acquaintances, especially with girls of better standards; he likes to drink and eat well. He plays the rôle of a well-to-do good fellow.

Another feature of his personality is a kind of boastfulness and ambition to be and seem important. Paralleling this are some masculine ambitions, which, however, do not seem very genuine, but more of a reactive nature; they evidently represent attempts to get rid of the sense of inferiority which his receptive dependent demanding attitudes have caused. This pseudo-masculinity manifests itself in one of his possible choices of profession—to join the Coast Guard. Near the end of the

analytic study he becomes aggressive toward the prison inmates and engages in a fierce argument. Only his fear of being
"licked" prevents him from accepting an invitation to a fist
fight with a more powerful prisoner. This rather smooth and
passive boy becomes full of powerless anger and self-deprecia-
tion on account of his cowardice. Through insight gained from
the analysis, he becomes more and more aware of his feminine
qualities. His sudden aggressiveness can be considered as a
reaction against his own passive tendencies. In this state of
mind in which the conflict, the protest of the ego against the
receptive tendencies, becomes stronger, the resistance against
the analysis manifestly increases. In the past his ego has more
or less renounced any desire for masculine activity and accepted
the oral receptiveness. The analysis now stirred up the ego's rejection, which, however, never really became strongly effective.
He feels that the analysis would drive him toward the danger
of becoming more active and aggressive, which attitude has
no great attraction for him and is basically foreign to his
nature. He prefers to break off the analysis and be transferred
to another jail because it is near his family and the K. family,
who in the past have treated him in generous and friendly
fashion. His last question after the final session—"Do you know
from my early history whether or not I was a sneaky kind of
fellow?"—reveals his inner situation. Evidently he wants a
negative answer in order to relieve his feelings about giving
in to the resistance and breaking off the analysis. In turn we
may ask: Was this a kind of defeat for him? Was it his acceptance of remaining a "sneaky fellow"?

His sense of inferiority has even a deeper origin than the
infantile demanding wishes; there is an unconscious passive
homosexual trend. The analysis could not probe this strongly
repressed layer; nevertheless, a few reliable signs became evident during the analysis. In identifying himself with little

children, he prefers little girls. The most enjoyable situation for him is to take care of little girls, which shows that the identification with a little girl is more suitable for the gratification of his passive receptive tendencies.

In one analytic session he began to talk of his phantasy of adopting a little girl. He fell into a hypnagogic state in which he saw himself at home for a couple of years. He made a great deal of money and was comfortably situated. He went to Dr. H.'s office with a little girl friend and told Dr. H. that he was going to adopt a little girl and Dr. H. told him where he could get one. Two weeks later he got a little girl, took her home, and arranged a little party. His home was opposite the home of the K.'s (a family with whom he was acquainted). Then the picture faded away. The girl was eight or nine years old (not far from his age when his brother was born). This little girl reminded him of one he knows in the small town where the K.'s live and who is really eight or nine years old. He may really some day adopt a little girl. He would like to have children, but not very little babies.

Here the analyst interrupts him and asks: "Why do you like children?"

"I don't know."

The analyst tells him that he probably identifies himself with the child and wants to take care of it as he wanted to be taken care of after he was thwarted in his receptive demands after the birth of his little brother. In his phantasy he adopts a little girl of nearly the same age as himself when his brother was born, and gives this girl all the attention which he wanted to get from his mother at that time. Very characteristic is his reaction to this interpretation.

"I thought that myself. But I would not have this fear of water which my mother had." (She was always afraid to let him take a boat out or go swimming.) Then he goes on to say that he would not be so apprehensive about children.

From this remark we can see that unconsciously he feels that, apart from his brother's birth, his mother's over-protective attitude in blocking his early boyish independent active ambitions was responsible for his softness and passivity. This factor we will discuss later in more detail. Let us return now to the continuation of the above analytic session.

After Henry's critical remarks about his mother's over-protectiveness, the analyst asks him: "Why do you think you want to adopt just a little girl and not a little boy?"

He answers very quickly: "I don't know. Every man prefers to have a girl, a woman a boy."

He is told that perhaps he can identify himself better with a little girl. This wish to adopt a child is based on his wish to enjoy through identification the situation of a spoiled little girl. His receptive wishes are after all not very boyish or manly. The identification with a girl is more suitable for gratifying this kind of longings. After this explanation there is a long silence.

Analyst: "What are you thinking of now?"

Of a little girl who was in their home last autumn. She was about ten or eleven. He took two pairs of ear-phones and gave her one of them so that she could listen to the radio. She was sitting on his lap listening while his brother and her brother were playing outside.

The analyst again points out how easily he can put himself in this little girl's place and how he enjoys her pleasure in listening to the radio together with her, one ear-phone on his ear and one on hers.

He continues: Yesterday he listened to the radio. He recognized it faintly as the same program that he heard a year ago. At first he recognized a little children's poem and then the music. Suddenly he begins to finger his shirt. He bought it in Canada for a dollar and a half. "A cheap-looking thing." In the States he can get a better one for that money. "It is too light and too soft." And then, seemingly without any connection, he asks: "Did you read the book, *Three Soldiers*?"

This sequence of association is very instructive and displays his central conflict. After the analyst's remarks had made him more conscious of his soft and passive nature, he suddenly begins to criticize his shirt, which is too soft and light, as a displacement of self-criticism to an external less painful spot. Not he, but his shirt is soft. Then he suddenly jumps to the idea of soldiers —to the opposite of being girlish. In the following part of the session he speaks of his wish to have money, to spend it in good hotels, to live in luxury, and then he goes on speaking about powder, toothpaste, cigarettes which he obtained from one of the better-off inmates of the prison.

There is no question that his mother's over-protectiveness in those years in which he made an attempt to overcome competition with his little brother by accepting the rôle of the adult had interfered with the development of his masculine trends. He complains bitterly, full of emotion, of how his mother had hid his bicycle or would not allow him to go swimming. He could not enjoy the advantages of being the older boy, but neither had he the privileges of the little baby. The outcome of this conflict was his excessive stealing, appropriating the receptive rights of the little child. Probably his constitutional masculinity was not strong enough to overcome by active independence the restrictive influence of the mother. After some faint attempts he regressed to the oral stage and gave up the satisfactions derived from active masculine accomplishments. He developed a technique to win other people's approbation and favors by the aid of little tricks, smoothness, and false gestures of generosity. The analyst had the opportunity to observe how well he succeeded in winning the benevolence of a so-called "patient"—a prisoner with whom he was in the hospital department of the jail and to whom he was of slight medical assistance. This patient soon went out of the prison and sent Henry cigarettes, eatables, writing- and reading-material and was even willing to offer him a job after his term was ended. This man took the trouble to write a letter to Dr. Healy soliciting the boy's transfer to another jail and made all kinds of promises to Henry himself.

One of Henry's phantasies shows best his emotional attitude toward the "patient" and himself: When he is sitting around during the day he often has half-dreams. The other day he phantasied that he went to work for the "patient" who was his friend in the jail. He worked for him, but got no salary, only food, clothes, and dwelling. Once they came out to the city of S. They called up L. (a friend of Henry's who is in the oil business) to come for them with his car. They went to K.'s house, the comfortable home of a girl friend, and spent the evening there. They stayed a few days in the house and then they went to New Jersey. There his employer died, but before that he gave him some papers. One of these papers was a will. A lawyer filed it for him. He was left eight thousand dollars, with the condition that he take care of his employer's aunt in Connecticut. He went to this aunt, but she did not need anything. Then he bought clothes, went back and lived in K.'s house. One day he took L. aside and made a proposal to him—to buy half of his interest in the oil business. Then he opened a new office, with a new method of bookkeeping, and was very successful. This phantasy shows better than anything else his entirely dependent and receptive attitude, his lack of confidence in accomplishing anything without the help of others.

His relation to the K. family is also very instructive. He became acquainted with the K. girl on the trolley car and was invited to her house. K.'s mother, a hospitable and kindly woman, invited him often to her house and allowed him to help a little in the home, which was more comfortable than his own. He developed a peculiar sentimental attitude toward this family and dreamed of becoming a member of it. However, one of his friends courted the K. girl and planned to marry her. It is very interesting that Henry did not feel any conscious jealousy toward this rather successful friend, but phantasied being taken by him as an employee in his business. He wishes that this friend's plan to marry their friend, the K. girl, will be successful and his next thought is about his hope that on Thanksgiving his mother will send him a whole roast chicken. Again we see the entire lack of competition and in the place of it the wish to be fed by the mother.

No doubt, in this over-compensation for the competitive spirit, guilt feelings play a great rôle, deriving from jealousy toward the little brother, but the main reason for this lack of masculine aggression is the fact that the only desirable competition for him involves passive receptivity. If his mother will feed him, if he can have his youngest brother's position, then he easily gives up competing with boys of his own age and does not care if his rival marries the girl whom he loves. In renouncing rivalry he goes even so far that in his phantasies he wants to be helped by his friend who is going to marry the K. girl. He phantasies that after he gets out of prison he may get a position in his friend's business.

His attitude toward women includes some idea of sentimental love, but basically it is an egocentric wish to be loved and to have casual physical intercourse. It is characteristic that in connection with the latter he has much more sense of guilt than in regard to stealing. Sexuality as a whole does not play a very important rôle in his life. There is an important narcissistic element in it. He seeks it chiefly to prove his own attractiveness. There are also signs of a rather strong oral dependence upon women whom he wants to use for his personal advantage. If he comes into a new city, he tries to get acquainted with girls to use them, as he says, as a stepping-stone for making other better connections.

Here we have to deal with a personality in which the oral receptive fixation is quite acceptable to the ego and determines the criminal behavior. Henry requires only certain rather superficial justifications for the acceptance of this passive receptive attitude. There are indications both of a sense of inferiority which originated in the receptive attitude and of a sense of guilt on account of the jealousy toward his brother, but he succeeds in eliminating these conflicts by complacent boastfulness and superficial generosity, and, furthermore, by putting himself in real situations of suffering in which he has justification for demanding. This need for punishment or suffering explains also the readiness with which he gave himself up and went into prison to be analyzed.

The analysis of three months' duration was far too short to rearrange these emotional patterns. He became conscious both of his receptiveness and of his defense reaction to it, but developed a very strong emotional resistance against the continuation of the analysis. One cannot foretell how much he will be able to free himself from the experiences of the analysis and will give in again to his old behavior patterns. There is some hope that he will not be able entirely to get rid of this insight which may block the blind repetition of his misbehavior.

A range of etiological questions must remain unanswered in this case. The mother's over-protective and partially restrictive attitude had undoubtedly a great influence on him. The younger brother's birth and presence in the family strongly contributed to the oral fixation, which was based both on his sense of deprivation and on the inhibition of the masculine independent tendencies. The relative weakness of the conflict or, to express it otherwise, the relative ease with which the ego accepted the passive attitude with nothing more than rather superficial conflicts makes the assumption probable that the oral receptive passive tendencies were constitutionally very strong. The attitude toward his father and later toward his stepfather is not sufficiently analyzed. So far as his father plays any rôle in his memories during the analysis, there are very few signs of aggressive attitudes directed to the father. Once he appropriated his stepfather's automobile, which would tend to show a certain identification wish with him. Similarly, in the transference he showed only very little competitive identification wish with the analyst, to whom he attributed almost exclusively the rôle of the mother. Only once or twice he spoke about wanting to do later on work for children something similar to what the analyst was trying to do for him. Otherwise he easily accepted the authority of the analyst and the passive rôle toward him.

Naturally, one cannot decide whether a continued analysis could not have brought to the surface more attempts at masculine identification, but even this could not essentially change the picture. The family situation, especially Henry's relation to his mother and younger brother, together with the constitutional factors, the importance of which cannot be estimated with certainty, are decisive in this case. Environmental influences as specific factors in the development of his stealing tendencies can be almost entirely disposed of. The question why the oral fixation in this case led to stealing and did not find its expression in neurotic symptoms remains unsolved.

Comparison of the case record with the material obtained in the thirty-eight psychoanalytic interviews shows, in general, the factual validity of these interviews. Moreover, the interpretations seem amply justified in the light of the record if we allow for the fact that emotional attitudes in childhood life count more than specific objective occurrences.

The original case history had been much added to through contacts with the family and by many letters received from Henry during the long periods that he has been in prison. These letters reflect his personality characteristics very thoroughly. They abound in self-condemnation, assertions of his intentions to reform, reproaches against his parents; but more than anything else he is always wanting something, begging for candy, cigarettes, eatables, or money to be sent to him. And he is forever requesting special favors, either in the form of changing him from one institution to another or having particular consideration for early parole.

The psychoanalytic material as given above cannot at all do justice to the excessive amount of demanding that went on during the sessions with the analyst. He was always wanting somebody—his mother, or the family of his girl friend, or Dr. H.—to do something for him.

The record contains many evidences of Henry's changeableness in employment, even when he was considered by an employer to be doing well; some of the changes, however, followed episodes of dishonesty. Earlier he had once stated to a psychiatrist that at night before he went to sleep he was accustomed to think about all the things that he wanted, and that his stealing was to satisfy these inner representations of desires.

Light is thrown on another of his characteristics that is brought out in the analysis by Henry's behavior on a certain occasion, behavior which his mother mentioned as being very curious. He often wrote to her begging her to visit him more frequently in prison. Once when she went there he hardly paid any attention to her because some other woman was in the visitor's room with a baby. Henry was entirely absorbed in the little child.

## EPILOGUE

After he refused to go further with the analysis, Henry was transferred as he requested to the county jail near his home, but he soon tired of this, giving as his reason the lack of occupation, and he asked to be transferred again, this time to the institution where he had been earlier and to which he had said that, above all places, he never wanted to return. After his release on parole about a year later he was much befriended by the parole department and a soft-hearted man ("the patient") of a good family whom he had met in the jail when he was being analyzed and who had become almost abnormally attached to him. Employment conditions were very bad, but the best possible was done for Henry, and a place was found for him to live and work with a religious organization. When he came out of prison Henry was in a very nervous condition and his irritability found expression in quarrels with the people in the organization. Perhaps some little injustices were done him, but he could see only his side. He left there twice, thus breaking parole rules, and tried to get employment elsewhere. Then he returned and the parole department generously obtained a new position for him, working for a family. Inside of a couple of weeks he rifled the house and departed for the West, where he engaged in an amateurly conducted hold-up of an office. Without trouble he was apprehended at some distance with a girl who had been his companion for a week or two. He was sentenced to the penitentiary.

It is worth noting that Henry's running away from the private family where he was well placed occurred when several friends were trying to do their best for him and when a promising plan was afoot to get him a position at doing the thing he most of all wanted to do—namely, working with children in an institution. Henry evidently had doubts how this plan would mature, but, more than all, he seemed to lack faith in himself, in his ability to stick to a job or to any plan for his future.

# CHAPTER EIGHT

## *Nobody's Son*

ALBERT DRETT was thirteen years old when he first came to the Guidance Center, and twenty-one years old when analysis was attempted. He was referred to the Center because, after being placed in a foster-home six months earlier by a children's agency and after a period of seeming very happy, he had repeated the runaway episodes which had been a common practice with him since he was seven years old.

Albert was the youngest of a large family of children. His mother died when he was an infant. Almost nothing is known of her and her family. His father is said to have been the black sheep of a good family. After the mother's death the children were distributed about; Albert was placed in an orphanage. At two years of age he was adopted by a veterinarian and his wife. This couple had much earlier adopted another boy who turned out well, and they had a daughter of their own who has likewise been successful. The family situation was very peculiar; evidently the man earlier had been a fairly good character, but during his later life degenerated greatly. In his stories at the clinic and even before this, Albert reported that this adoptive father was alcoholic and a sex pervert. Other sources of information tended to corroborate this. The adoptive mother was much older than her husband, both of them now being well past fifty. She was a frail, harassed woman, unable

255

successfully to meet the situation. A few years later she left her husband.

In some ways and especially when younger, Albert was fairly well treated in this family; for example, he was given music lessons, which he much enjoyed. But the woman was too worn to give him much affection and the last few years after he had become troublesome the adoptive father on occasion brutally whipped him. Albert stated that when he was younger this man had engaged in minor sex play with him and that later, when he went back to visit, the man made definite homosexual advances.

Information about Albert's early history was obtainable from other sources than the family, and the adoptive mother herself apparently attempted to give accurate data. As a very young child he was notably restless and overactive, but appeard cheerful, happy, and optimistic, always attractive, likable, and seeking affection. His school-teachers later spoke of his restlessness, changeableness, and lack of ability for good continuous performance. He had to repeat a couple of grades in spite of his obvious intelligence. His mother repeatedly challenged physicians with questions concerning his mental normality. After Albert's appearance in a juvenile court at twelve years for mischievously breaking into a building with companions, his father beat him severely and took him to a psychopathic hospital for diagnosis. It was there that the boy told of the man's characteristics and in turn this adoptive father told the boy for the first time directly that he was adopted, that his own father was alcoholic and that his own mother, long dead, had been no good. The children's agency took the boy from the hospital for placing.

Examined at the Guidance Center when thirteen years old Albert proved to have normal physical development, with no signs of somatic disorder; however, there were indications of some sexual precocity. At the hospital previously it had been noted that there were suggestions of probable pituitary hyper-functioning. Psychological testing again showed average general intelligence—I.Q. 96. Extremely variable mental attitudes were evidenced and the results on scholastic tests were very irregular. Albert had reached only the fifth grade.

Albert had run away from home many times during the previous years, sometimes staying away three or four days or even longer. He took small sums of money to aid him on his travels, but for the most part he found friendly truck-drivers with whom he could ride and who furnished him with food. He often slept out of doors. After these excursions he returned home, seeming very penitent and affectionate. By people outside of the family he was spoken of as being very pleasing in his manners, as having an outstanding interest in music, but as being always changeable and showing incapacity for sustained attention in any direction. Already at twelve years he was demonstrative toward girls and they in turn were attracted to him.

### PSYCHOANALYTIC MATERIAL

Albert's history is unquestionably the saddest of all which have been studied by us. Yet his criminal acts are not so much direct expressions of unconscious impulses; they are rather the secondary results of real need, of hunger and cold, of situations in which he became involved by the combination of external and internal factors. He has to serve a sentence of seven years, and this fact has proved a serious handicap in securing his co-operation for uncovering deep unconscious material. Thinking about his problem, he always ran against the stone wall of the unchangeable hard fact: seven more years in prison and after that being on the street without help, relatives, or friends, with a criminal record and with little chance to find employment and build up a constructive life.

Analytic material, which was obtained during one month, chiefly consisted in Albert's telling the analyst his extremely sad life-story, at first in the form of a dry, chronological report and gradually allowing to come to the surface the repressed emotions of fear, humiliation, and mainly the deeply buried craving for a mother whom he never knew and for whom he never found a real substitute. At the beginning he was extremely mistrustful and thought that the analyst wanted to perform a dangerous painful brain operation, but soon this mistrust disappeared and Albert dared to give more insight into his intimate emotions. This confessional attitude came to an end, however, as soon as the unearthed conflicts became stronger than he could stand in his present circumstances in the prison, where he will spend seven more years without the least hope that he will have any advantage from the painful analytic procedure which forces him to face his hopeless cravings.

From his story we learn that he was one year old when his mother died. He was the last of eleven brothers and sisters, whom he never saw again and whose whereabouts he does not know, except that the oldest brother lives in California. He was adopted by a veterinarian, Mr. P., who had a daughter. The early period of his life which he spent with this family consisted of a series of extremely traumatic events. He says he was brutally mistreated by the stepfather, who approached him sexually several times. Albert now makes the accusation that Mr. P. had no other interest in him than to use him sexually and suspects that that was the only reason that he took him and brought him up. According to Albert, he was taken out of this family after he was cruelly beaten because of his resistance to the stepfather's homosexual approaches. He was then twelve years old. He was sent for examination

to a psychopathic hospital, where his stepfather visited him
and told him for the first time that he was not his real father.
Albert asserts that he always felt somehow that Mrs. P. was
not his real mother. From this time on, after he learned about
his own family, he was persecuted by the desire to find the
members of his family.

After leaving the house of his adoptive parents, he went,
often of his own accord, from one foster-home to another;
between twelve and seventeen years he changed his home at
least fifteen or twenty times. He could not stay anywhere. An
uncontrollable wanderlust compelled him always to leave the
places whether he was treated well or badly. After a few
changes he came to the K. family. Here he found finally real
love and interest. He never mentions this family but in the
tones of greatest warmth, love, and deep attachment. It would
have seemed that in this family he could at last have found a
real home, but it proved otherwise. It is only natural that the
adolescent boy, with his accumulated longing since early
childhood for a loving motherly person, would develop a
violent attachment to Mrs. K., and this soon assumed a definitely sexual character. Mrs. K. responded in like fashion and
an extremely conflictive relation developed between the two.
They embraced and kissed each other, and when he went to
bed, Mrs. K. regularly came to kiss him goodnight. They
never went farther than this, but on one occasion he lay beside
her on her bed. Mrs. K. was extremely jealous of his interest
in girls and tried with all her means to keep him from such
contacts. Albert was entirely conscious that he loved Mrs. K.
as a woman and as a mother at the same time and was torn
by inner remorse. During this period he had sexual relations
with two different girls, yet could not emancipate himself
from Mrs. K. Time and again he ran away to end this unbearable emotional conflict, returned, and ran away again.

When he left the home of the K.'s, he tramped around awhile and was driven back by hunger and cold, but also by the deep craving for Mrs. K. He found a mother, but too late, at the time when he had become a man. This conflicting combination of the infantile never-satisfied need for a mother and the adolescent wish for a woman, he was unable to solve.

It is not difficult to visualize from his colorful dramatic reports the violent inner fight which the boy had to go through during the years which he spent with the K. family, with other families for short periods, or on the road. All of his criminal acts he committed during his periods of tramping his way from town to town after he left the home of the K. family. But apart from this flight motive to escape from the unbearable conflict in relation to Mrs. K., perhaps an even more important emotional factor is responsible for his compulsive wanderlust. This second factor is entirely repressed; it is the deeply buried but never abandoned hope to find a real substitute for his mother. During one of the interviews he expressed his mystical belief that after death one finds persons that one loved and lost in life. In his wanderings he is searching for his mother, whose phantasied picture he sometimes vividly hallucinated in the jail. This phantastic search for the mother found rational expression in his consciousness as the wish to find the members of his family. Twice he attempted to get to California to find his oldest brother, the only one whose whereabouts he knew.

These two factors—his conflictive love for Mrs. K. and a secret unconscious hope to find a mother—are responsible for his restless desire for change, which does not allow him to stay in one place and keep his jobs. After a short futile attempt to remain in one place he usually suddenly and impulsively leaves with the pretense of some seemingly rational reason and finds himself on the road without food, money, and shelter and it is because of this situation that he breaks into a house.

On one occasion, for example, he left the K. home because he did not want to continue in school, where he got low marks. Everyone, even the head master, assured him that he had made very good progress. Nevertheless he was deaf to all arguments and suddenly left. This happened in the early summer. He found a job on a farm, but left it soon and hitch-hiked to a Southern state. It took him three weeks to return to the K. family, who welcomed him back. In the course of a year he left and returned three times. One time when he had just returned from his wanderings to the home town of the K.'s, instead of going back to them, he broke into an empty cottage. He said he did not want to appear at home in the condition in which he was. He wanted warmth and food. In the cottage he found frozen beans and a can of sardines. After he ate, instead of going home, he went to a neighboring town where he knew another family. He wandered six miles in deep snow, and when he arrived his feet were frozen. As a result he had to stay in bed for three weeks. After his feet got better, he found a job as a manual laborer. He accepted the job in order to pay this family for the board and care they gave him. After he earned enough, he paid for his board and went on to another state. Then he experienced the typical fate of the American tramp, spending three nights in different "flop houses," because one cannot stay longer without paying. Finally he was committed to a correctional school, from which he ran away to the K. family, who again took him back on the condition that he get a job and pay for his board. He found work in a factory and for three or four days everything went well. Then he quit the job, but did not confess it at home. At the end of the week, when he should have paid for his board, he stole the money from the K.'s (in order to pay it to them), but instead he spent it. After this episode he was not taken back by the K. family.

His periodic day-dreams of finding his own home have a significance similar to that of his wanderings. He visualizes different houses, working out in phantasy all the details. He rejects one picture for another and tries to create the picture of a house which pleases him the most. These phantasies correspond to his attempts to visualize the unknown mother's face, to find a face which is most similar to his phantasy of his mother.

The longing for his own home, which in the unconscious is linked up with his wish for a mother, is behind his wish to become an architect. Even in jail he takes a correspondence course in architecture. He mails the blueprint lessons and receives them back corrected.

Apart from wandering and architecture, music is his other passion. Nevertheless, owing to some external but probably also internal motives, he always used to interrupt his studies and find excuses for not continuing the music lessons. The short analysis was unable to reveal the emotional factors responsible for this self-thwarting tendency which checked his musical career. In phantasy he often reverts to music and in his future plans, study of music is one of his permanent desires, alternating with plans to become an architect. He loves sentimental love-songs and on one occasion he sang to the analyst with much feeling the extremely touching song, "The Light in My Mother's Eyes."

The emotional linkage between *mother, music,* and *home* becomes impressively manifest during the analytic interviews, music and the craving for a home substituting in consciousness for the repressed longing for his mother. He does not dare to face this consciously, because he is not able to admit the futility of it all, since it would necessitate a final renunciation.

The emotional factors responsible for his continual changing of homes and jobs became clear in the perspective of the analytic material. His whole life is centered on the search for a mother whom he never can find, and the reality always proves unsatisfactory in comparison with the phantasy and secret hopes, which he never dares to confess to himself consciously. In Mrs. K.'s home finally he comes nearest to the illusion of realization, but it is too late; not the little boy, but an adolescent finds the mother. He finds her and at the same time experiences the violent attacks of awakened adolescent sexuality, thus becoming involved in an insoluble conflict.

The criminal career of this boy is obviously not the direct expression of unconscious impulses which would lead immediately to criminal acts, such as aggressiveness, in order to overcompensate a deep sense of inferiority, which motive we have found to predominate in the cases of Vorland and Perez. The flight from an unbearable love situation and the unconscious search for a mother are the deep emotional impulses which do not allow him to settle down and through the inexorable logic of events finally drive him out to the road. The criminal deeds are largely acts of self-preservation and the ultimate consequences of the external situation to which he is driven by these unconscious forces. Thus we arrive at the paradoxical fact that this boy's criminality is the result of impulses which are considered highly respectable and desirable—the flight from the incestuous love for his foster-mother and the never-satisfied longing of the little boy for his mother.

There is only one aggressive criminal act in his case history which might suggest the presence of irrational unconscious factors other than self-preservation. Once he succeeded, after much trouble, in arriving in California in search of his brother, but could not locate him. After this futile expedition he returned in an obviously very desperate state of mind to the home town of the K.'s. Instead of going to the K.'s he broke into a house in which a lonely woman lived. He tied and gagged her, took her money, and ran away. It seems that at the last moment he did not dare to expose himself again to the unbearable situation with Mrs. K., and under the pressure of desperation and thwarting his longing turned into an aggressive spiteful desire to take by force something which was denied to him.

The analytical insight into the deep sources of his failure in life came not only as an intellectual but as an emotional revelation to Albert during this short analytic exploration. His emotional reaction to the analyst's interpretation was the most dramatic proof of its correctness. With elemental force all the deeply hidden sentimental longings for his mother broke through, and Albert bitterly wept through the night after the session in which he understood the motive of his wanderlust and his seemingly contradictory insatiable longing for his own home. A deep depression overcame him, which lasted for several days.

It was a touching experience to observe how this unhappy creature tried to work himself out of his desperation by phantastic plans for the future when he would leave the prison; in his phantasies he went into detailed calculation of the cost of building a house, the money for which he will get by constructing a new type of racing car. He is a speedy driver and has no fear. He thinks he has good chances to win races. In listening to his phantasies the analyst could not help tacitly admitting to himself that this boy unquestionably possessed one important emotional requisite for becoming a record-breaker in automobile races—he had not much to lose in risking his life.

# CHAPTER NINE

## *Unsuccessful Attempts*

THIS group includes four cases in which we failed to win co-operation for analytic study or therapy. Three of these were adolescents; the fourth, a pronounced schizoid personality, possibly a case of incipient schizophrenia, was twenty when analysis was attempted. With this latter boy, Karl Van Horn, the analyst did not succeed in establishing any contact whatsoever in two sessions. Karl had a long criminal career, which started rather suddenly at twelve years of age when he began associating with a corner gang of boys and commenced stealing. At that time attempted psychotherapy had to be given up because of the boy's sulky attitude and lack of co-operation. Every effort was made to give him new interests and new companions, but the boy would not respond. There were intermittent spurts of good behavior during the next few years, always followed by relapses. After committing several burglaries with companions, he was sent to a correctional school. From there he soon ran away, stole an automobile, and was sent to the reformatory. In this institution he maintained that he liked cell life better than the correctional school. He was in the reformatory when it was proposed to him that he try to aid himself through psychoanalysis. He appeared to welcome the chance. During the first interview he spoke hardly at all; in the second he absolutely refused to proceed, saying that he simply could not talk. Since there was suggestion of incipient schizophrenia, further attempts at continuing the analysis were abandoned.

Stanley Sadowski was sixteen years old when his analysis was attempted. His case history shows a long list of delinquencies and frequent appearances in court for minor burglaries, other stealing, and running away from home. At fifteen he made his way through the South to the Pacific coast, once at least, while away, serving a short sentence for stealing. Very little analytic material was gained in three interviews with Stanley. He seemingly took hold of the idea of analysis very well, but for some reason, perhaps because his coming to the office would be noted by his fellows, he came no more.

Andrew Roberts was eleven years old when first seen at the Guidance Center, and fifteen years old when analysis was attempted. Andrew has had an extraordinary career of delinquency since he was six or seven years old. It began with lying and petty pilfering; soon he was stealing from neighbors and engaging in other dishonesties, such as defrauding boys when he sold newspapers for them. Later he grew shrewder in his dishonesty, always showing a great deal of enterprise in this as well as in other ways, and began rather clever swindling operations.

The analytic exploration of this fifteen-year-old boy was discontinued with the fourth interview. Andrew's attitude toward his own problems and his future gave no promise of co-operation. There was no urge to reform and he displayed an extremely infantile personality, entirely dominated by the pleasure principle. The slight interest which he displayed in the first four sessions was only the expression of childish curiosity; it was fun for him to demonstrate to the analyst his smartness, sophistication, intelligence, and cynicism. No signs of a deeper inner conflict could be discovered. Andrew maintained that his only problem was obtaining money. He wanted to have a good time and could not resist temptation. No inhibiting forces, except the fear of detection, were present in him. He phantasies the free life of a tramp, roaming in the woods, securing food by shooting, living the life of a primitive, but he does nothing of the sort. In the city he enjoys mainly shows and movies.

There was only one trend which showed possibilities of serving as a basis of later sublimation—namely, a seemingly genuine interest in geology. He has some knowledge of stones and crystals and some scattered information about paleontology.

The association material, which was entirely of a superficial nature, allowed one only to surmise the deeper emotional reactions toward his stepfather and toward his mother, against whom he made accusations of drinking and immorality.

It is not impossible, however, that with a long preparatory period, following the principles of child-analysis, one could win his co-operation for further analytic work, but this preparatory period alone probably would require a considerable length of time, quite disproportionate to that which was available for our research program.

John Mansart, fifteen years of age when first seen at the Guidance Center, was eighteen years old when analysis was attempted.

At marriage his parents were each about twenty-five years old and John was born within a year. His mother had already discovered that her husband was a drinking man and dishonest. When John was about a year old, the mother left her husband and with her child lived with relatives in Boston, going to work to support herself and the boy. Her husband's family sympathized with her; he went elsewhere to live. Some years later he obtained a divorce and remarried. He had practically nothing to do with his son until the latter was twelve, when he took him from the boarding-home where his mother was then maintaining him. She always felt her responsibilities deeply, but on account of her work was unable to be much with the boy. Twice she placed him in church institutional schools.

The first trouble with John came when he was six years old; several times he stayed out late at night with companions. Then at eight years he associated with a group of boys who engaged in petty stealing. After some months of this he was placed in a church school. At fourteen, when John was living with his father and the second wife, he was caught shoplifting and taken to court. He had run away from his father's home several times to go to his mother, but was dishonest while with her. After being placed on probation he stole from employers. Then he was placed successively in two very good foster-homes, where more accurate knowledge was gained of his behavior tendencies. At first he was known only to lie and be deceitful and then came suspicions of petty stealing, which were finally proved. The boy was doing so extremely well in school, however, and had made such a good name for himself in the community, that a second good foster-home was readily found for him. There he seemed to improve even more, but after a year or so, people in the town found indications that he was stealing from stores. It was then discovered that he had hidden away a most extraordinary assortment of small articles obtained by shoplifting. He had accumulated scores of things which, for the most part, seemed of no use to him; they were simply articles that he could readily steal. A couple of dozen unread books, for example, on all sorts of subjects were found. Also he had stolen and consumed large quantities of candy. Besides this he had misappropriated an automobile, hiding it in the woods until detected. Naturally, he had to be removed from the community. While being tried in another place, and continuing with his education, he stole an automobile and started off with it, but was arrested and placed on probation in an adult court. This was just after he refused to continue with his analysis.

In about a dozen earlier interviews with a psychiatrist and many conversations with a skilled visitor from the placing agency, John always appeared superficially frank. The main burden of his story was that he had begun stealing with other boys and experienced pleasurable returns from it; stealing had become a habit. His thoughts frequently turned to stealing even when he did not engage in it. When confronted by the fact that he stole so many apparently useless things, he still answered that it was the result of his habit. His lying and deceiving were all in self-defense. He could not see that his unsatisfactory family life had any connection with his stealing, nor did he think that sex stress, which he experienced much, had any relationship to it. He said that at times he felt encouraged and then again that he was fighting a losing battle, but he never failed to assert confidence in his own ability to stop stealing. He sees the contradiction in his character and has prayed a great deal about this. He is very ambitious for success. Thus John could never bring himself to go deeply into his difficulties; he always asserted his desire for independence and insisted that he could manage his own troubles.

Unquestionably the most interesting aspect of this case is that John engaged in the most excessive irrational stealing when he was otherwise doing very well. Especially in the second foster-home his career seemed highly promising. He was well regarded by his teachers, he showed active powers of leadership in church and school organizations; he was apparently deeply interested in religion. Associates of the same age looked up to him, he had close companionship with some very fine older people, and apparently he loved his foster-home. Letters written later to the foster-mother were not only full of contrition, but expressed much gratitude and affection for the splendid way in which he had been treated by her and her husband. His desire for superiority and recognition was perhaps over-accented, but he easily won his way to this in athletics through his great strength. Observers said that he "loved the limelight." That he felt some inferiority is clear because he invented a wonderful sister about whom he told phantastic tales of histrionic achievement. He endeared himself to people by his courtesy and unusual thoughtfulness during this period of foster-home placement. Naturally girls were very much taken by him and he had normal heterosexual relationships. For several months one exceedingly fine girl saw much of him and apparently there was a strong attachment between them, and it was for the sake of showing off to this girl that he took an automobile and successfully hid it for some time.

John Mansart was accepted for a preliminary analytic investigation, after which it was to be decided whether he should continue. He was eighteen years old, but his mental attitudes corresponded more to those of early adolescence. During a trial period of three weeks the analyst was unable to obtain any real co-operation on his part. Even though his interest was from time to time awakened, he never had any continuing urge to get insight into the nature of his difficulties and showed great disinclination to go on with the analysis. Thus the analytical material which was obtained is extremely incoherent and does not even suffice for reconstructing the most predominant dynamic relationships. He offered the typical picture of the emotional conflicts of adolescence, with the most outstanding motive of an extreme inner uncertainty about himself, the typical adolescent urge for prestige denying the undercurrent dependency, which is a natural consequence of uncertainty and lack of self-confidence. In the center of the psychological picture stood his very strong longing to be loved, praised, and reassured by authorities.

Even during this short period he was able to discover the definite relationship between his compulsive urge for stealing and his deep inner discontent connected with the divorce of his parents, the lack of a permanent home and parental care. He was so extremely dependent on external appraisal and reassurance that whenever he was unjustly accused, he stole with the motivation: "Why shouldn't I steal, if they believe it anyhow? Why should I control myself if I do not get any praise for it?" Since he was six years old, there were only two years during which he did not steal; that was when he lived on a farm where the foster-parent praised him and showed him extreme confidence, and apparently much affection. He claims that in order to live up to their confidence he did not steal. But apart from this period he felt that he never received much affection or love, that he was always suspected and therefore had no reason to stop his habit of stealing. In his own home he had been considered "a piece of furniture."

The analytic material is in every respect incomplete and does not allow the reconstruction of the dynamic relations and the origin of his stealing tendencies. This much became apparent: his strongest motive in stealing was the urge to compensate for the love, attention, and parental care which he missed in his childhood, together with a certain revenge element for this emotional deprivation. The other factors which must have been involved could not be clarified during this short investigatory period.

Mansart, Sadowski, and Roberts exemplify the difficulties of analysis of the adolescent. This age seems to be ill-suited for analytical investigation and therapy. The young adolescent is not inclined to find a solution for his difficulties through the inner changes which the painstaking task of psychoanalysis requires. The acute current problems of this period drive youth to repeated—and in the pathological cases often futile—trials to work out the problems of life in reality situations, in action. This attitude was especially clear in the case of John Mansart, who concluded, after the very first insight that he received through analysis, that now he knew enough about himself and that he would be able by himself to solve his problems. This optimism of adolescents, which is so valuable for the successful outgrowing of their difficulties in all those fairly healthy cases in which adolescence means really only a temporary disturbance, is one of the great obstacles to the analysis of the severely neurotic.

These three attempts with adolescents in which we failed to obtain an emotional contact sufficiently strong to serve as a basis for analytic therapy or investigation should not be interpreted as indicating that they might not possibly have been approachable at all by the method if the technique of child-analysis had been utilized. The application of this latter method, however, lies outside the scope of our present study, since our primary aim was not to experiment with analytic technique but rather to gain deep psychologic insight in the greatest possible number of cases in the time at our disposal.

CHAPTER TEN

# The Interplay of Social and
# Psychological Factors

THE problem of delinquency and criminality cannot be solved
from either the psychological or the sociological point of view
alone. Criminal acts are not always committed by certain
individuals who can be defined and characterized psychologically or in terms of personality as specifically inclined to crime,
but neither are criminal acts restricted to certain social groups
which can be characterized and defined sociologically. Of
course in the last analysis every criminal act must be explained
as a psychological process ending in a certain type of motor
activity, but both personality and sociological factors are active
at the same time; either of them may be predominant in one
case, negligible in another. A great range of quite different
types of personalities under certain given social situations drift
toward a criminal career. On the other hand, there are certain
personalities for whom criminal activity is so deep an emotional need that they indulge in it under either good or bad
external circumstances.

We felt certain that from our analytic studies we would be
able to understand those real motives which actually determined the criminal behavior of a certain few individuals, and
we have given in detail, step by step, the course of develop-
ments which resulted in a criminal career. Only such a precise
approach to the problem of criminality by the investigation of
individual cases is able to rid this complicated field of its pres-

ent confusion of concepts. Social research, no matter how care-fully and critically carried out, especially serves to contribute to this confusion if those actual causal chains are not known which determine the development of a criminal career. Thus, for example, elaborate statistical investigations, such as Shaw's [1] in Chicago, have shown that vastly greater propor-tions of delinquents come from certain areas of a city than from others. These criminal centers often supply twenty times as many criminals as other districts. The study of these crim-inal centers shows that they are characterized by lower social standards and are usually the places called slums, where the new immigrants settle. This geographical distribution of crime corresponds simply to social stratification and is due to the fact that individuals belonging to certain social strata usually live together—for example, the lowest social groups are in the neglected and consequently the cheaper parts of the city. This statistical result means nothing more than the numerical cor-roboration of a fact which is well known to every policeman and inhabitant in the city and does not need further explana-tion. Criminality means violating the social order which is defined by the law and, therefore, it is evident that those portions of the population will have the greatest inclination to break these rules which have the least interest in upholding them—that is, either the discontented elements or those who for various reasons have not yet accepted the standards of the community and hence consider its rules as a pressure.

Such a statement contributes literally nothing to a deeper knowledge of the sources of criminality and adds nothing to what we already know by common sense. Recently different sociologists show more interest in the psychological milieu of criminal areas, and recognize that this can only be studied by obtaining an intimate insight into individual criminal person-

[1] C. R. Shaw: *Delinquency Areas.* University of Chicago Press.

alities. An example of such an attempt is Saul D. Alinsky's "A Sociological Technique in Clinical Criminology" (The American Prison Association 1934 Report) in which he tries to obtain such an intimate insight into the psychological and ideological background of criminal areas by establishing rapport with individual criminals. The extremely short case histories quoted by him however do not illustrate the effectiveness of his method, and we must wait for further publications of detailed case histories gained by this "sociological technique".

Science begins and is needed where common sense fails. It is obvious that even in the worst slums a part of the population is not criminal. The influence of environment on the individual takes place in the form of a certain selection. Influences which induce individuals to break the law may be greater in certain social strata than in others, but work always according to an unknown selective principle which is inherent in the character trends of the individual exposed to these influences. It is also evident that the more powerful the social factor, the greater the number of individuals who will yield to it, but, on the other hand, if the individual through his character tendencies is especially predisposed to crime, he may become criminal even under the most favorable social circumstances.

A complete analysis of the etiology of crime necessarily must consist in the simultaneous study of both social and psychological factors. The most obscure problem, however—that of the nature of the selective principle according to which the environmental influences work—can be solved only by psychological investigation. The first question is: What is the origin of those character trends which make an individual receptive to the criminal influences of the environment? Can we speak of individuals peculiarly predisposed to criminality—in general of a "criminal personality"?

The knowledge of the human personality which the psychoanalytic method has given enables us to answer certain fundamental aspects of these questions with considerable reliability. It has shown that those behavior tendencies which make people suitable to live in community life are acquired during the individual's early developmental periods, and that the inherited instinctual drives do not possess originally any qualities which would guarantee social behavior. Psychoanalysis has shown that social life is based on certain acquired restrictions of erotic and destructive tendencies and that these restrictions are reinforced through what Freud called the reality principle. Whereas the small child's mental processes are guided by the pleasure principle—that is to say, by the tendency to gratify immediately every need and to avoid pain—the adult learns to endure temporary dissatisfactions and even pain and to postpone certain gratifications in order to secure important satisfactions. This more far-seeing attitude of controlling intelligently the instinctual demands in accordance with the requirements of the given external situation is the reality principle. It is evidently nothing else than an improved pleasure principle, because in the end it is able to improve the final balance between pain and pleasure in securing a greater amount of pleasure and avoiding more pain. For the self-imposed restrictions and renunciations, the individual is compensated by the gains which he obtains as a result of these sacrifices. These gains may be of a positive or negative nature, such as obtaining various types of rewards from the environment or avoidance of such painful experiences as punishment and losing the respect and love of others.

Social behavior represents a complicated balance between gratifications and renunciations. It is easy to understand that the greater the sacrifices and restrictions an individual has to bear, the more unstable will be this equilibrium and, conversely, an individual who has the possibility of gratifying a greater amount of his subjective needs, no matter what the nature of these needs may be, will be more willing to accept certain restrictions necessitated by collective life.[1] The specific capacity of the ego for enduring restrictions and deprivations is, however, dependent upon many factors and is too complicated a phenomenon to be described exhaustively by this simple formulation. Apart from the amount of gratifications which compensate for restrictions, the ability to sublimate and modify unsocial tendencies plays an important rôle.

Nevertheless, discontent always is prone to induce the individual to give up those restrictions which he accepted only in order to secure certain gratifications. To renounce personal freedom if satisfactions are not forthcoming is evidently more difficult than to renounce it in order to get something in exchange. Therefore, the original unadjusted nature of man is more apt to break through and to overthrow social restrictions in the discontented strata of the population.

This psychological insight alone is sufficient to prove that a real cure of society's disease called crime cannot be solved without considering the social bases. The more that subjective needs are permitted gratification by social institutions and the greater the number participating in these advantages, the more readily individuals will accept the social order.

On the other hand, our psychoanalytic insight into individual cases has shown that it would be entirely false to assume that only economic factors are responsible for the discontent which is apt to disturb the equilibrium between gratifications and social restrictions, achieved with such difficulty.

Emotional factors of all kinds have been found active in

[1] These considerations follow ideas which have been set forth by Alexander and Staub: *The Criminal, the Judge and the Public* (New York: Macmillan; 1931).

creating inner tensions which the individual attempts to relieve by criminal acts. In such cases the rational, mostly economic purpose runs parallel with the irrational emotional and mainly unconscious motives. Thus we found that stealing, apart from its rational aim, often expresses revenge or offers a symbolic rather than a real compensation for deprivations that may be emotional and not necessarily material. Acts of violence or robberies in which risks are taken often serve the emotional purpose of reinstating the impaired inner prestige, inasmuch as they give the perpetrator the feeling of bravery and self-reliance. Such acts are demonstrations of toughness and aggressiveness that hide the inner weakness and insecurity which the perpetrator does not want to admit even to himself. Emotional factors of this kind together with rational purposes of gain often lead to criminal behavior in cases in which one of these factors alone would not suffice to bring about criminal activity; combined, however, they represent a powerful driving force to criminality. This explains why the majority of criminals belong not only to the economically disfavored class, but at the same time also to the group of emotionally unsatisfied individuals.

These few general observations are sufficient to demonstrate that, apart from the social situation, the personality problems of the criminal must be considered in order to understand his behavior. That the psychology of the adolescent or adult criminal may be comprehended, naturally the whole personality-development from early childhood on must be reconstructed. In all of the cases we have investigated, the criminality of the adult was the direct continuation of the delinquency of the child, which fact alone places the delinquent child immediately in the center of the problem of criminality. Moreover, if there is such a thing as a personality with criminal inclinations, it must necessarily develop in childhood, when all the important character trends are formed. We may call personalities with criminal inclinations all those individuals who have acquired during their development such character trends as make them more receptive to the unfavorable influences of the social environment. These character trends are responsible for the selective nature of the environmental influences to which we have already referred. As we have stated before, the universal basis of criminal inclinations is the instability in the psychological balance between social restrictions and gratifications. It is evident that the distribution of satisfactions and deprivations in the early periods of life is decisive in its influence on the stability of this balance. The crucial problem, however, which is not solved by this general statement, but requires patient investigation of many individual cases, is the knowledge of those specific emotional factors and experiences which disturb this balance. It was to be expected that early deprivations undoubtedly would diminish the resistance of the ego against the tension of repressed tendencies, but long indulgence in certain gratifications, which later in the course of the development necessarily have to be abandoned, may also have a similar effect. In this respect it is most interesting to compare the case of Richard Vorland with the case of Ferdinand Perez. In the former case we saw serious emotional deprivations from the eighth year on, whereas in Perez's case there was a continuous extreme spoiling by the mother and older sisters, lasting all through childhood.

As different psychoanalysts have found before, so our observations show that there are certain definable character trends and psychological factors which make the individual more susceptible to influences of the environment in the direction of criminality. These character trends develop chiefly under the influence of the very first environment of the child—namely, the family, especially of course, the child-parent relationship. Particularly in American literature on crime there is much said about the influence of the social environment upon character-formation. "Social environment," however, is too vague a term to be useful for a more precise description of the post-natal influences which determine the character-development of an individual.

In the first place, it is necessary to differentiate the closer family environment (child-parent and sibling relationships) from the social environment in the broader sense, which begins to exert its influence in a later period of the individual's development—namely, after the child comes in closer contact with others than members of his family. But even when these social contacts develop, the family, no matter whether the child's own or a foster-family, retains, for a long time, a predominating rôle in the formation of character. This distinction between family and social milieu in the broader sense is therefore important because when the social environment is mentioned ordinarily, only this broader milieu is meant. Naturally the parents and the whole family also represent a definite sociological factor. On the other hand, the clinical study of individual cases does not leave any doubt about the fact that the emotional relationships between members of the family are incomparably stronger determinants of character-formation of the child than the position of the family in a certain social group. The neurosis of one of the parents or disturbance of the emotional attitudes between father and mother is, for example, of pre-eminent importance. The influence of such matters on the child's personality-development is vastly greater than the fact that the father belongs to the intellectual class or is a manual worker, is native-born or has recently immigrated.

Just these deeper environmental factors affecting character-development, however, are necessarily neglected in most statistical studies, where only the superficial but more easily obtainable data regarding sociological and racial identifications are considered.

A schematic view of the different etiological factors active in personality-development may serve to clarify the involved causal relations in this field.

### DETERMINING FACTORS IN PERSONALITY-FORMATION

1. Congenital equipment (hereditary and intrauterine influences).          Constitution.
2. Early acquired reactive tendencies.[1]
3. Family influences.               Post-natal
4. Influence of the social environment in a broader  development.
    sense.
5. General ideological trends in a given civilization.

1. We have to consider the congenital equipment and may call it constitution. We know little about it, but we have to assume its presence and importance on the basis of empirical observations which do not allow the assumption that all human beings are born alike. All later post-natal factors act upon this constitutional substratum, which probably determines certain general characteristics of the instinctual life.

2. The early influences of the extra-uterine existence can be differentiated from the later ones through their more impersonal nature. They consist mainly in the handling of the child's early biological functions in the field of nutrition and excretion. The influence of these processes is also considerably obscure and what we know about it is based more on reconstructions than direct observational establishment of cause and

---

[1] This corresponds to Freud's "disposition." We prefer not to translate it from the German as equivalent to the English word "disposition," which has an ambiguous significance.

effect. But certainly there are reactive tendencies which are acquired very early and which are to be contrasted with "constitution."

3. Then come the personal influences of the members of the family. These are the best-studied and probably are the most important factors in personality-development. Emotional experiences in relation to the parents and siblings are unquestionably decisive for later social behavior, since the family is a kind of society, and adjustment to this first society forms the conditioning pattern of later behavior.

4. With the more or less defined character trends which develop under the influence of these three categories of factors —constitutional, early acquired reactive tendencies, and family influences—the child enters the social environment in the broader sense. The selective principle according to which the later environmental influences act consists in the end-result of all the three above-mentioned previously determining factors. Which individual will be influenced toward delinquency in a given environment is dependent upon those character trends which are part of the personality equipment at any given time. Bad examples, deprivations, and discontent of every kind induce to antisocial behavior only a certain percentage of individuals who live in a similar environment—namely, those whose acquired and constitutional character trends are susceptible to these influences.

5. We feel that it is justified to distinguish, apart from the influences of the closer social environment (for example, the neighborhood), factors of an even more general nature, such as are represented by the leading ideological trends in a given civilization. If we compare the criminal personalities which we have investigated in America with Alexander's and Staub's studies made in Germany, we cannot but be impressed by certain outstanding differences. The most impressive of these is

the heroic exhibitionistic evaluation of criminal deeds in America; this much more than in Europe plays an important part in formation of motives for breaking the law. In spite of official condemnation, not only instinctively but even consciously, the public views criminality with a sort of adolescent hero-worship. At the same time machine civilization with its mechanizing and levelling tendencies strangulates individuality and compels the individual to become a part of the collective unit. Criminality remains one of those few outlets left through which the individual can express his spite against this pressure and emphasize his masculine sovereignty. It is a pathological attempt to regain a lost freedom. One of the most constant factors which lead to criminal behavior, especially pronounced in the cases of Vorland, Perez, and Tome, is the fact that criminal behavior alone serves to save the face of these fundamentally inhibited boys. The tendency to display one's masculinity by showing disrespect for the law is a reaction to the restrictions of the instinctual life which lead to a deep sense of inferiority. This serves as a permanent stimulus to the wish to compensate for inner weakness by toughness and aggressiveness.

This excessive craving for prestige to be achieved by the display of masculinity, independence, activity, and aggressiveness has deep sources in the ideological atmosphere of American civilization. The ideological basis of American democracy, an individualistic philosophy of life, is personified in the ideal of the self-made man, who is independent of external help, who is successful in the free competition of equal chances. These ideals of the pioneer period appear in almost tragic contradiction to the superhuman equalizing and anti-individualistic forces of present machine civilization. Under the instigation of this still prevalent individualistic philosophy the individual is driven to fight the increasingly difficult battle of individual success and expression of individuality. This is a hopeless battle because the example of the pioneer ancestors cannot be approached any longer under the changed condition of an overorganized industrial civilization. This conflict between the traditional individualistic philosophy of success and the real possibilities of present life explains the frequency and the intensity of the prestige motive as the unconscious background of criminal careers in America.

The preponderance of this psychological mechanism (inner prestige motive) in the American scene justifies its further discussion. Criminal activity as an over-compensatory reaction to an internally felt weakness is only one example of a general dynamic phenomenon of mental life—namely, that overt behavior frequently is a reaction to a diametrically opposed unconscious attitude and serves for its denial. Thus it was an interesting but not at all unexpected finding that the urge for reckless stealing or robbery is frequent in individuals who have a strong but repressed need for dependence, the infantile wish to be supported by others. Taking by force in such cases is a denial of a wish to be given things. It satisfies the wish for possession without the humiliation which is caused by the helpless longing for receiving everything from others. These criminals have no confidence that they can earn their living and support themselves, but neither can they accept the humiliating feeling of dependence on others. Stealing remains the only recourse. Rather than receive, they take by force what they need and what they wish to possess. They expose themselves to danger and this gives them a false sense of power and accomplishment.

Some of our cases gave us a deep insight into the sources of this dependent receptive attitude that causes both the lack of confidence in oneself and also a disinclination for the continuous and systematic efforts that are necessary in a self-supporting scheme of life. There is no question but that this receptive trend is an infantile phenomenon. It corresponds to the emotional attitude of the young child who is entirely dependent on his parents. Some individuals never are able to outgrow this dependent emotional attitude (fixation); others return to it at the first failure in life (regression).

There are three factors that we found active in the causation of a fixation or regression to this infantile dependence and receptiveness: (1) early intimidations of the instinctive life (fear and sense of guilt); (2) spoiling; (3) early deprivations.

1. Early conflicts connected with the first manifestations of the active masculine impulse are apt to drive the child back to the dependent receptive attitude. Early rivalry with the brothers and especially the Œpidus conflict between son and father cause guilt reactions and fears which become linked up with active and aggressive manifestations. If the first expressions of masculinity, activity, and competition have been blocked and associated with fear and guilt, the whole later development in the direction of activity and independence becomes inhibited, and in turn the opposite tendency to return to the pre-Œdipal infantile passive dependence gains the upper hand. It is self-evident that in an adult or even in an adolescent boy such a strong infantile craving for dependence must necessarily lead to a severe conflict that destroys self-confidence and self-esteem (narcissistic trauma). Criminality, especially stealing or robbery, is, then, an attempt to regain the lost self-esteem by a kind of pseudo-masculinity, but at the same time the criminality offers means of self-support and avoidance of the systematic effort involved in working. These emotional factors, fear and guilt, which are responsible for the early inhibition of the active masculine trends and for the consequent regression to infantile dependence, we call early intimidations. In the development of David Diedrich, Richard

Vorland, and Elmer Tome, they play a predominant rôle.

2. Whereas intimidations are apt to lead to regressions, a fixation to the infantile dependent attitude is most frequently caused by spoiling. It is only natural that the child pampered and preferred by the parents and older siblings will consider it his natural right to be loved and supported by everybody through all his life. Such a claim can seldom be successfully realized in later life, nor can it be accepted by the adult ego without an inner conflict. Long indulgence makes it difficult to abandon the dependent attitude, and yet the adult portion of the personality reacts with a sense of inferiority to these infantile claims. Thus in the ego a split is created between the wish for the comfortable dependent situation and the ambition for independence, the latter being reinforced by the attitude of the environment, which is no longer willing to allow the same privileges to the adolescent or adult as it had allowed to the child.

A clear example of this type of conflict we described in the case of Ferdinand Perez.

3. These two factors, the early intimidations of the instinctive life and spoiling, are both prone to produce an *internal conflict,* a split between two different attitudes in the personality—namely, infantile dependence and the claims of the adult ego. A third factor can be fairly distinctly differentiated: it is the early deprivations of childhood that may perpetuate an *external conflict* between the individual and his environment. We found that criminal behavior in some cases is a direct expression of a protest against certain deprivations, a reaction of spite against certain members of the family, the expression of jealousy, envy, hostile competition, all of which are strengthened by early sufferings or the lack of love and support on the part of the adults. Often delinquency originates from the stubborn wish to compensate for previous deprivations. In cases

where infantile claims to be loved and cared for never have been satisfied, the individual, even as an adult, may stubbornly hang on to these infantile claims. Conflict with the environment is unavoidable, and this explains why in these cases so often the spiteful attitude toward the environment is accentuated. Criminal activity in such cases often is an expression of this antagonism to the environment, rather than representing a method of attempt to solve an inner conflict, such as restoring inner prestige and denying inner weakness. But, we must add, intense hostilities in such cases frequently create strong guilt feelings, which in turn lead to an unconscious need for punishment.

All these psychological factors that we found active in our criminal cases are constantly present also in psychoneurotics. Of course, as has been already stated, we are conscious of the fact that such personality factors in many cases of criminality are of secondary importance—namely, in all cases in which the social situation is mainly responsible for the criminal behavior. On the other hand, our examples show that frequently we encounter cases in which the criminal behavior is largely determined by unconscious psychological factors similar to those found in the psychoneuroses. In all these cases we have to face a question of primary importance: What is responsible for the fact that the same emotional conflict which in certain cases finds expression in psychoneurotic symptoms, in other cases leads to criminal behavior?

The main difference which our investigation was able to establish between the developmental history of psychoneuroses and criminal careers is the greater emphasis in criminals on certain conscious and rational motives which are co-determinants of their behavior and which they utilize for covering up the underlying and usually more powerful unconscious emotional motives. As we see, many criminals steal not only out of need but also in order to avoid being helped, while at the same time they cannot endure to be helped on account of an over-strong but inwardly rejected dependence, or they steal in revenge or in order to compensate for earlier deprivations. They will, however, only be aware of and emphasize the conscious rational motive of need, which alone seems to explain their action. In most cases where actual deprivations due to social circumstances are present, these can serve easily for rationalization of their criminal activity, and the underlying motives, the emotional conflict arising from the family situation, can thus remain unconscious. The rational conscious motives run parallel with the repressed unconscious motives, but may entirely overshadow them. If the social situation gives justification for discontent and the expression of an antisocial attitude, the earlier emotional conflict in the family is more prone to be expressed as delinquent conduct. In other words, if the earlier emotional dissatisfaction in the family situation is combined with social discontent, antisocial behavior rather than neurotic symptom-formation is likely to result.

The chief difference between neurosis and criminal behavior is that in neurosis the emotional conflict results in symbolic gratifications of unsatisfied urges, whereas in criminal behavior it leads to overt misdeeds. Those needs which are frustrated by economic conditions belong usually to the sphere of self-preservation and, like hunger, cannot be satisfied as easily by the symbolic gratifications of phantasy as can the emotional tensions of love and hate. The emotional conflicts and deprivations of childhood, the resentments against parents and siblings, find a powerful ally in resentment against the social situation, and this combined emotional tension seeks a realistic expression in criminal acts and cannot be relieved by mere phantasy products that are exhibited in neurotic symptoms.

In summary, where actual motives of need coincide with

parallel emotional conflict situations, there is a greater likelihood of criminal behavior than of neurosis because rational needs can hardly be satisfied by the symbolic gratifications which the neurotic symptoms supply. Of course, this formula does not include all cases, because we often see the tendency to act out neurotic conflicts in reality in individuals who have no reason for social discontent; and, vice versa, we see the development of neurosis in many socially handicapped individuals who have ample opportunity and reason to transform their neurotic conflict into an external conflict with society.

Thus one cannot discard an earlier assumption of Alexander that certain unacquired bases of the instinctive life (constitution), apart from environmental influences, must be partly responsible for the fact that similar emotional conflicts may, depending on the make-up of the individual, result either in criminality or in neurosis.[1] The introverted nature of the neurotic, his readiness to content himself with gratifications in phantasy and to renounce real satisfaction, seems to be founded on some constitutional factor. And, on the other hand, certain individuals are characterized by a more robust expansive instinctual life which contents itself only with outgoing behavior.

In the case of Henry Elton we are inclined to attribute great importance to constitutional factors. His reaction to the birth of the younger brother is typical and explains the strong regression to infantile dependence and to a receptive, parasitic attitude; but such a reaction to the birth of a younger child in the family is extremely common. Neither the family situation nor the later environmental influences can explain why this regression led to such stubborn criminal behavior.

Thus, aside from the influence of psychological experiences which are painful, we cannot entirely disregard certain funda-

[1] Franz Alexander: "The Neurotic Character," *International Journal of Psycho-Analysis*, Vol. XI (1930).

mental constitutional characteristics. At the same time our studies compel us to appreciate also the significance of the external social situation. There is no sense in searching for deeper emotional motives for stealing when an individual is near starvation, because hunger alone sufficiently explains such deeds without assuming the presence of any such unconscious motives as early thwartings in the expectations of love or hatred against the rivals in the family. Undoubtedly, such unconscious forces of emotional discontent do enhance the dynamic power of rational motives which derive from the social situation and thus do increase the probability of antisocial behavior.

The interrelationships between unconscious emotional and conscious, rational, external (mostly economic) motives in the determination of criminality have been of primary importance for the formulation of our views.

The dynamic relations between neurosis and crime were, however, not less impressive. It could be observed during the analysis of Richard Vorland that after his criminal behavior had been blocked by the analysis and ceased to be an outlet for emotional conflicts, a depression developed in the place of the criminal behavior. Two others, David Diedrich and Sigrid Amenson, confessed during the analysis that the criminal activity relieved them from a kind of free-floating anxiety and restlessness which had a typically neurotic character. The real sufferings and deprivations in life make it possible to act out aggressive and destructive tendencies and at the same time relieve the need for punishment. The criminal behavior serves the same purpose as a neurotic symptom in gratifying repressed urges and at the same time it is also a source of suffering which satisfies the claims of the guilty conscience. This explains why some criminals will develop neurotic symptoms in place of their criminal activity if they reform externally before the underlying emotional conflict is solved.

In conclusion, we may say that an unfavorable social situation makes it easier for the individual to displace emotional conflicts which were created in family life with reactions against the social order and to relieve accumulated disappointments and hostilities of every kind in the form of antisocial behavior. Thus, the manifest conflicts with the social environment become the open battlefield of underlying, invisible unconscious conflicts belonging to the past experiences of life.

It would be erroneous to deny the reality and importance of the more tangible conscious conflicts deriving from the actual situation or to consider them always as mere excuses for relieving unconscious aggressions in the form of antisocial behavior. Naturally there are many cases in which there are no momentous external reasons for criminal behavior, and on the other hand there are many individuals who have real reason for revolt and yet accept social order. Early post-natal experiences, especially the emotional conflicts in family life, the social situation, and in addition certain constitutional characteristics are together responsible for these differences. This last factor, the constitution, we must consider as an unknown quantity as long as biology is not able to supply further information. In our present studies we have tried to analyze the relative importance of the psychological development and the social situation by selecting cases of different types—individuals with a reasonably favorable social background and those who had suffered from neglect.

# CHAPTER ELEVEN

## *Practical Conclusions*

IT IS only too evident that the present general social program for dealing with or preventing criminality is so poorly conceived that it is in very considerable measure an utter failure. The methods which have so far been developed evince a very real incapacity on the part of society for reforming offenders or even for checking careers of criminality when they are seen developing. No fact is any clearer than that the public is paying a terrible price for delinquency and crime. Only during periods of incarceration, itself expensive enough, is there freedom from the aggressive costly activities of many offenders. More light is needed from all directions to show what better measures can be undertaken for the prevention of criminality.

In attempting, as we have done, to explore the causations of certain types of delinquent careers, we are pursuing a path that science, particularly in medicine, recognizes as offering the greatest promise of showing new ways to therapeutic achievement. It is true that sometimes such research involves studies of chronic ailments that at a late stage cannot be cured, but nevertheless the only way to understand for earlier curative purposes the nature of any particular type of disease or the susceptibility of any given type of individual to that disease is to investigate thoroughly all the factors according to the best methods of etiology, the science of causes.

For at least a couple of decades we have known that there

are individuals normal physically and mentally according to any ordinary criteria, who experience internal mental or emotional conflicts, largely unconscious, which drive them toward delinquency and crime in spite of suffering. The ordinarily conceived laws of relative pleasure-gain and pain-loss seem not to be active in such cases. Evidently, then, other deeper dynamic issues are at work, indeed sometimes to the extent that punishment itself may not seem something to be avoided—as a matter of fact, punishment occasionally appears even to be sought.

This introduces the whole question of the deterrent effects of punishment. It is generally considered that police methods and court procedures and penal sentences have a deterring effect and undoubtedly to some extent this is true. But all who have studied large numbers of offenders know very many cases in which punishment does not check criminal tendencies. In several of the cases we present here nothing of the sort has proved a deterrent. Physical and mental suffering have been a common experience of the individual, beginning with punishments administered by the family and later through other sources. In most of the cases the individual has been brought face to face with the law through arrests, court appearances, probation, correctional and reformatory treatment; and in a number of instances the offender has received prison sentences, with all the hardships involved. Neither what he has experienced himself nor what he has witnessed of the punishment of others has checked his antisocial activities.

With full intelligence and reasoning ability, with more than ordinary access to the knowledge of what happens to the transgressor, these individuals have continued transgressing. It is thus evident that why these offenders have continued in their careers is a matter for scientific investigation of underlying motives and drives; and the fact that they have been so willing to enter into a long study of themselves proves their own ignorance, confusion, and questioning concerning the springs of their conduct.

More than this, it is plain from our cases that some individuals, given chances for a normally pleasurable life after making a start in the paths of delinquency, find themselves unable to cease their delinquent trends under the very environmental circumstances which they themselves in full consciousness declare to be most desirable. These case histories demonstrate that any ordinarily or even extraordinarily good environmental changes may not bring about the desired checking of antisocial impulses when from early years unconscious motivations or drives have existed. The overwhelming influences of such inner forces not only are inimical to the interests of society but also thwart any common or conscious modes of pleasure-finding.

So far as the family situation is concerned, the eleven cases show great variation. Seven had no delinquent siblings; two were the only children in the family; two had siblings who were delinquent, in one instance mildly and in the other severely so. Of the group, four would not continue the analysis. Three of these, two with deep-set peculiarities in personality make-up and one definitely diagnosed as an abnormal personality, were adopted children. Two of these had lived in homes where other adopted children were non-delinquent. The fourth had splendid personality assets, but a most unfortunate background for family life. That only two had delinquent siblings would seem to indicate that the problems were largely peculiar to the individual and to his inner mental life.

It is an interesting conjecture whether, with the better methods which are now used at the Guidance Center and in other guidance clinics, more could have been uncovered and accomplished with some of these individuals. The primary investigations, most representative of that earlier period, were conducted through social and psychiatric studies which did not presume, with the resources at hand, to be delving into or treating deeper causations. Perhaps the therapy that in many instances can be carried out by the more modern co-operative effort of psychiatrists and skilled psychiatric social workers might have availed in some of these cases. But it must be acknowledged that even now, with these better methods more attainable, very rarely are such difficult offenders accepted for intensive treatment—they are generally under the law turned over to the standard reformative agencies, which, at least in these cases, very frequently fail to reform.

Without any reiteration on our part of the specific issues brought out by the analysis in these different cases, professional and other readers can form their own opinions concerning what might have been the most promising point of attack upon the problems of mental life and the environmental conditioning factors these individual cases presented. Certainly there was need for modification of both.

All that can be finally stated is that in seven cases, if there had been intensive, prolonged work with these individuals and their families upon the basis of psychoanalytic understandings and interpretations, extremely difficult and costly years of misconduct might possibly have been averted—but nothing more certain can be added to this very uncertain statement.

With regard to the other cases, four of them were not accessible either to psychoanalytical therapy or exploration because we did not succeed in securing their co-operation. One of them was probably a border-line case of psychosis, three of them were adolescent (one of them was in the early post-adolescent period; psychologically, however, fully in that of puberty). It is not impossible that these cases could have been successfully handled therapeutically with the technique of child- or, more precisely, adolescent-analysis (Melanie Klein's, Anna Freud's, and Aichorn's technique), which approach, however, from the beginning we excluded from our present study. Most probably such cases could be really successfully treated only in institutions where they would receive both psychotherapy and schooling in combination.

It is only fair to say that the extraordinary repetition of offenses and the dire results exhibited in these instances have by no means obtained in all cases where we have known delinquent trends to arise upon the basis of mental conflicts. Many successes of psychiatry aided by good social therapy could be recorded from various guidance clinics. Here we are deliberately presenting very costly failures of earlier non-psychoanalytic attempts at treatment, together with a later and deeper study of causations, in order that there may be more awareness of the likelihood of failure in such cases and greater efforts at preventive therapy.

What could be done at earlier ages, in and outside of an institution, by prolonged psychotherapy with such difficult cases, particularly by child-analysis? Practically all the cases in this study began to show antisocial tendencies at a very early age— nearly all of them before they were ten years old. Undoubtedly they needed deeper analysis of their underlying emotional difficulties; perhaps the procedure of child-analysis, if it could have been obtained for them, might have availed to change their destiny. It is not possible to answer this question, because we have no knowledge of any such serious attempts having been made in America, where so many social conditioning factors exist which are fraught with danger to the young person who for any reason is inclined to accept the standards of delinquent behavior. With all the costs involved it would unquestionably be greatly worth while to undertake such treatment, making proper provision for after-care and especially for modifying family attitudes when the individual, as nearly always, has to be returned to family life. The expense would be nothing as compared with the social costs of long continuance in delinquency and the careers of criminality that are brought to light in our present studies.

One of the main questions unsolved is concerned with the criteria for selecting those young offenders for whom the arduous procedure of psychoanalysis is an essential prerequisite of reform. Experimentation with a series of cases would go far toward solving this problem. What a vastly important investigation of this major social problem might be undertaken if there were funds available for a definitive research in the comparative values of different forms of the treatment of delinquents!

Coming now to the question of psychoanalytic treatment of older offenders, we have no inclination to minimize the difficulties of this, especially as we have observed them during this study. In the first place, such analysis is very time-consuming, requiring expert service in each case over a period of many months. It is obvious that comparatively few cases could be analyzed in any center. But, on the other hand, it might be argued that if only a small number of cases were selected for the prevention of some of the most costly careers, the expense in time and effort would be thoroughly warranted.

Before giving indication of what would seem to be necessary to insure favorable results, some of the practical difficulties, none of them by any means insurmountable, should be reviewed.

We found that convenience of access to an incarcerated offender is a minor matter that can be easily arranged for when the authorities are co-operative. But another situation loomed up that was unexpected. The attitude of guards who were in contact with the prisoner counted much. Instead of giving encouragement to what was hoped might prove to be a therapeutic procedure, these officers with their various backgrounds of prejudices and sentiments either sneered at the idea of psychoanalysis, of which they knew nothing, or advised the prisoner not to go through with it, or attempted in petty ways to make it difficult for him to keep his appointments, or even teased him by intimating that he must be mentally abnormal if he was seeing a psychiatrist. It was very amusing, however, to note that in the case of one of our young men, Perez, who had somehow, we believe unfairly, achieved the reputation in the prison system of being tricky and dishonest, the opinion of the guards concerning analysis was radically changed. During the course of the analysis this young fellow found a considerable sum of money which had been left in a mattress by another prisoner; instead of keeping it, as he might well have done, he turned it over to the authorities. Then the opinion spread that his character was being changed. Frequently also the attitudes of other prisoners had to be combated. They either ridiculed the offender for being analyzed, or passed the word about that he was crazy, or in some cases they were jealous of him as having special privileges. Prison life has its social circle, upon which the prisoner is dependent in matters of reputation, response, and security. As composed only of other prisoners and the guards, with merely slight contacts coming from the outside world, the life situation is abnormally narrow. The whole atmosphere is charged with suspicion and jealousy built up on preconceived ideas and on inadequate outlets for emotions, as well as on the lack of adequate mental interests.

Perhaps, too, public opinion in some quarters might interfere with psychoanalytic treatment—the objections would be founded on the unconscious sadistic attitudes toward prisoners that are so often expressed in the idea that a prisoner is a person to be punished, that life should be made hard for him. Above all things, the offender is not to be coddled, and more than likely the attempt to gain deeper understanding of motivations would be regarded as coddling.

Considering how psychoanalysis of an offender might possibly be successfully utilized for his rehabilitation or reformation, it is obvious that by the time adult life has been reached or nearly reached there are added difficulties, among which are the following:

1. Socially an inferiority situation has been piling up as the result of natural attitudes taken toward the offender's behavior, by society and particularly by the law. This is deeply felt by the offender and his family. The reputation achieved by the criminal gives him much less than an equal chance with his fellows after release from incarceration.

2. In almost all cases undesirable associations with other lawbreakers have been steadily growing, often through the comradeships formed within penal institutions. Such associations become more and more difficult to break, and their continuance after the offender has served his sentence is a great factor in further law-breaking.

3. The offender, as the result of habit-formation, tends most readily to identify himself with the criminal population, and so very easily turns to the notion of repeating his offenses. Indeed, the psychological considerations of habit-formation as related to ideas and emotional attitudes show that there may be great barriers to success in avoiding criminality.

4. The relation of the offender to the law itself or to authority constituted under the law creates another difficulty. If the individual is at a highly critical period in character-development, or in the full mood to reform, he may be utterly discouraged by the fact that he has years more to serve.

But the conditions militating against the chances of rehabilitation obtain with variations for all sentenced offenders. Our point here is that these conditions cannot be abolished by psychoanalytic treatment. Nor can we expect that even those whose essential needs are only to be met by psychotherapy and probably only by psychoanalysis are by this treatment rendered capable of enduring vicissitudes—ego and affectional deprivations—which no ordinary, non-analyzed criminal can tolerate. In the light of the fact that incarcerated offenders of the type under discussion have a double burden, internal and external, we may consider what is necessary for the possible successful carrying out of their treatment by psychoanalysis. Extreme external difficulties are apt to throw back even a very successfully analyzed individual, especially if he encounters unusual external difficulties immediately after his analysis has been finished. It would be erroneous to attribute to the psychoanalytic treatment a magical power of omnipotence unparalleled in the whole field of medicine and to expect that a successful analysis could enable formerly severe neurotic individuals to cope with all kinds of life situations, even the most unusually pathogenetic.

In the first place, some sort of institutional provisions are necessary that will permit the offender to be analyzed under advantageous conditions. A hospital is not necessary, but rather some form of segregation where all in authority and the other offenders will be in sympathy with what is being undertaken.

Secondly, it is equally obvious that there must be an indeterminate sentence. At the right time the analyzed offender should have the opportunity to prove on parole the power of any new character-formation that may have been derived from insight gained into the causes of his previous antisocial behavior.

Thirdly, under the conditions and surveillance of strict parole the offender must have opportunities for living under normal social conditions, for employment, and for social contacts that may prove constructive for the possible rehabilitation of his conduct tendencies. It will be noted in our own studies that we report that several of these common-sense conditions were not obtainable. The economic depression made it absolutely impossible for employment to be found for those who were analyzed while not in institutions, as well as for those who were released after analysis. It was a most unfortunate period to enter upon this study; we made every effort to do something for these young men, but with tens of thousands of others out of work nothing could be done for them, who so badly needed funds and employment.

In the train of such economic restrictions there arose the unsatisfactory situation that these individuals, though some of them had the serious intention of breaking away from all the poor influences of their past life, had perforce to return to the living-conditions and associations that had earlier proved so hazardous. They had anything but a fair chance to profit by their psychoanalysis.

The others, who remained in prison, were equally handicapped because of the obvious discouragements of their surroundings and because when they had the spirit to make themselves over they were met only by further frustrations.

But there is another important matter for consideration: We are thoroughly convinced that following upon even a fairly complete analysis, implying insight gained by the offender and deep changes in the emotional life, there is eminent necessity in many cases for a reconstructive period. Insight and emotional change alone can hardly offer great expectation of success in the case of an individual who has been so definitely handicapped in preparation for life, even by the forms of treatment that he has received at the hands of society, which tend to make him less and less likely to adapt normally to ordinary social demands. Difficulties are bound to beset him, difficulties peculiar to any individual who has a record of crime.

Quite in addition to the direct aid that many paroled prisoners need in order to become self-supporting and to obtain the minimum decencies of life, understanding guidance and encouragement are essential to keep them steadied toward new goals. It is evident that a period is required for assimilating or incorporating into their personality and behavior trends the insight which they have gained. One of us saw Elton on the day that he was released from prison, a year after analysis with him had been attempted. The situation, although with some exaggeration, was typical. The young man was nervous and actually trembling as he faced the world anew; he seemed like a man blinded by the light after having been long in a dark dungeon. It was only too evident that he needed to be regarded as a convalescent patient, without strength to meet the world, quite unfit to adjust himself to life—and yet, with no home to go to and without any strong hand to guide him, there was nothing to do about it except have him go to the small job which the parole department obtained for him. One could almost sense that he was likely to fail on parole. Of course this particular man is especially weak in some of his personality characteristics and had only had the very first introduction to a therapeutic analysis, the completion of which would have required at least a year, but probably a considerably longer period of intensive daily work. But for many of those whose deep-lying emotional conflicts are the motivating forces of their delinquency, practical personal reconstructive help will be required following even a complete and successful analysis. On the other hand, we must fully recognize that such factual assistance alone may accomplish nothing. Our case studies will prove the failure of environmental advantages as well as of the usual prescriptions of probation or of the different forms of correctional and penal treatment. For this type of case it is the solution of inner conflicts that makes it possible for external opportunities to be of any essential benefit.

Long ago the Directors of the Judge Baker Foundation[1] became convinced that only a commission of experts could solve the problem of giving adequate protection to society through effectively checking delinquent and criminal careers. Such experts, after thorough studies of individual offenders, might be in a position scientifically to prescribe the nature and the length of treatment. Other careful students in this field have contended for this same scheme of procedure. Under this plan the court would find the individual guilty and then he would be turned over to such a commission, which would be responsible for deciding upon treatment. That many offenders would then receive much longer terms to some sort of confinement and that some of them would need almost permanent segregation goes without saying, because all studies show that short terms or early releases on parole are very frequently ineffective—although perhaps no more so than full terms served without thoroughly reconstructive measures for the individual being undertaken.

We cannot discuss here the implications of the duties and prescriptions of such a commission in handling other types of offenders, but for those who, like the cases we give, are so obviously driven by unconscious motivation, there can be but one answer. For modification of their antisocial tendencies it is absolutely essential that they gain insight through exploration and analysis of their own early experiences and attitudes, and that afterwards they must live for a period under specifically reconstructive conditions. To speak of the expense of this as being prohibitive is to neglect to compare the fact that

1 Vide: William Healy and Augusta F. Bronner: *Delinquents and Criminals—Their Making and Unmaking.* New York: The Macmillan Company; 1926.

such individuals without reformative treatment are great economic burdens to society, representing costs that are many times greater than that of the treatment proposed.

We were very fortunate in having the opportunity to carry on this study as a purely scientific effort to contribute to knowledge concerning some special types of very difficult cases. The inquiry has been primarily into the causation of antisocial behavior. The therapeutic possibilities of psychoanalysis in this field cannot yet be estimated on the basis of this study, in which because of the limited time (ten months for the whole study) only one of the cases could be subjected to a fairly complete therapeutic analysis and only three or four others to an analytic therapy which, though incomplete, could effect some limited yet definite changes in their personality. That even these incomplete therapeutic analyses have been carried out under the above discussed external difficulties should also be considered. (In the rest of our cases we could use the analytic technique only for genetic exploration without expecting any permanent therapeutic results.) Our experience makes us feel that until opportunities are afforded for manipulating the environment in favor of success with such types of offenders through providing a convalescent reconstructive period the possibilities of any psycho-therapy cannot be justly evaluated.

The main conclusion of this whole study is that investigation of the individual by psychoanalytic technique brings out a very great deal that was not known and could not be known through even good case studies. And there can be no doubt that these unknown factors were dynamic in producing the antisocial trends—the individual himself during his analysis makes it plain to us. These factors vary greatly from case to case, and it would be difficult to make more generalizations about them than those formulated in the previous chapter.

As advances are made in understanding the general principles of the development of personality and character it is to be hoped that much more information of what really is at work in the individual forming his conduct trends can be surmised or interpreted from shorter good case studies, and that some of the dynamic issues can then be met more readily than by complete psychoanalysis, even sometimes by modifying the social environment. Thus may be developed somewhat of an answer to the problem of how to meet the exigencies of the situation, since many cases for various reasons cannot be analyzed. From such studies as we have presented there may be, on the other hand, some intimation of the types of offenders and careers which for understanding and therapy require psychoanalysis. Our hope is for continuance of psychoanalytic research not only into causation but also into the possibilities of adequate preventive treatment at any age for the prevention of such costly careers as those exhibited by the offenders we have studied.

# Index

PATTERSON SMITH REPRINT SERIES IN
CRIMINOLOGY, LAW ENFORCEMENT, AND SOCIAL PROBLEMS